Underrepresentation
and the
Question of
Diversity:

Women and Minorities
in the Community College

❧

Underrepresentation and the Question of Diversity:

Women and Minorities in the Community College

BY ROSEMARY GILLETT-KARAM

SUANNE D. ROUECHE

JOHN E. ROUECHE

THE COMMUNITY COLLEGE PRESS

A DIVISION OF THE AMERICAN ASSOCIATION

OF COMMUNITY AND JUNIOR COLLEGES

PUBLISHED BY THE COMMUNITY COLLEGE PRESS, A DIVISION
OF THE AMERICAN ASSOCIATION OF COMMUNITY AND
JUNIOR COLLEGES
National Center for Higher Education
One Dupont Circle, N.W., Suite 410
Washington, D.C. 20036
(202) 728-0200

ISBN-0-87117-225-9
Library of Congress Catalog Card Number: 91-70325

CONTENTS

PREFACE

Twenty years ago, American Association of Community and Junior Colleges (AACJC) President Edmund J. Gleazer, Jr. observed that the greatest challenge facing American community colleges in the future was the challenge of making good on the promise of the open door. An open door for everybody and anybody who applies or who can profit from college instruction is a mission that some simply take for granted. That mission brings into higher education, in the community college, a population comparable to that of an intensive care unit—with the full array of emergencies, problems, and desires to be better, to be healthy. People in an emergency room represent every aspect of life, every level of educational background; that heterogeneity and that aspect of emergency probably is not represented anywhere else except in the American community college. And this condition runs contrary to the dominant view of higher education in America.

Historically, colleges and universities have specialized in admissions processes and selections designed to eliminate from consideration students who have problems. Factors typically used in the selection process—SAT scores, high school GPAs, level of family income, and level of educational attainment of parent—yield a more success-oriented, goal-oriented, self-directed, and motivated student body. This selective admissions process is designed to produce the best and the brightest, the most talented, most gifted, most positive student body with the highest parental expectations. It also identifies those students who have been successful in other arenas.

Community colleges, however, with their open-door admissions policies, attempt to accommodate everyone who applies. Yet we know college reputations are almost irrevocably tied to how selective colleges are—that is, how difficult it is to meet their entrance requirements. For example, *U.S. News & World Report* ranks and rates colleges based on their selectivity. They reason that if a college takes only the best and the brightest students, then obviously it must be excellent. Thus, in America, the mission of the community college requires that it run counter to the common stereotype of what makes a college a good college. If a college takes everybody, if its standards for admission are completely flexible, then it must not be much of a college—it must be a welfare organization. Critics of community colleges, such as Zwerling (1976) and Brint and Karabel (1989), are quick to point to the most damaging aspect of the community college—the promise, the dream offered, and still the goal unachievable. They claim that the mission is more missionary, more revivalist, than egalitarian. Because community colleges have been identified as "democracy's college" and "the people's college," they have been accused of hyping and ritualizing their mission while offering little substantive change. Critics say that most community college students don't do well, a severe social criticism at best.

One point needs to be made, however: Many community college students are first-generation college students who come to school without the support of family, spouse, friends, or the working world. Thus, to pay attention to the needs of this "intensive care unit," we must get past social criticism and acknowledge that in many ways community colleges face a "mission impossible." The heterogeneity of the students who enroll in American community colleges represents a challenge of enormous proportions. Although community colleges have not yet demonstrated success with this high-risk population, they have been serious in their efforts. Over the last 20 years, the enormity of the challenge posed by racially diverse and heterogeneous groups of students has reached almost crisis proportions. The complexity of student diversity that Gleazer talked about in 1969 pales in comparison to the complexity and reality of current demographic and societal data and to the forecast for the year 2000.

COMMUNITY COLLEGES: THE EGALITARIAN MISSION

The American community college and American democracy are inexorably linked, and as the decline of communism unfolds, we are more cognizant than ever that democracy is an ideal global cultural goal. People everywhere prefer to be liberated from dictatorships, authoritarianism, and elitism. The revolutions in Eastern European countries are high praise indeed for America because what others seek to do is to emulate our own revolutionary break with a superordinate elitist power. The affirmation of the fundamental dignity of the individual—the notion of classical liberalism or anti-authoritarianism, is a theme resounding in Eastern Europe. This indicates that whatever happens in America works, no matter what our criticism of it is; other people want democracy because it is a naturally responsive system.

People's chances and opportunities are limited without the benefit of education. Today, the fulfillment of the American dream that every generation should have the chance to exceed the attainment of the prior generation is inexplicably tied to an individual's skills and educational achievement. Currently in this country, White populations are stable or even decreasing in terms of percentage of the total population, while the Hispanic and Black populations are growing rapidly. This demographic reality represents an important shift in the new millenium: Whereas in the past America has been composed of a mostly Anglo-European population, no single majority group will predominate in the future. Although they are growing in numbers, racial-ethnic minority groups (whom demographers are calling "the new majority") tend to be underrepresented in higher education and in the business and political arenas as well. They represent a uniquely sanguine set of problems: for many of these minorities poverty is a way of life, the educational drop-out rate is high, and crime and drug use are rampant. Who addresses these problems? Who provides access to the American dream of greater opportunity? Who is equipped to do so? Probably the American community college.

If community colleges are going to be the colleges that specialize in taking the "hard-to-get-well," then the burden falls to college programs, college faculty, and college leaders. In the next 10 or 20 years, community colleges will bear much of the responsibility for addressing the impending crises of the future; for that task, we must have better-prepared and better-motivated students. We must do a better job of orientation, placement, and remediation. We must have faculty who understand the developmental nature of our original mission, men and women who are sympathetic with it and who themselves represent and model behavior for the "new majority student." We must expect problems and no quick-fix, easy solutions.

We need to recommend cultural awareness. The magic of the American dream is that a person can be anything he or she wants to be through motivation and a work ethic. As a society, we cannot afford for people to drop out and eventually fill our state penitentiaries, our welfare rolls, and our halfway houses. Colleges must do more to make certain that people who have not been successful in the past develop the skills, qualities, and acumen to be successful in the future.

We need to be more inclusive. Merely hiring people who are more representative of color or ethnicity is in itself insidious unless the college makes certain that quality of selection is not compromised.

The real challenge of the 1990s will be to add new faculty and staff who have better skills, better qualities, better hearts, better caring about students than we have had in the last 20 years. Our bottom line is always that we build quality and nothing less than that. Quality is the heart and soul of the institution. It is going to take more talented, more committed faculty and staff to get the outcomes that we all seek. What are the roles for the future, the issues? Can they work? What are the new directions? The common thread among students is that they are going to have more problems, not fewer. We've got to have better faculty who also are more representative of students. Can we do that? Can we be equal and excellent at the same time? The mindsets of people who look at these questions will determine and drive our responses. Unless we bring harmony, we're going to have a society cut in half. And community colleges have been thrust by society into being the bridge between where we are now and where we can envision we ought to be. If we don't do that job, a whole society is in jeopardy.

THE CHALLENGES OF THE 1990S

American community colleges are at the brink of an important era in history. The third milennium rapidly approaches, and the decade of the 1990s is a watershed period. As we face our challenges and opportunities, as we confront our destiny, we are aware of the issues of underrepresentation and underutilization of women and racial-ethnic minorities in higher education. Remembering that the foundation of community college education is egalitarianism guides our goals for the coming decade: It would be antithetical to the nature and mission of the community college not to recognize the discrimination of the past and not to seek to redress the injustices of underrepresentation. The challenge of representation is a historical mission of American citizens; the American revolution was fought over that right. Representation is the very core of our republic, and it provides the basis for our democracy. Obviously, this fact is an embedded assumption of American culture. Lack of representation violates the premises on which this nation was founded.

This book focuses on the lack of representation, or underrepresentation, of women and members of racial and ethnic minorities in community college leadership. Some would say that these two groups cannot and should not be linked, that they are too different to be discussed together, and that research does an injustice to individuality by creating a posture on groups. This is not the intent of this study. Our assumption is that controversy surrounds the representation of both groups in higher education and in other fields as well. Moreover, we postulate that the examples of challenge demonstrated by underrepresented groups do have similarities and commonalities. Finally, we make note of the fact that debate and discussion are mixed, at best, about the possible outcomes for women and minority groups. In each of these instances, our goal is to present the data, highlight the situation as it is, celebrate breakthroughs, and offer suggestions and strategies that allow progress toward full representation of women and members of racial-ethnic minorities in American community colleges.

In Chapter One, "Finding Equality in Egalitarian Educational Institutions," the premise of the book—that community colleges have not met their responsibilities to women and members of racial-ethnic minorities—is examined. We discuss the mission of the Truman Commission and the community college commitment to egalitarian education as a backdrop for issues of exclusionary practices and the imminent need to represent women and members of ethnic and racial minorities at all levels of community college life. We see the 1990s as an emerging "Era of Developing Diversity," in which cultural pluralism will be valued and rewarded. We discuss overcoming perceptions and structural barriers to full representation as community college CEOs respond to culture of conformity, selection of sameness, position perfection, and reproduction of self concepts—all obstacles for women and minorities. Diversity, pluralism, cultural pluralism, and multiculturalism are. defined, and Ravitch comments on the differences between multiculturalism and particularism. Finally, seven recommendations are made toward the achievement of diversity and multiculturalism in community colleges.

Chapter Two, "Confronting the Language of Diversity," examines the debates over diversity, cultural pluralism, and multiculturalism from the perspective of debates over equality and inequality, the meaning of justice, the critical importance of embedding culture, and American democracy and pluralism. Finding equality in egalitarian systems is not as simple as one would imagine, and only by confronting those concepts that have become bywords of politicians and educators can we gain some insight into the enormity of the dilemma that confronts researchers on cultural diversity and its impact on American institutions. The very language we use is ambiguous and complex; finding explicit meaning in relation to the issue of representation demands that we examine that language and its conceptual meanings as they relate to the issues of diversity.

In Chapter Three, "Women: Expression and Experience in Academic Literature," we look at the historical and philosophical premises on which the "woman question" rests. Much of the exclusivity of history lies in the fact that the record and voice of our past is the record and voice of men. By probing the literature and research about women, we can more adequately understand the insights that women's studies have to offer about the contributions, strengths, and differences of women. We discuss Carol Gilligan's *In A Different Voice* (1982), the classic that has irrevocably changed the single-view emphases of researchers, both male and female. The role of women in education and leadership, and in community college education in particular, is examined from recent discoveries by Desjardins (1989a and 1989b) and Gillett-Karam (1988).

Chapter Four, "Minorities: Expression and Experience in Academic Literature," looks carefully at the dilemmas and controversies that surround the issues of racial and ethnic minorities in America. Terms such as ethnicity, minority, prejudice, and discrimination are defined. We analyze the immigrant and ethnic traditions in America and offer theories of racial and ethnic relations. We also describe the legal and educational histories of Blacks, Native Americans, Hispanics, Puerto Ricans, Cubans, and Asian Americans. Although the emphasis of this chapter is sociological, it is so because the experiences of racial and ethnic groups in America are not always included in standard community college curriculum and texts.

Chapter Five, "Affirmative Action: Then and Now," examines the issues and politics of social movements and the challenges to the status quo or equilibrium in politics and society. While the 1950s and 1960s were a period in which great social change took place and in which extension of fundamental civil liberties was pervasive, by the 1970s we began to see retrenchment and a desire to return to "less costly" policies. Affirmative action has been and still is a principle that garners great support and great derision. We inspect the challenges to affirmative action, presenting both the neoconservative and the liberal views of the topic. We review the role of the Supreme Court and discuss how the relationship between affirmative action and representation on community college campuses is confirmed by the exemplary role played by the California community colleges and their state mandate, known as AB 1725.

Chapter Six, "Inclusionary Practices: Highlighting Exemplary Programs," points out the Challenge-Rechallenge Framework and spotlights the achievements of the many organizations, programs, and policies now in place throughout the United States. In most instances, the programs that we discuss are those we have seen first-hand. The Minority Fellows Program (sponsored by the League for Innovation in the Community College and the Community College Leadership Program at The University of Texas at Austin), the Leaders for the Eighties, the American Association of Women in Community and Junior Colleges (AAWCJC), the National Council on Black American Affairs and the Presidents' Roundtable, the National Community College Hispanic Council, the Hispanic Association of Colleges and Universities (HACU), the Texas Association for Chicanos in Higher Education (TACHE), and the Minority Affairs Commission of AACJC provide examples of the networks for women and minorities. College programs that encourage inclusionary practices for underrepresented groups are featured.

Chapter Seven, "What the Leaders Are Saying: The Voices of Diversity," provides us with the "voices" of women and racial-ethnic minority leaders of community colleges. In their discussions, we hear about their desires for inclusionary practices and greater representation and about the institution and operationalization of practices that work in their colleges.

Chapter Eight, "Getting There from Where You Are: Increasing Representation and Recognition," provides a timeline for transforming institutions, with major consideration of the critical natures of leadership and mission, campus culture and climate, the teaching-learning environment, student retention, hiring, and curriculum needs. It concludes with suggested strategies for implementation.

ACKNOWLEDGEMENTS

Writing a book about controversial subject matter raises the questions of stridency and imposition of opinion. In this book we intend neither an irascible voice nor a subjective one. The message of representation is itself a subject of great emotion and passion; after all, it is the language of revolution in America. Justice, as Solomon (1990) would suggest, involves our concern for others and our compassion over righting wrongs easily recognized as disharmonious to the community and state in which we live. In addition the very nature of the community college cries out for the demonstration of egalitarianism; to suggest that exclusionary practices are acceptable in such a milieu is to suggest something antithetical to the mission of the community college.

Fortunately, there are many who feel that the inclusion and full representation of women and minorities are fundamental principles on which that most unique experience of American higher education, the community college, must stand. The following individuals, and others who are quoted in this book, share this goal and commitment. We wish to recognize these individuals in a special way for their vision and support of this undertaking: Dale Parnell, president, AACJC; Terry O'Banion, executive director, League for Innovation in the Community College; Donald Phelps, chancellor, Los Angeles Community College District; Jim Hudgins, president, Midlands Technical College; Robert McCabe, president, and Tessa Tagle, vice president, Medical Center Campus, Mardee Jenrette, director, Teaching Learning Center, and Eduardo Padron, vice president, Wolfson Campus, all of Miami-Dade Community College District; Tom Barton, president, Greenville Technical College; Paul Elsner, chancellor, Alfredo de los Santos, vice chancellor, Raul Cardenas, president, South Mountain Community College, and Carolyn Desjardins, director, Leadership Institute, all of the Maricopa County Community College District; Al Fernandez, chancellor, Coast Community College District; Judith Valles, president, Golden West College; Tom Fryer, chancellor, and Geraldine Kaspar, director of human resources and affirmative action, Foothill-DeAnza

Community College District; Sandy Acebo, vice president of instruction, and Carolyn Fountenberry, affirmative action chair, DeAnza College; Pam Fisher, vice chancellor, Yosemite Community College District; Sharon Yaap, president, AAWCJC; Marjorie Blaha, chancellor, Los Rios Community College District; and David Mertes, chancellor, California Community Colleges.

There are also those closer to home who have provided daily support, nurturing, and invaluable aid. Eli Eric Peña, now at Texas Southmost College, ably served as a research associate and wise counsel to this study. Sheryl Fielder's generous hard work and dedication to a sometimes impossible task—keeping up with revisions and having the patience to suffer "just one more change"—have made her a legend in her own time. Her keen eye for details has made us look good. Both Alex Chaniotis and Christina Alonso helped translate the frequently indecipherable notes of the authors, and Christina took on the daily responsibility of making the "library run." Lisa May Cortez and Lisa Gutierrez were always quick to sniff out panic and distress and offered their assistance at many critical moments in the research and writing stages. Ruth Thompson, whose National Institute for Staff and Organizational Development (NISOD) responsibilities demand 110 percent of her time, never failed to make even more time for us. Libby Lord provided continuity and sanity in an environment that was often chaotic; her steady guidance and sage advice kept our eyes on the path. Reid Watson demonstrated his astute instinct for protecting our need for privacy to write and for accommodating our need for companionship when writing became too onerous.

Definitive research ideas came from Charlotte Biggerstaff's (1990) dissertation on transformational leadership and culture, and Rex Peebles guided our thoughts through the ideas of MacIntyre, Sandel, Rawls and other political philosophers whose ideas were then re-examined by Solomon. Steinfels, Omi and Winant, and Feagin, political scientists and sociologists, have written works of tremendous importance and impact, and we are indebted for their insightful stimuli. Finally, Gilligan's (1987) breakthrough in the theory of moral development and Green's (1988,

1989) critical examination of the needs of minorities in education today were critical to this text.

Rosemary Gillett-Karam
Suanne D. Roueche
John E. Roueche
Austin, Texas
January 1991

CHAPTER ONE

❧

FINDING EQUALITY IN EGALITARIAN EDUCATIONAL INSTITUTIONS

❧

There are over 1,200 American community colleges—
90 percent of them are headed by White men;
and almost 90 percent of their faculties are also White.

&.

Who attends community college, who teaches in college, and who administers college? Since the 1970s, educational research has addressed these questions that focus on identifying the constituencies of higher education. For example, a plethora of materials describe the nontraditional student and advocate the necessity of building developmental skills for the "underprepared student." For over a generation, academicians and policy makers have given special attention to the needs of the academically underprepared in American community colleges. Recently, we have begun to learn more and more about the nature of leadership in the American community college, and some research is beginning to surface concerning the teachers of community colleges.

The recent emphasis on community college constituencies has made us aware of an irrefutable fact: women and members of racial-ethnic minorities are underrepresented in higher education. Neither minority students, minority teachers, nor minority administrators in American community colleges are represented in numbers equivalent to those in the general population. This underrepresentation demands our immediate attention and calls for positive action.

Population statistics and projections emphasize the importance of a more representative cohort of women and minorities teaching and administering in community colleges. Population trends for the twenty-first century predict a decrease in the percentage of Whites and a rapid increase in the percentage of Hispanics and Blacks in America. Hodgkinson (1985) tells us that by the year 2020, the U.S. population is expected to grow from 242 million to 265 million, and the largest increases will be among Hispanics and Blacks. At present, one-fifth of our population is Hispanic and Black; by the year 2020, Hispanics and Blacks will represent one-third of the population, and in certain states these groups will comprise half of the total population. Moreover, as large cohorts of faculty and administrators reach retirement, we can anticipate faculty and administrative shortages. Our future, therefore, is one in which change is inevitable—community colleges must respond positively to these challenges to avoid future repercussions. We must respond to these questions:

- Are American community colleges making good on their promises to educate all of the people?
- Are American community colleges egalitarian in their recruitment, hiring, and promotion procedures?
- Are women and members of racial-ethnic minorities excluded or included in the constituencies of American community colleges?

THE TRUMAN COMMISSION: COMMUNITY COLLEGES DEMAND EGALITARIANISM

Although the junior college had its origins in the first half of the twentieth century, it was not until the latter 1940s that the idea of the comprehensive community college was truly born. Then, through presidential leadership, the Truman Commission applied the principles of egalitarianism to education. For the first time in our history, all people were enfranchised to be educated beyond secondary school. We might say that the underlying premise of community college education is the democratization of higher education; it is providing all people, within their own communities, access to education beyond high school. Today, there are more than 1,200 community colleges dedicated, ostensibly, to the mission of providing an opportunity for higher education to all people. The community colleges of America make the idea of serving the "public good" real—community colleges are dedicated to educating and serving everyone, regardless of educational background, skills, handicap, gender, culture, or economic status.

But this movement to break down barriers to education has not always been on guard against the resurrection of those same obstacles and barriers. America is no stranger to demographic changes and, as an open-access nation, its ethnic and minority populations are rapidly increasing. Data demonstrate that the path of access for these populations is the community college. Community colleges provide opportunities to fulfill the dreams embedded in our national values and identity; these opportunities are dependent on the promises of egalitarianism and democracy.

We must recognize that community colleges have not met their responsibilities to minorities as students, faculty, and administrators. Minorities' representation in these institutions does not reflect, by a long shot, their proportional representation in society. Minorities who are in the pipeline, who are at the threshold of entry into careers, who are being trained to take over positions of authority and leadership, are few in number, and rather than growing in proportion to minority population statistics, the number of minorities in this pipeline has only declined. A 1987 report of the Education Commission of the States said that "progress toward full participation of minorities in higher education has become distressingly stalled" (p. 1). Perhaps we should go a step further and report that our data indicate that we are more than stalled; we are going backward. Decreasing participation only means that the pipeline of expectations is also drying up.

We must argue for policy changes—not only because such an argument is morally right, but because our personal futures and the well-being of our nation depend on these changes. For example, consider that by the year 1992 it will take three workers to support each retiree, and one of the three will be either Black or Hispanic (Hodgkinson, 1985). Will this work force be capable of supporting and contributing to this system?

5

If we want to continue to count on retirement benefits, we must pay attention to immediate realities: If a third of our nation is undereducated and if the groups overrepresented in that third are also underrepresented in present educational institutions, then we may reason that these groups cannot contribute to our future security and well-being. We have reciprocal dependency on future generations—what we do today affects what others do after us. We cannot afford to disenfranchise those who will represent a large number of the "contributors" to our retirement.

THE HISTORY OF EXCLUSIONARY PRACTICES

We know a great deal about the exclusionary practices of American government and American education, and we have labeled these practices acts of segregation and discrimination. Whether the practices affect civil liberties or freedom of opportunity, most educators agree that segregation and discrimination on the basis of gender, handicap, or minority status are inappropriate behaviors in a democratic system.

Community colleges were established to redress the grievances brought about by the practices of elitist or meritocratic educational systems. An almost fanatical zeal accompanied the early days of this uniquely American form of higher education—the "people's college." Some who write about this period refer to "the movement" and focus on the "missionary zeal" of the early founders and leaders of community colleges. That missionary spirit took to the community the message that college can be of service to everyone. Thus, the community college's "mission" is to accomplish what almost no other American institution has done without legal directive: to create and implement inclusionary practices that fulfill the promise of a democracy.

The promise of American democracy, stated simply, is "rule by the people." In practice, however, rule by the people actually means rule by some of the people to the exclusion of others. That was not, and is not, the intent of democracy. The community college has recognized this chasm between what is and what should be and has chosen to represent the idea that all people should have access to education and the opportunity to succeed. And the community college works diligently to make good on those ideas.

Three eras can be identified in which, as community colleges evolved, they created and implemented inclusionary practices. The first era was in the 1970s, the era of recognizing differences and meeting needs. During this period, community colleges focused on meeting societal needs emanating from shifts in national policies and attitudes. The practices and social norms of the past were challenged, and in the changing social milieu, the community college became the vehicle by which "the people" (the nontraditional students of higher education) would be prepared to meet these challenges.

In the 1980s, the era of developing programs, community colleges emphasized meeting the special needs of their nontraditional students. Developmental programs were instituted to accommodate the needs of students with basic skills deficiencies; colleges worked to institute programs that retained students, regardless of their needs.

In the 1990s, a new emphasis is emerging, which could be called the era of developing diversity for community colleges. This era focuses on the avowed mission of the community college: that, as a mirror of society, the college will recognize racial-ethnic and gender diversity and work to include members of ethnic minorities and women in all leadership roles, including faculty, administration, and support staff.

This evolving era, in which new leadership must be developed for a rapidly changing nation and world, once again places the community college at the forefront of higher education in meeting the future needs of our society. As the AACJC Commission on the Future of Community Colleges has noted:

> There is a clear and pressing need to increase diversity among community college leadership. Currently, 10 percent of community college chief executive officers are women (121 of 1,222), as are 35 percent of all administrators. There are 37 Black, 32 Hispanic, and 8 Asian chief executive officers in the nation's community colleges. Blacks and Hispanics are underrepresented among all administrative and faculty groups... a

special effort should be made to recruit leaders from among minority and female populations (1988, p. 42).

Many researchers are critically examining the future of leadership in American colleges and universities. Some have suggested that the community college is the only educational institution that has success-fully responded to the issue of underrepresentation and underutilization of women and members of minorities in positions of leadership (Green, 1989). Although the numbers of women and members of minorities in positions of leadership in the community college is higher than in senior institutions, the real number remains very low. Roueche, Baker, and Rose (1989) point to this critical awareness in their work *Shared Vision*. They discuss leadership concerns and implications for the future. By exam-ining the challenges of—and our expectations for—the future, by overcoming the obstacles of underrepresentation, and by examining exemplary leadership behaviors of present chief executive officers who are women and members of ethnic minorities, community colleges can develop a core of leaders who will lead with vision and passion in the twenty-first century.

CHALLENGES AND EXPECTATIONS

The most serious challenges we face in the twenty-first century relate to: the reasons for the small number of women and minorities in present positions of leadership in community colleges; and the need to remove the mental, societal, and educational obstacles that inhibit their access to leadership positions. Most educators agree that new leadership is necessary to meet the needs of changing external and internal forces in community colleges. We must look to the untapped resources and creativity that women and minorities can bring to leadership.

Overcoming perceptions affected by societal and structural barriers is critical. Traditionally, women and minorities have been excluded from participation and decision making; thus, our norms represent the codes and behaviors of only a limited portion of our society. Continuing to allow discriminatory practices to diminish and cloak the attributes, behaviors, customs, and values of a great segment of our society misrepresents the natural order of that society. This phenomenon would never be tolerated by a natural order that seeks diversity as an expected manifestation of life. We must look to those who provide us with new paradigms to understand and to lead our society.

In 1982 Carol Gilligan debunked one of the critical theories of moral development by pointing out that the stages of development of men and women grew out of separate, but equally important, behaviors. Neither behavior was aberrant, just different. Following this paradigm, we extend Gilligan's philosophy to women and minorities as they pattern their leadership behaviors. We must expand our thinking and turn away from the misconceptions and prejudices that have limited women and minorities' access to positions of leadership in American community colleges. As Wilson and Melendez (1988) point out, intolerance of diversity spawns problems between the majority and minorities. For example, nonmajority attributes should not be misinterpreted (Cronin, 1984); confidence should not be misread as arrogance because we switch the actor of the attribute; energy and tenacity should not be seen as aggressiveness, nor risk-taking as nonconformity, nor a sense of humor as a lack of seriousness simply because a leader is a woman or a member of a minority group. Rather, we must look to the present leaders who represent this new constituency of leadership and listen to their voices to provide us with new behaviors and attributes of leadership and vision.

OBSTACLES OF UNDERREPRESENTATION

From our research on leadership, we find we can predict leadership behavior. The attributes of leadership that are derived from the characteristics of the transformational leadership model (Roueche, Baker, and Rose, 1989) posit the concepts of vision, influence/empowerment, motivation, people orientation, and values as the conceptual bases of the leader-follower relationship. The leader has the ability to arouse, engage, and satisfy the needs of the follower (Burns, 1978); in the same vein, the follower brings commitment to the leader. Where the leader has vision and a sense of future direction, the follower identifies with the leader's vision and buys into that direction. To the extent that the leader inspires and motivates, the follower has imagination and new insights. When the leader demonstrates that he or she values the pre-eminence of people, the followers believe they can make a difference. The outcome of this behavior, then, is that the follower is educated to lead; the leader helps make the follower into a future leader.

This model was used in a nationwide study of leadership in American community colleges to identify the characteristics and attributes of exemplary CEOs. Analyzing the variables of gender and ethnicity of this dominant group, Gillett-Karam (1988) produced the following results:

- *Percentages of Women and Minorities.* In actual numbers, women and minorities represented a very small percentage of the whole group of American community college CEOs: women accounted for about 7 percent of the group; minorities accounted for less than 3 percent. National figures show women holding 10 percent and minorities holding 5 percent of the CEO positions in American community colleges.
- *Age Variations of Women and Minorities.* There were significant gaps between the ages of women and minorities and the ages of men of the dominant group entering administrative and executive positions. Women demonstrated a gap of six years' difference for entry into first administrative position and a seven-year delay for achievement of first executive position. Minorities demonstrated a delay of almost four years difference for entry into first administrative position and also a four-year gap for achievement of first executive position.
- *Years in Present Position.* Tenure, or average length of time spent in present position, was 12 years for the male dominant group; for women it was 3.8 years, and for the minority group it was 5.6 years.
- *Positions Prior to Present CEO Position.* One-third of the male dominant group held the position of president or CEO prior to

their present position; one-fourth of the women had previously been presidents of community colleges, and one-half of the members of minority groups had previously held the position of president.

• *Entry Work Position.* Women and minorities reported backgrounds and previous work experiences that included teaching experience in public schools and colleges and universities; the traditional male group did not. Also, women and minorities began their administrative experience as department heads or division chairs 50 percent more often than did the comparison group.

IDENTIFIERS/INDICATORS OF UNDERREPRESENTATION

The differences demonstrated by data collection identify the underrepresentation and underutilization of women and minorities in positions of leadership in American community colleges. Studies of leadership demonstrate that leadership is not affected by gender or ethnicity. The same convictions, care, and concern about leadership abilities were expressed by all the exemplary leaders we studied: these leaders' practices have been recognized not only by their communities but also by their peers and academic researchers. The concerns of these leaders speak to the problems of underrepresentation:

> The value of cultural diversity and the tremendous contribution that can be made by different perspectives are the major themes that should be stressed throughout the community college movement; it is not sameness that defines us, but cultural diversity. The more we value differences, and the more we understand diversity, the greater our cohesiveness and strength as a college, a community, and a nation (Jerry Sue Owens, president, Lakewood Community College, Minnesota).

The issues of underrepresentation seem to converge in the concept of diversity and the values that support that concept. If an intolerance of diversity is valued by society, then the benefits and potential of new ideas and vision are undermined. The CEOs we studied were aware of the limitations created by the phenomena of culture of conformity and selection of sameness, the element of position perfection, and the reproduction of self concept. We used these terms to address the difficulties that women and members of minorities encounter in hiring, screening processes, job aspiration, and job advancement.

Culture of conformity refers to the practices of honoring and emulating only the traits of previous leaders, or to institutional rules that exclude and diminish the importance of exception or diversity; in essence, the concept refers most directly to exclusionary practices that inhibit civil rights legislation and affirmative action principles. Donald Phelps, chancellor, Los Angeles Community College District, reminds us:

> If affirmative action is no longer purposeful, then it does not allow for the nurturing of the idea of providing opportunity. This idea can easily fall out of favor and be eliminated from the consciousness of employers.

Selection of sameness and the concept of position perfection refer to screening and hiring processes that dogmatically follow requisites that "prove" that women and minority candidates are neither as highly qualified nor as acceptable as White males. Jerry Sue Owens states:

> Women and minorities are not moving up in the administrative pipeline, and presidents are not finding new opportunities to use their networks to promote new leadership. This lack of opportunity has to do with screening committees. The committees are not representative of the diverse populations found in community colleges; and they often apply a subtle racism by demanding that the best person for the job is the most published, is the best educated, has the most proven track record, and has the most exemplary qualifications that are highly competitive against any standard of performance. This is the selection of sameness concept in which a conscious decision is made to screen out women and members of minorities.

The concept of reproduction of self is another manifestation of culture of conformity or selection of sameness. This concept speaks to the idea that people who are in positions of leadership or who are seeking job applicants want those who replace them or those whom they hire to look exactly like them, speak like them, and act like them. This reproduction of self pre-empts the broadening of our pool of aspirants to leadership positions. As Flora Mancuso Edwards, president of Middlesex County College in New Jersey, states:

> The history of the professional pool and the requirements and dynamics involved in deciding who can enter that pool is basically modelled on White, male behavior. For the long view, when a Black or Hispanic physics instructor is a common sight, then, too, will a Black or Hispanic president be a common sight.

There is still another aspect to barriers in the hiring process and the attempt to identify gender and ethnicity issues of underrepresentation; these are the views that are manifested in the single-mistake syndrome, the double-edged sword idea, tokenism, and alienation.

The single-mistake syndrome has its origins in the folklore of cultural pluralism and should be acknowledged as such because it is the perception that if a woman or a member of a racial-ethnic minority has made a mistake, that mistake is proof that the whole group is not competent. There is, in the folklore, a whole series of statements along the lines of "I told you so," "I knew they couldn't do it," or "We shouldn't have taken the risk" that are aimed at racial-ethnic minorities and women and their new positions of leadership. This kind of thinking and perception is steeped in bias. The question becomes: Is it all right, is it permissible, for women or members of racial-ethnic minorities to make a mistake, to be risk takers, to be change agents, as they fill positions of leadership in the American community college? Of course they should be able to make mistakes, and they should be able to survive their mistakes and grow. However, this "I told you so, they can't do it" perception remains part of social reality.

Another set of obstacles to women and minorities in positions of leadership is related to the idea of the double-edged sword. This idea raises the question of personal identity and personal style of leadership: Can one identify strongly with one's gender or one's own ethnicity? That question plagues many leaders in terms of their relationship to their college, to their colleagues, and to their community. Is it all right to represent yourself in terms of your own personality and in terms of your cultural development, and is it all right to honor those things? If members of minorities or women exhibit such characteristics stridently, they are often denounced. The double-edged sword is this attempt to walk the fine line between presentation as self and presentation as leader for all.

The concept of tokenism exists not only in the minds of the women and racial-ethnic minority members who are leaders, but also in the minds of those who see such nontraditional leaders and confront them. This is the idea that if women or members of racial-ethnic minorities have attained positions of leadership, they have done so by virtue of a quota or "set-aside" system; that without affirmative action, "they" would never be leaders. This belief is one with which leaders must constantly contend, which they must acknowledge and dispel.

Finally, the issue of alienation cannot be ignored because it frequently limits the growth of new leaders. In an environment inundated by a history of racism, or a "good ol' boy network," alienation is a distinct possibility. The product of alienation is, of course, the disenchantment of the leader with the position, the disenchantment of the leader with the challenge to change, and the eventual resignation or desire to leave that place in which the alienation exists.

Leaders who are commanding our attention, therefore, refer to those positive benefits of resources, talents, and diversity that women and members of minority groups can bring to the community colleges of America. According to Eduardo Padron, vice president of the Wolfson Campus at Miami-Dade Community College, Florida:

> I feel we underestimate the tremendous resources that members of ethnic minorities and women can provide to leadership. Our student body for the year 2000 needs such role models because students continue to represent diversity

and differences. Women and minorities as applicants to jobs are not unidimensional in their thinking or creativity; they are individuals who can lead and inspire all groups—they deal well in a multidimensional society. Boards, screening committees, and organizational associations need to become sensitive to these resources that are neglected and misunderstood.

DEFINING DIVERSITY

The issues of underrepresentation of women and racial-ethnic minorities lead us to question our present understanding of culture and diversity and to examine the role of the community college. The era of developing diversity refers to the critical role of community colleges, who must be pacesetters for multicultural identity. As technological advancements require a more sophisticated work force, as American demography challenges pre-existing political, social, and economic patterns, as diminishing national boundaries bring the world's peoples closer together, our educational systems must prepare and be prepared for diversity. They must prepare for differences, for the distinct, for the dissimilar, the various, the alternative—and in doing so must find advantages and value in diversity. Community colleges should be at the forefront of these shifting views, providing the higher education necessary to confront a changing world.

Diversity is a term that focuses on the ideas of pluralism, cultural diversity, and multiculturalism. Each of these terms suggests that "the one, like-minded view" of culture may be challenged by different and equally contributory views of culture; that, in fact, two or more cultures can coexist without one being qualitatively "better" than the other. Although diversity suggests difference and distinctiveness, pluralism asks different groups "to explore, understand, and try to appreciate one another's cultural experiences and heritage" (Green, 1989, p. xvi). This understanding leads to multiculturalism, or the transcendence over ethnocentrism, and to the enjoyment of the contributions of the many, instead of the one.

Diane Ravitch, in her article "Multiculturalism Yes, Particularism No" summarizes the argument for multiculturalism:

> The debate over multiculturalism follows a generation of scholarship that has enriched our knowledge about the historical experiences of women, Blacks, and members of other minority groups in various societies. As a result of the new scholarship, our schools and our institutions of learning have in recent years begun to embrace what Catharine R. Stimpson of Rutgers University has called "cultural democracy," a recognition that we must listen to "a diversity of voices" to understand our past and present (Ravitch, 1990, p. A-52).

But Ravitch warns of the competing danger of particularism, which demands loyalty to a particular group and disparages any commonalities among groups. Particularists reject the ideas of accommodation and interaction and espouse a version of history in which "everyone is either the descendant of victims or of oppressors."

> The pluralist approach to teaching culture accords with traditional academic ethics, in that students learn to approach their subject with a critical eye. They learn about the subject, and they know that they may criticize its strengths and weaknesses without offending the professor. For example, in a traditional academic setting, the object of learning about Confucianism or Islam or Judaism is to study its history and philosophy, not to become an adherent of the faith. By contrast, particularism has spurred a separatist ethic in higher education. In the particularist classroom, students are taught to believe in the subject, immerse themselves in its truths, and to champion them against skeptics. They are taught to believe, not to doubt or criticize (p. A-52).

CONCLUSION

Community colleges must express doubt and criticism, especially around the issues of exclusion and underrepresentation. They must be cautious about the negative effects of particularism and assert the positive effects of pluralism and multiculturalism. We suggest, therefore, that by valuing diversity, pluralism, and multiculturalism, community colleges will take a leadership role in higher education and will develop commitments to:

- Recognize the value of diversity that promotes broad, multiple views
- Represent and utilize women and members of racial-ethnic minorities in positions of leadership equivalent to their representation in the population
- Develop strategies and procedures that achieve full participation and full representation of women and minorities in community colleges as students, teachers, and administrators
- Acknowledge individual differences around campus culture and climate, and create a system for dispute and grievance resolution
- Designate and develop curricula that acknowledge and reward diversity in individuals, groups, and cultures
- Begin with the here and now, and with the acceptance that success and quality are achievable goals

CHAPTER TWO

❧

CONFRONTING
THE LANGUAGE OF DIVERSITY

❧

The pervasive gap between our aims and
what we actually do is a kind of moral dry rot
which eats away at the emotional and
rational bases of democratic beliefs
(Harry S Truman, Committee on Civil Rights, 1944).

✒

The language used in discussing diversity, pluralism, and multiculturalism is difficult at best and confusing at worst. Issues and ideas are
presented here that relate to the debate and critical thinking surrounding
the concepts of equality, justice, culture, and pluralism.

Finding equality in so-called "egalitarian" systems is not as easy or
as predictable as might be imagined. Often when we ask questions
concerning equality, we do so because we see inequality—in social
settings, in economic distinctions, and in educational attainments.
Inequality and unfairness are terms that raise the consciousness of people
in a democratic society because they reason that in a democracy all
people should have equivalent opportunity. Leahy (1983) points out that
children, as well as adults, ask basic questions about wealth, poverty, and
fairness, and that those questions are reflected in governmental policies
aimed at one or another aspect of inequality.

If we were to accumulate all the questions raised, we could refer to
the collective American consciousness of inequality. We might reveal, for
example, that American attitudes about social welfare and other equality-
related policies have an inconsistent and sometimes seemingly
contradictory quality. During the New Deal, for example, American

government policies focused on "redistributive" justice, programs that sought to redistribute wealth and welfare to achieve benefits for the public good. During the 1950s and 1960s, a social movement focused on extending civil liberties and civil rights of citizens. Now we see the curtailment of such programs and a return to a more entrepreneurial, individualistic political culture in which the individual reasserts a competitive, marketplace mentality for growth, and in which the private good is seen to supersede the public good.

More specifically, Americans have previously accepted the idea that minorities have suffered from discrimination. They have maintained an abstract commitment to equal opportunity, yet have demonstrated opposition to specific policies designed to implement equal opportunity, such as busing to desegregate schools or affirmative action programs. Kluegel and Smith (1986) suggest that although Americans highly value equal citizenship rights and democratic politics in the abstract, the right of the wealthy to wield disproportionate economic and political power is unchallenged in practice. In a study of Americans' perceptions and beliefs (including their inconsistencies and contradictions) about social and economic inequality, these researchers found that attitudes toward inequality are influenced by three major aspects of current American social, economic, and political environments: a stable, dominant ideology; individuals' economic and social status; and specific beliefs and attitudes.

First, beliefs and attitudes concerning inequality reflect the stable influence of the existing stratification system; Kluegel and Smith call this the "logic of opportunity syllogism" because it provides a deductive argument that justifies inequality of economic outcomes. The major premise in the argument is that opportunity for advancement based on hard work is plentiful. From this premise, three deductions follow. First, individuals are personally responsible for their own fate; where one ends up in the distribution of rewards of the system depends on the effort one puts into acquiring and applying the necessary skills and attitudes, or depends on the native talent with which one begins. And, as a consequence, because individual outcomes are proportional to individual inputs (talent and effort), the resulting unequal distribution of economic rewards is, on the whole, equitable and fair.

Second, attitudes about inequality are shaped by a person's objective position in the stratification system. One's economic and social status provides a basis for assessing the relationship between self-interest and support or opposition to particular inequality-related policies. It also influences personal experiences of various kinds, such as affluence or poverty, or fair and unfair treatment, which may lead to generalizations about inequality and its bases and effects.

Third, attitudes about inequality are shaped by "social liberalism," or an acceptance of social and political equality between Whites or men and groups such as Blacks, Hispanics, or women, without the bases of economic inequality being called into question. These attitudes reflect recent social and political changes, such as the massive movement of women into the labor force, the dismantling of legalized racial segregation, and an awakening to the presence of poverty in the midst of affluence. Thus, in recent decades, specific attitudes and beliefs may have changed substantially in a liberal direction—for example, the right to an old age with a decent standard of living and basic medical care through Social Security and Medicare has become so widely accepted that the mention of benefit reductions elicits strong public protests. Also, recent survey data demonstrate marked reductions in traditional racial and gender prejudices (Miller, Miller, and Schneider, 1980).

But we also recognize limitations on these concepts. We know that the effects of political trends are multiple and are not exclusively limited to increases in social liberalism. Recent intergroup conflict over inequality, even as it has won increasing general acceptance of minority rights, has produced negative emotional responses based on race. This fact seems to have the greatest consequence around policies that benefit certain minorities. Kluegel and Smith (1986) maintain that it is the prevalence of these three factors that produces the inconsistency, fluctuation, and seeming contradiction in attitudes toward inequality and related policy found in the American public. Welfare programs are seen as unnecessary in a stratification system that people believe provides ample opportunity to better oneself by individual efforts. Even when such programs are approved, they are predicated on the assumption of individual responsibility and on the necessity of economic inequality.

To achieve public acceptance, inequality-related policy must accommodate both the liberal orientation that provides the impetus for the policy's existence and the conservative implications of the dominant ideology or culture. This need for accommodation is particularly strong because conservative and liberal beliefs and attitudes are often found within the same person. The absence of consistency at the level of the individual often proves to be a problem. Our liberal tendency may demand support for dependent children in poverty, but the dominant ideology distrusts the personal character of parents or welfare mothers because they abused their opportunities to succeed.

Thus, ambivalent orientations to inequality, produced by the coexistence of liberal and conservative beliefs and attitudes within the same person, do not necessarily require resolution toward consistency. People may allow their beliefs to remain inconsistent to reduce cognitive effort—the so-called "cognitive miser" rather than the "cognitive seeker" aspect to human personality (Taylor, 1981)—as long as important goals are not threatened by inconsistency. Social liberalism is not logically integrated with the dominant ideology. It is "layered on" and available to shape attitudes and behaviors in particular situations in ways that are potentially inconsistent with the consequences of the dominant ideology. Humans are seen as seekers of cognitive efficiency rather than complete consistency; they use heuristics, or short-cut methods, that efficiently produce reasonably good solutions to problems, rather than rationally considering all relevant evidence to achieve complete consistency in opinions and judgments (Nisbett and Ross, 1980).

JUSTICE: FROM VENGEANCE TO SOCIAL CONTRACT TO PASSION

The ideas of justice have been critical to philosophers throughout history. Plato, in *The Republic*, presents justice not only as an ideal, but also as a personal virtue and the central virtue that defines the good life.

And, although justice was, to Plato, an exercise of civic virtue—that is, concerned with the harmonious working of the community and the well-being of the state—he notes its frequent use as a synonym for vengeance and revenge. Both Plato and his student Aristotle rejected this idea; they emphasized instead that justice connotes fairness and equity.

Aristotle in *Nicomachean Ethics* distinguishes between justice as the whole of virtue and justice as a particular part of virtue. In the former sense, justice is understood as what is lawful, and the just person is equivalent to the moral person; in the latter sense, justice is understood as what is fair or equal, and the just person is one who takes his or her proper share. It is this definition of justice as a part of virtue that Aristotle further divides into distributive justice, corrective justice, and justice in exchange. Each of these forms of justice, Aristotle claims, can be understood as concerned with achieving equality. The concern of distributive justice is equality between equals; corrective justice is concerned with equality between punishment and crime; and justice in exchange is concerned with equality between whatever goods are exchanged. Aristotle's views of justice clarify the distinctions of justice without developing any particular conception of justice. The task of conceptualizing justice, then, has preoccupied the attention of philosophers and governments since Aristotle's time.

Thus, a liberal concept of justice can be distinguished from a libertarian concept of justice (in which justice is the ultimate moral ideal) and from a socialist concept of justice (in which social equality is the ultimate moral ideal) inasmuch as it attempts to combine economic and political liberty into one ultimate moral ideal. A liberal conception of justice is derived from the idea that rational agents would freely agree to abide by the requirements of justice—the social contract as a hypothetical agreement. The "contractual" approach to justice is derived from Kant, who claimed that a civil state ought to be founded on an original contract satisfying the requirement of freedom (the freedom of each person to seek happiness in whatever way he or she sees fit so long as that person does not infringe on the freedom of others), equality (the equal right of each person to coerce others to use their freedom in a way that harmonizes with one's own freedom), and independence (that independence of each citizen that is necessarily presupposed by the free agreement of the original contract [Sterba, 1980, p. 5]). The original contract does not have to exist as fact; laws of the civil state presuppose such a contract and allow citizens the right to reach any degree of rank earned through labor, industry, and good fortune.

Rawls (1971) argues that principles of justice are those principles that free and rational persons, concerned about advancing their own interests, would accept in an initial position of equality; this is Kant's "original position." Rawls adds his own condition—the "veil of ignorance," which deprives persons of information about their own particular characteristics or social positions so that they will not be biased in choosing principles of justice; behind the veil of ignorance, people do not "know" their race, sex, or socioeconomic status. The informational restriction helps ensure that the principles chosen will not place avoidable restrictions on the individual's freedom to choose or revise his or her life plan. The choice of the principles of justice, to Rawls, is construed as an ideal social contract that underscores those principles established by Kant: it becomes the rational collective choice of people, it emphasizes commitment and agreement on principles that can be enforced, and it emphasizes voluntary agreement that assumes the cooperation of all members of society.

In *A Theory of Justice*, Rawls (1971) pursues two main goals: to fix a small but powerful set of principles of justice that underlie and explain the considered moral judgments we make about particular actions, policies, laws, and institutions; and to offer a theory of justice that is deontological, meaning that under this theory, good and right are dependent and "right" supersedes the good (Rawls, 1971; Sterba, 1980; Buchanan, 1981). Rawls's principles of justice include two particular concepts of justice, liberty, and fair opportunity, and one general concept of justice, the differ-ence principle. According to Rawls, liberty means that each person is to have an equal right to the most extensive basic liberty compatible with a similar liberty for others; this is the principle of greatest equal liberty. Fair opportunity means that social and economic inequalities are to be arranged so that they are both reasonably expected to be to everybody's advantage and attached to positions and offices open to all; this is the principle of equality of fair opportunity. In Rawls's general concept of justice, the "difference principle," all social goods—liberty and opportunity, income and wealth, and the bases of self-respect—are to be distributed equally unless an unequal distribution of any or all of these goods is to the advantage of the least favored.

To Rawls, the primary subject of justice is the basic structure of society (the Constitution, private ownership of the means of production, competitive markets, and the monogamous family) because it exerts a pervasive and profound influence on an individual's life prospects. If the primary subject of justice is the basic structure, then the primary problem of justice is to formulate and justify a set of principles that a just, basic structure must satisfy. These principles specify how the basic structure is to distribute prospects of what Rawls calls primary goods (the basic liberties, power, authority, opportunities, income, and wealth). Although the first and second principles require equality, the difference principle allows inequalities as long as the total system of institutions maximizes the life prospects of the "worst-off."

Rational persons are characterized by Rawls as those desiring to maximize their share of primary goods, because these goods enable them to implement effectively the widest range of life plans and because at least some of the goods, such as freedom of speech and of conscience, facilitate the freedom to choose and revise one's life plan or conception of the good. The maximin argument, the rational strategy in the original position, allows choice over principles that "maximize the minimum share of primary goods one can receive as a member of society, and insure the greatest minimal share" (Rawls, 1971, p. 152). The principles of justice protect an individual's basic liberties and opportunities and ensure an adequate minimum of goods, such as wealth and income; thus, Rawls argues, the rational thing is to choose, rather than to gamble, with one's life prospects. In particular, Rawls contends that it would be irrational to reject his principles and allow one's life prospects to be determined by what would maximize utility, since utility maximization might allow severe deprivation or even slavery for some, as long as this contributed sufficiently to the welfare of others (Buchanan, 1981).

Rawls is criticized by many. Some criticize his conceptualization of hypothetical agreement and the original position (Dworkin, 1977). Others criticize him and claim that justice cannot be primary in the deontological sense and that we must venture beyond that idea to a conception of community that marks the limits of justice (Sandel, 1982). Others see Rawls as the personification of the theory of moral development from a justice/rights perspective (Gilligan, 1982). Perhaps Rawls's most deliberate critic is Solomon (1990), who raises the question of justice in all its historical forms (including justice as vengeance, as social justice concerned with the distribution of wealth, and as a virtue of institutions, not individuals). He is especially critical of theories of justice that emphasize rationality and right and denigrate emotion, compassion, caring, and moral sentiment. According to Solomon:

> For most of us, the inequities and inequalities of wealth and freedom are not as objectionable as the cavalier, uncaring, and insensitive attitudes toward the poor and the desperate and the needy on the part of those who have so much. Justice is up to all of us. It is a personal virtue, an open and receptive but (com)passionate mind toward the world (p. 28).

Solomon maintains that the American experience of freedom and prosperity should be accompanied by a passion for justice—justice that is personally felt.

> Justice is not a set of principles or policies; it is first of all a way of participating in the world, a way of being with other people, a set of feelings of affection and affiliations—not "reason"—that links us with other people. Without cultivation of these feelings, even the unattractive ones, the principles of justice are nothing but abstract ideals (p. 32).

Solomon rejects both the notion of human life as brutish and selfish and the moderating need for contractual obligation to force people to cooperate. The state of nature argument and the social contract argument juxtapose emotion and reason and allow people distance from "unnatural emotions." Solomon claims, rather, that justice is a passion to be cultivated, not an abstract set of principles to be formulated. The desire for justice begins with the promptings of some basic negative emotions such as envy, jealousy, or resentment, a sense of being personally cheated or neglected, or the desire to get even—but also, with basic feelings of sharing, compassion, sympathy, and generosity. Whatever one's principles of justice, they are meaningless without that fundamental human sense of caring and the ability to understand and personally care about the well-being of others (p. 33). Somewhere along the path, Solomon believes the Platonic and Aristotelian concept of justice as integrated with one's sense of the good life, and the premise that the most important element in moral education is the cultivation of the emotions, have been lost. We have overemphasized performance and the cognitive while neglecting the affective and the emotional. Justice requires knowledge and understanding, concern and curiosity—our natural reaction to and sentiments for homeless, needy, or desperate people arise out of their similarities to us, invoking our sympathies and the urgency to do something. This is the heart of justice. Plato would say that justice is not a social convention, but that which is found in the soul. According to Solomon, there has been almost universal agreement on certain points concerning justice: (1) justice is not a matter of "might makes right;" (2) irrelevant considerations—such as issues of gender or cultural background—should not enter into deliberations of justice; and (3) the most obvious way to reconcile the demand for equal treatment with attention to differences is to insist on equal standards. But Solomon argues that "whatever is relevant to the evaluation in question becomes awkward when we try to apply the same criterion to everyone (because these standards include many choices as criteria, including equality, just reward of effort or performance, ability, need, market value, rights, the public good, duties and responsibilities, risk and uncertainty, seniority, loyalty, moral virtue, and tradition). Therefore, we must know which standards to use. His point is that there is no possible formula and no theory that facilitates justice when there are so many standards and when the dimensions of justice are based solely on reason and hypothetical agreement. To Solomon, justice is contextual and virtually always involves contraditions and conflict.

It is not that there is no justice, but that we look for it in the wrong places. Justice is to be found in our sense that there are wrongs to be righted; justice is that vital sense of engagement in the world in which the dimensions of justice coalesce in judgments based not on rational formula or theory but on experience and emotion—on the moral sentiments (pp. 173-176).

CULTURE

Sathe (1983) identified almost 200 different definitions of culture. Definitions of culture range from those applied to organizations, in which culture is defined as a phenomenon or property of a formalized organization, to those applied to society, in which culture is a system of collectively accepted meanings that operate for a given group at a given time and interpret a group's situation to its members.

Pettigrew (1979) views culture as an amalgam of beliefs, ideology, language, ritual, and myth. Mitroff and Kilmann (1984) define culture as a set of shared philosophies, ideologies, values, beliefs, expectations, attitudes, assumptions, and norms that are learned by living in and becoming a part of a specific organization. Sathe (1983) described culture as a set of important understandings, often unstated, that members of a community share. Albrecht (1987) sees culture as a pattern of accepted habits, values, and rules—most of which are so deeply internalized that they are unconscious or semiconscious. Deal and Kennedy (1983) see culture as a core set of assumptions, understandings, and implicit rules that govern day-to-day behavior in the workplace. Finally, Jelinek, Smircich, and Hirsch (1983) stress that culture is both product and process, the shaper of human interaction and the outcome of it, continually created and recreated by people's ongoing interactions.

In higher education, studies of culture reveal similar analyses (Biggerstaff, 1990), with emphasis placed on culture as a metaphor or simile. A college's culture is a "saga;" it evolves out of a set of beliefs and values tied together in the form of a story that chronicles an institution's history (Clark, 1972). As an "interconnected web," a college's culture can only be understood by looking beyond structure and natural law and into individual interpretations of interconnections (Tierney, 1988). And as an "invisible tapestry of windows," colleges are interpreted as places where institutional saga, heroes, symbols, and rituals serve as "windows" on academic culture (Masland, 1985).

It is Schein (1985b), however, who provides the most comprehensive definition of organizational culture. According to Schein, culture is a pattern of basic assumptions that are invented, discovered, or developed by a given group as it learns to cope with its problems of external adaptation and internal integration. This pattern has worked well enough to be considered valid and, therefore, to be taught to new members as the correct way to perceive, think, and feel in relation to those problems (p. 9). Kuh and Whitt (1988) are also responsible for a comprehensive and operative definition of culture as it applies to an academic setting. They believe culture is "the collective, mutually shaping patterns of norms, values, practices, beliefs, and assumptions that guide the behavior of individuals and groups in an institute of higher education and provide a frame of reference within which to interpret the meaning of events and actions on and off campus" (pp. 12-13).

PROPERTIES OF CULTURE: UNIQUENESS, ADAPTATION, STRENGTH, AND HEALTH

The nature of society is to distinguish itself—to be unique—and to establish internally and externally understood boundaries. Kuh and Whitt (1988) see this property of culture in an institutional setting as the development and refinement of an institutional mission that represents a conscious effort to establish an identity apart from that of any similar institution. Moreover, culture is constantly evolving through the interaction and socialization of individuals to their particular environment (Jelinek, Smircich, and Hirsch, 1983). Culture has a naturalistic, adaptive tendency to organize itself into what Smircich (1983) calls an unconscious infrastructure or paradigm—over time, the paradigm becomes a framework for creating additional meaning and for further understanding behavior within particular frames of reference. Adaptive quality varies from institution to institution, in a continuum ranging from highly fluid to highly static. Static cultures resist change, fix uniform standards of behavior, maintain membership, simplify values, and clearly define norms (Albrecht, 1987). More fluid cultures are receptive to change and frequently modify internal structures, change their membership, and accommodate conflicting norms and values.

Organizations are characterized by the relative strength or weakness of their culture. Generally, the greater the number and power of shared assumptions, beliefs, and values, the stronger the culture. Moreover, strong cultures are healthier, or better identified, than weak ones. Gregory (1983) points out, for example, that ethnocentrism—the tendency to evaluate phenomena from a singular cultural position—can lead to internal conflict and a de-emphasis on innovation. Furthermore, he contends that complex organizations are more appropriately viewed as heterogeneous, cross-cultural contexts that change over time rather than as stable, homogeneous cultures. Given this value for distinction of individuals and groups within organizations, the strength and health of a culture need not necessarily imply that the "native view" must be socialized to conform to the dominant belief system. Rather, accommodation of variant assumptions has the potential for adding desirable dimensions to a healthy organization. Acceptance of diversity can prevent stagnation and rigidity in the face of imminent change.

LEVELS OF CULTURE: ARTIFACTS, VALUES, AND ASSUMPTIONS

Discerning levels of culture aids in understanding how culture influences collective perceptions and behaviors. According to Schein (1985b), there are three levels of culture that are important in helping leaders achieve high levels of success in integration and adaptation in their institutions: artifacts, values, and assumptions.

Artifacts are the visible representations of culture and include sagas, myths, and stories; rituals, rites, and ceremonies; norms, rules, procedures, and language. Sagas are generally factual accounts of an organization's or leader's past that relate group or leader accomplishments in heroic fashion, binding them to beliefs or actions (Masland, 1985). Myths are usually fabricated illusions of events that never really occurred; they serve to explain origins or transformations of principles, structures, or processes (Kuh and Whitt, 1988). Norms are unwritten rules that guide behavior and elaborate on an organization's values and beliefs by clarifying what is expected of members. They cause conformity to social, not objective, reality (Mitroff and Kilmann, 1984). The stronger the consensus around acceptable behavior, the greater the sanctions against those who violate norms. Rituals, rites, and ceremonies are also important artifacts of culture. Finally, language systems provide conceptual communication symbols and a structure for internal integration of artifacts.

Values reveal how people explain and rationalize what they say and do as a group. Values justify behaviors, help people make sense of their artifacts, and may link artifacts and assumptions (Schein, 1985b). Rokeach (1968) believes that a value is a single belief that transcendentally guides actions and judgments across specific objects and situations and beyond immediate goals to more ultimate end-states of existence. Goodstein (1983) points out that organizational values become modal (a logical structure) when they are espoused by most members as appropriate to a given situation and are promulgated as truth. Organizational members generally have a set of beliefs about what constitutes appropriate behavior or inappropriate behavior and generally agree that these beliefs can be ordered in importance. Schein points out, however, that a sense of group value does not evolve until individuals have tested and debated their personal values in a situation that has resulted in a collectively shared solution to a problem. When this happens, values become part of an organization's ideology and philosophy. Values are yardsticks for guiding actions, developing attitudes, justifying behavior, and judging others.

Values are critical to organizational and personal functioning, and there are various dimensions by which values can be differentiated (varying degrees of awareness of values, transience or permanence of values, or the generalizability or specificity of values). Because values are multidimensional, they may demonstrate congruity or conflict. Clark (1983) suggests that value conflicts are generally more prevalent in academic organizations than in corporations largely because belief systems in academia exist at various levels—the enterprise itself, the academic profession, and the individual discipline. The degree to which organizational members hold congruent or conflicting values about the nature of education in general, and about an institution or discipline in particular, can have a profound bearing on the success of efforts to develop a common organizational culture. When subcultures evolve at any of these levels, the dominant culture is threatened. The degree of congruity or conflict around specific values often determines the strength of an organization's value system and its power to socialize members in a common direction.

As values become entrenched as preferential ways of doing things, they begin to form patterns that govern attitudes and behaviors. Congruence of values leads to consistent decision making and problem solving. The more consistency, the more values become unconsciously accepted and taken for granted. This transformation process is a lengthy one and eventually leads to the creation of assumptions. Assumptions are the deepest level of cultural values; because they are taken for granted, seldom articulated, and nearly impossible to identify, they become ultimate and nondebatable. Argyris and Schon (1974) call them "theories in use." They are internalized beliefs and values. Because of their nature, assumptions often create problems for organizations. Sathe (1985) and Schein (1985b) concur that conflict arises when assumptions held by one individual or group do not conform with the assumptions held by the culture in general. These conflicts are unresolvable without an understanding of organizational assumptions, which Schein deciphered in a comparative study of cultures in the southwest United States in 1961. He claimed that cultural paradigms form around assumptions that raise epistemological questions, such as the nature of man, of reality and truth, and of human activity and human relationships. Schein believes that answers to these questions reveal the underlying assumptions of culture. A culture can measure its strength to the extent that these assumptions appear to be compatible and consistent. Organizations that have conflicting assumptions in any of these categories are weak or are still forming.

Cultural formation and development is built on the accumulation of artifacts, values, and assumptions that occur over long periods of time and result in collective experiences or socialization processes that embed and transmit cultural experiences to future generations. External and internal issues influence the formation and development of culture. External issues are those that focus on the environment and the ability of both the leader and constituent groups to survive within it. External adaptation (for example, to national, regional, local, and professional cultures) involves creating the core mission, achieving consensus around values and goals, arriving at agreement around measurements for success, and evolving adaptive strategies for necessary change. As external issues are confronted and understood, so must issues of internal integration be addressed. Internal integration involves the sense of bonding and cohesion of group behavior; this involves defining group language and boundaries, establishing power bases, determining rules for intimacy, formulating criteria for rewards and punishment, and creating ideologies (Schein, 1985b). Nadler and Tushman (1988) enumerate four critical internal factors affecting organizational culture: leadership behavior; strategic definition; structure; and human resource systems. Thus, leaders are said to make sense of organizational complexity and then provide direction for its membership.

Many researchers see the development of culture centered almost exclusively around "influential" people—those who shape culture by virtue of their authority, power, or role. But others look to "conditions" affecting the development of culture: confrontation, workability, feasibility, and positive value orientations; stability of membership; isolation from alternative belief systems; and opportunities for interaction across divergent boundaries, establishing a world view.

SOCIALIZATION PROCESSES

Pascale (1985) explains that organizations embody paradoxical orientations toward individuals and groups. On the one hand, the American view of the world is "intellectually and culturally opposed to the manipulation of individuals for organizational purposes" (p. 28); and on the other hand, organizations expect social uniformity for effective performance. In academic institutions, the likelihood is that subcultures will arise and compete with the dominant culture; thus, the challenge for organizations is to reconcile the dominant culture with the subculture through socialization around common orientations with the need for individual expression. Socialization becomes the process for informing and educating members of an organization; it distinguishes between conformity and autonomy, and it provides a rationale to encourage both. If organizations understand that the individual has critical needs in a social context—including inclusion and identity, control and influence, and acceptance and intimacy (Schein, 1985b)—they must demonstrate interest in satisfying these needs to a desirable degree before individuals can, in turn, support the organization. Individuals must be motivated to support the organization; if they are not, the organization will not thrive. The more an organization rewards individuals in ways that meet the expectancy requirements of primary individual needs, the greater the likelihood that members will be inclined toward group cohesion (Bass, 1983). Individual emotions, cognitions, wants, and needs must be satisfied, accommodated, and allowed expression for social unity and growth of culture. But an organization must also serve the internal integration needs of its various groups. As groups seek solutions to problems, catalytic "marker events" or critical incidents (Schein, 1985b; Flanagan, 1954) frequently precipitate the growth and development of common understandings and norms. These in turn lead to participative problem solving as the cycle begins again, accumulating new artifacts, values, and assumptions. Socialization is a key process in the legitimization of culture. It is at this level of organization, where external and internal adaptations are made, that leadership matters most.

LEADERS AND CULTURE

Burns (1978) would say that leadership can transform an organization. Pfeffer (1981) claims that leaders are those who capture group history and bring symbolic and actual meaning to establish common frames of reference and shared understanding. Often, conflicts between incoming and current members of organizations cause dysfunction around the idea of adaptive culture and socialization. When this occurs, unfreezing, changing, and refreezing of attitudes, values, and behaviors are required (Lewin, 1951). Disengagement from pre-existing attachments and redirection of belief systems, time, and commitment are requisites for adaptation to a "new" organizational culture. If culture is to stabilize an organization's external and internal environments, then transmission of culture to the organization's members must occur. Leaders have a responsibility to facilitate this stabilization. The imperative focus of their responsibility is to their followers. To some degree, organizational culture can be created, influenced, and even transformed by culturally sensitive leaders. Peters and Waterman (1982) demonstrate that it is not incongruous that naturalistic cultural development is subject to intervention and redirection under certain conditions. They postulate that organizations are dependent on excellent leadership for effectiveness; and thus, leaders are capable of manipulating, influencing, and embedding culture.

The literature abounds with discussions of the role and importance of the situational/contingency/transformational leader whose vision of an institution or organization is linked to task, action, role expectation, environment, and the readiness and willingness of followers to be motivated in ways that are consistent with the demands of all environments. Framed within the definition of this type of leadership is the assumption that leaders alter their behavior to fit the situation. For example, in the life-cycle theory of leadership (Hersey and Blanchard, 1972), consideration is given to the level of maturity of the followers, such that the relevant degree of appropriate task-oriented or relationship-oriented leader behavior will apply. The situational variable of leadership focuses on follower readiness, development, or maturity. The leader's actions, therefore, are proscribed by followers and may change according to whether the situation demands attention to task and theory, or relationships. *Teaching as Leading* (Baker, Roueche, and Gillett-Karam, 1990) uses both path-goal theory (House and Mitchell, 1971) and life-cycle theory to explain the special relationships and environment of the classroom interaction between teacher and students. On the one hand, the teacher as leader influences the path to the educational goal; on the other, the teacher/leader is influenced by the readiness and maturity of the student in regard to the level of independence-dependence, passivity-activity, task-relationship orientations that they, as situational teacher/leaders, must pursue to meet students' needs.

To exchange the follower's role with the cultural role is not a perfect solution, but life-cycle theory can be adapted to organizational culture largely because it attends to developmental aspects and properties. Organizational cultures can be perceived according to their level of maturity, and leadership behavior can be modified appropriately. Moreover, cultural evolution, growth, and transformation require leaders who understand such cycles and who can empower organizational members to work with environmental change or ambiguity. Bass (1985) and Burns (1978) call these leaders transformational. These are the leaders who reach to the "nature" of their followers to arouse and satisfy higher-order needs. Roueche, Baker, and Rose (1989), in a study of transformational leadership among American community college presidents, found that such leaders have five basic orientations around vision, people, motivation, empowerment, and values. Excellent community college leaders envision and plan for the growth of a college culture; they influence and are influenced by their institutional members; they value, respect, and reward their followers as individuals; they model leaderly behavior and seek to empower others; and they demonstrate strong personal values and honor the intellectual and individual development of others.

Leaders have been studied because of the role they play in creating organizations. "Founders" (Schein, 1983) envision and communicate assumptions as originators of organizations; depending on the extent to which others share their vision and assumptions, these leaders are thought to, at least, initiate organizational culture. The growth and management of this culture is critical; transformational leaders must fully engage and empower followers to pursue the goals of the organization. Schein (1985a) believes that founders have fairly stable cultures, but he also asserts that as organizations become more complex and differentiated, subcultures may exert conflicting forces on the dominant culture. Under these conditions, the role of the founder is to accommodate for diversity and to integrate new patterns into the fabric of the organizational culture. Failure of the leader to do so leads to organizational dysfunction—momentum, cohesiveness, and natural adaptive growth are stymied as crises in values and conflicts over basic assumptions occur. Peters and Waterman (1982) noted that excellent companies with strong cultures are characterized by flexibility and homogeneity, while paradoxically allowing heterogeneous features such as openness, tolerance for failure, and concern for individuals. They foster creativity and innovation, and they thrive on chaos!

However, not all leaders survive periods of turbulence and change—often leaders are replaced during such times. Leadership succession becomes a triggering mechanism for cultural adaptation of organizations as the "transitional" leader modifies the culture and reinstitutes a different set of values and behaviors. Such leaders are critically challenged to consider the uniqueness of their situations (including those conditions that are most resistant to change) and to commit to an alternative vision for the future. Moreover, they must mobilize follower commitment, trust, and acceptance.

Tichy and Devanna (1986) and Schein (1985a) propose guidelines for transforming an organizational culture. Where Tichy and Devanna concentrate on identifying the "gate keepers" of the current culture, Schein focuses on stages of the organizational life cycle (early growth, midlife, maturity) and the greater difficulties encountered among mature systems. Thus, the leader is called on to become teacher and coach; reducing barriers to successful goal achievement is the critical change the teacher as leader makes when confronting unsuccessful classroom or critical student incidents—the reaction is to alter the dominant behavior almost immediately and confront and reduce obstacles that prevent student development. So, too, does the transformational leader, and, indeed, the transitional leader needs to provide access and retraining for cultural change; new artifacts, values, and assumptions become the tools of this practitioner. Thus, leadership may be measured for its products and its processes: It can be symbolic, as leaders manipulate cultural artifacts so they are commonly understood and accepted among the followers.

PLURALISM

Robert Dahl, the political scientist whose name is irrevocably linked with the concept of pluralism and democracy, maintains that democratic theory is transformational. Historically, the first transformation came from the Greek ideal of democracy and the city-state—from the idea and practice of rule by the few to the idea and practice of rule by the many. From the city-state to the nation-state, the ideas of democracy flourished as a second transformation of democracy was embedded into the principles and ideals of the modern nation-state. It is this idea of democracy that is today universally popular but not universally understood.

Dahl's concept of democracy takes into account both adversarial and sympathetic criticisms of democracy. Dahl contends that the advocates of democratic theory must also be aware of the "shadow theory of democracy" (Dahl, 1989, p. 3). Critical and key problems are concealed in the explicit theories of democracy, Dahl maintains, which can be explained by illustrating the use of the word *demokratia*. Claims can be made concerning the self-evidency of this word, which means rule by the people (*demos* means people, and *kratia* means rule or authority). But we are immediately confronted by questions, such as who ought to make up the people and what does it mean for them to rule? In the city-state the obvious answer was the Athenian or the Spartan; but in the nation-state the answer is not so obvious or simple. Are people in local communities of nation-states entitled to self-government? Does government presuppose consent or consensus? Is there not ambiguity in the

40

issue of "who are the people who actually rule?" History, of course, demonstrates that in both the city-state and the nation-state the *demos* are a small minority of the adult population; since ancient times, some persons have been excluded as unqualified. Exclusions invariably seem to be justified on the grounds that the *demos* include everyone qualified to participate in ruling; the hidden assumption is that only some people are competent to rule. Thus, what we see is more of a guardianship of the people, and whereas democracy meant at one time a small, intimate, participatory city-state, today it is gigantic, impersonal, and indirect.

Dahl's notion is, in fact, that democracy is today a unique process of making collective and binding decisions that are not exclusionary. We offer the following criteria, or standards, to express the assumptions of modern democratic theory.

Effective Participation: Citizens ought to have an adequate and equal opportunity for expressing their preferences as to the final outcome. They must have adequate and equal opportunities for placing questions on the agenda and for endorsing one outcome rather than another.

Equality at the Decisive Stage: Each citizen must be ensured an equal opportunity to express a choice that will be counted as equal in weight to the choice expressed by any other citizen. In determining outcomes, these and only these choices must be taken into account.

Enlightened Understanding: To know what they want, or to know what is best, the people must be enlightened. Each citizen ought to have adequate and equal opportunities for discovering and validating (within the time permitted by the need for a decision) the choice on the matter to be decided that would best serve the citizen's interests.

Control of the Agenda: The people must have the exclusive opportunity to decide how matters are to be placed on the agenda for decision through the democratic process. Citizens have the final say; they are sovereign.

Citizenship and Inclusion: The *demos* should include all adults subject to the binding collective decisions of the association; no one subject to the rules of the *demos* should be excluded.

Thus, the ideas and practices of democracy are justified by certain values, including human freedom, human development, and the protection and advancement of shared human interests. But democracy also presupposes equality, the intrinsic moral equality of all persons, the quality expressed by the presumption that adult persons are entitled to personal autonomy in determining what is best for themselves, and political equality among citizens. Thus, an association between democracy and equality leads to a powerful moral conclusion: If freedom, self-development, and the advancement of shared interests are good ends, and if persons are intrinsically equal in their moral worth, then opportunities for attaining these goods should be distributed equally to all persons. The democratic process is attached to historical conditions and historically conditioned human beings. Its possibilities and its limits are highly dependent on existing and emergent social structures and consciousness. And because the democratic vision is so daring in its promise, it forever invites us to look beyond and to break through the existing limits of structures and consciousness—to continue its transformations.

CONCLUSION

In each of the discussions of equality, justice, culture, and pluralism, the frameworks for current and critical thinking about these topics have been explored and presented to help us understand the nature of diversity and cultural pluralism. There are, of course, lessons to be learned from these discussions that affect the issue of representation of women and minorities in community colleges across the nation.

Community colleges committed to the objectives of egalitarianism and opportunity in education must measure and evaluate these ideas for themselves and determine the bases for planning and strategies for implementing inclusionary practices on their campuses. Such colleges, in their efforts to make administration, faculty, and students aware of issues of diversity and cultural pluralism, may use these concepts to begin discussions of the meaning of equality, justice, and campus culture.

Community colleges that strive to meet the demands of challenging external and internal situations can, in the words of Solomon (1990), take pride in their "passion for justice." But community colleges and their various constituencies must also realize the challenges of cultural differences, cultural stagnation, and cultural development in their attempt to embed multiculturalism in their own campuses.

CHAPTER THREE

&

WOMEN: EXPRESSION AND EXPERIENCE IN ACADEMIC LITERATURE

&

Herodotus was perhaps the first to point out that history is an inclusive study of great men—the stories of conquerers and heroes—not a reflection of common men. Later, anthropologists and educators pointed out the need to study others, or the "ethnoi." From this beginning, in the nineteenth century, researchers turned to examining and studying the masses, common men and women. Sociological researchers Malinowski, Mead, and Pestalozzi were remarkable, because they were involved in lifetime research that celebrated the lives and achievements of "other" cultures and classes. In his classic pedagogical work, *Leonard and Gertrude*, Pestalozzi (1903) presents Gertrude as the model of the good educator who understands how to establish schools in connection with the life of the home. Gertrude is presented as an example on which to base the principles of education; her character and activities set the example for a new order (Martin, 1982). But what is perhaps most remarkable about Pestalozzi's work is that it marks a break with traditional views of women by educators. In Rousseau's work *Emile*, Sophie, the female counterpart to the hero, is presented as the prototypic woman who makes no contribution to education; her experiences are rejected as aberrant compared to the model behavior of Emile, and therefore as deficient in the educational realm.

This dichotomy of thinking that opposes Gertrude and Sophie is significant and symbolic. It is significant because it mirrors the expression and experience of literature and research regarding women and minorities in America. And it is symbolic because this dichotomy represents an example of the critical thinking about women in education for hundreds of years. For the most part, until the mid-1960s, standard educational theory, practice, and future planning excluded women and minorities—rarely did we see a "Gertrude" emerge who personified the unique needs and contributions of these two groups. In the pages that follow, the concepts of reductionism, deficit models, and similar phenomena will be acknowledged and reported as illustrative of the lack of insight that we, as a society and as researchers, have demonstrated regarding these groups. These discussions have particular relevance to the community college, which has been the single greatest recipient of these populations in higher education, primarily because the community college's major *raison d'etre* has been pluralism and egalitarianism.

In the following pages, the expressions (research, history, prevailing views) and experiences (documentation, reports, new research, studies) will be presented. We begin with the literature and research about women; these data are presented as philosophical and methodological inquiry. In the next chapter, we examine the prevailing views and historical context of research about minorities. Although the two chapters are separated, the issues surrounding the status of research and knowledge about women and minorities are similar. In both cases, research has tended to treat each group as aberrant or deficient. Much of what we purport to know, we know about the dominant White, male culture; much of what we need to know about women and minorities is emerging in a climate that is now anxious to learn about these groups and their contributions to society.

RESEARCH AND WOMEN'S STUDIES

Kanter (1977), in *Men and Women of the Corporation*, examined how consciousness and behavior are formed by the positions people hold in organizations and demonstrated that both men and women are the products of the circumstances that define and set their role-positions. Kanter recognized that most organizational studies discussing women were reductionist: Women were seen as different, inexact, or deficient in the characteristics that described leaders and managers of the corporation. Her inquiry discusses how forms of work organization, and the conceptions of roles and distributions of people within them, shape behavioral outcomes. Kanter believes we have gotten "hooked" on the individual model:

> Something has been holding women back (occupational segregation). That something was usually assumed to be located in the differences between men and women as individuals: their training for different worlds; the nature of sexual relationships, which make women unable to compete with men and men unable to aggress against women; the "tracks" they were put on in school or at play; and even, in the most biologically reductionist version of the argument, "natural" dispositions of the sexes. Conclusions like these have become standard explanations for familiar statistics about discrimination. They form the basis for the "individual" model of work behavior. Whether one leans toward the more social or the more biological side of the argument, both add up to an assumption that the factors producing inequities at work are somehow carried inside the individual person (p. 261).

The thrust of Kanter's book is to present an alternative to the individual model. Kanter has demonstrated that what appear to be "sex differences" in work behaviors are really responses to structural conditions (promotion rates, ladder steps, career paths, and individual prospects). Individual models absolve the system of responsibility; they do not emphasize the joint interests of all those in the organization. Attention to these issues would require organizations—not people—to change. Kanter states, "If we understand more fully the structural conditions that impact on human behavior in organizations, we can then choose more appropriate policies and programs to improve the quality of worklife and promote equal opportunity" (p. 264).

Kanter is supported by Burns (1978), who states:

> In some cultures women are cut off from power positions as well as from the stepping stones and access routes that reach toward leadership. This leadership bias persists despite the political influence of the likes of Eleanor Roosevelt, Golda Meir, Indira Gandhi, or Margaret Thatcher. The male bias is

reflected in the false conception of leadership as mere command or control. As leadership comes properly to be seen as a process of leaders engaging and mobilizing the human needs and aspirations of followers, women will be more readily recognized as leaders and men will change their own leadership styles (p. 50).

Kanter and Burns, therefore, in both substance and theory are able to focus on culture, socialization, and psychological perceptions of reality that account for differences between the sexes, not on specific gender differences that allegedly account for the roles of both women and men in society. But the inquiry and generalizations that are reflected in Kanter's work are unique; they do not reflect contemporary biases and deficit theories about women. Such biases and theories can be traced back to the philosophical foundations of society.

THE PHILOSOPHERS SET THE STAGE

Philosophers since ancient times have been in conflict over the role of women in society and in the world. Gender, seen as a reason for role differentiation, was also examined for "place-in-the-world" status. Theorists argued over the relevance of women in their theories of knowledge. When they asked, "How do we know?" their "we" was almost always the male "we;" the omission of women was deliberate.

The two most important philosophers of the ancient world, Plato and Aristotle, viewed women from totally different perspectives. Plato saw his wise leader as male or female and offered both equal educational opportunities to become a philosopher king or a philosopher queen. Virtue, to Plato, was not dependent on sex but on knowledge. To examine one's life, to become just, and to do so through education were all the prescriptions either men or women needed to attain the position of leader.

While Plato sought transcendence of the soul, be it male or female, Aristotle was contemptuous of the female and questioned whether women had souls. French (1985) states that the strongest indication that there was a matriarchal tradition in ancient Greece seems to be the negative evidence of the extreme rage and vituperation directed at women by generations of Greek writers, including Aristotle (p. 111). Aristotle's view of women was based on his theory of the animal nature of man. Because a woman had less "vital heat" than a man, she was seen as a deficient model of the animal world. Researchers have labeled this the "nature" argument about women; it is based in Aristotle's mistaken notion that women were biologically inferior beings. Aristotle stated, "We should look on the female as being, as it were, a deformity, though one which occurs in the ordinary course of nature" (Peck, 1953, p. 37).

Freud concurred with Aristotle, while borrowing liberally from Plato in other matters, by viewing females as defective males (Hunter College Women's Studies Collective, 1983, p. 63). The biological factor of women's differences has been seen as critical by many thinkers throughout history, and they are too numerous to mention here. The importance of this factor is that biological data are used to draw conclusions of an evaluative kind about women. Aristotle believed that the function of a woman was to bear children, whereas the function of a man was rational activity. He had a hierarchical view of human society; he thought it right and proper for men to rule over women. To Aristotle, women, slaves, and children lacked the ability to deliberate.

We now recognize such "theories" of intelligence or reasoning ability that are based on simplistic biological comparisons to be false. But for much of the subsequent history from Aristotle's time, these views persisted and were solidified. Holmstrom (1986) comments, "A distinct woman's nature contains a sex bias that takes man as the norm and women as 'the other' to use de Beauvoir's term; such theories are pseudo-scientific rationalizations of cultural prejudices" (p. 51).

Even from the spiritual realm of the Christian church, views about women reflected the Aristotelian view. The church hierarchy was dependent on a male presence that taught that women were helpmates to men, as indicated by their essential nature. Moreover, the church taught parables about the nature of women, such as the story of Eve, who was held up as the agent bringing original sin to the world. Finally, the church maintained that women lacked the intellectual commitment necessary for true faith. These ideas were refined and continued throughout the sixteenth century. Daly (1973) suggests that the church's view of the animal nature of woman was critical to the philosophies that would develop during the Enlightenment, noting, "It seems strange that even the church, whose major objective was the spiritual guidance of humankind, was attuned to the more physical aspect of women's nature" (p. 363). By the seventeenth and eighteenth centuries, the Enlightenment philosophers, such as Locke, Hobbes, Montesquieu, Rousseau, and Hume, deliberately rejected notions of original sin and of the innate inferiority of some men compared with others. They emphasized instead the essential equality of mankind and the importance of liberty and freedom. This liberal tradition provided the foundation for the development of the United States of America (Dahl, 1966). And, although the idea applies to the notion of the ideal democratic society and government, it does not apply equally to the notion of the economic activity of society. Liberalism did not require economic institutions to be democratic. And for some groups of people living in the United States, liberalism did not require freedom and the guarantees of a government responsive to their needs. These groups included slaves, women, and Native Americans. They could not vote. They could not own property. They were regarded as silent by those with hegemony. Again, even in the liberal tradition the philosophers were divided.

Rousseau, for example, openly argued that the liberal principles of the Enlightenment must not be applied to women. Women, he said, must learn to submit to man's will and find happiness in doing so. Rousseau used Aristotle's "nature" argument to demonstrate that women must be obedient to men (Okin, 1979). Because Rousseau considered freedom the essence of being human, he viewed women as less than fully human. He argued that women should disappear from public life and live within the four walls of their homes. While Rousseau was expounding these ideas, Mary Wollstonecraft began her written attack on his work, claiming that women ought to have education; she argued that the principles of freedom and equality were indeed as valid for women as for men. Wollstonecraft's *The Vindication of the Rights of Women*, written in 1792, was, however, an anomaly in her time. But the questions she raised and the solutions she offered led to the inquiry by and liberation of women like Abigail Adams and Harriet Taylor Mills.

Solomon (1985) writes that most women in colonial America were expected to know their place and to accept their husband's authority over them. But these ideas, evoked by Rousseau, were challenged by Locke. Locke believed that the infant mind was like an empty slate—ideas and sensations from the environment were impressed on it, thus molding the individual's personality. In his thinking, there was no difference in intelligence based on gender. Solomon suggests that this notion had a huge psychological impact on the treatment of women as "Locke's ideas began slowly to undermine the assumption of the immutability of female inferiority" (Solomon, 1985, p. 5).

It is Hume, however, who brought the most balanced treatment of moral theory to the age of philosophical "enlightenment." Hume made morality a matter of cultivating the character traits that give a person inward peace of mind and consciousness of integrity (Millar, 1985). Hume saw human reason as authored by self-interest, instrumental reason, and frivolous factors, including historical chance, custom, and tradition. Hume emphasized the role of feeling in moral judgment. Agreeing with the rationalists that when we use our reason we appeal to universal rules, he nevertheless pointed out that there are many universal rules of morality. He claimed that morality rests ultimately on sentiment, on a special motivating feeling we come to have once we have exercised our capacity for sympathy with others' feelings. We also learn to overcome emotional conflicts that arise when the wants of others and of the individual clash. Morality is the outcome of a search for ways of eliminating contradictions in the "passions" of sympathetic persons who are aware of both their own and others' desires and needs (Baier, 1987). To Hume, the human heart, as well as human reason, is needed for the understanding of morality.

Modern theorists and philosophers (Baier, 1987; Gilligan, 1982) would agree that the human heart's responses are to particular persons, not to universal and abstract principles of justice. When Hume lists the natural moral virtues, his favorite example is parental love and solicitude. The good person, the possessor of the natural virtues, is the one who is a safe companion, an easy friend, a gentle master (Selby-Bigge and Nidditch, 1978). The virtues that he lists are contained in relationships and in social contexts, such as the ability to earn and keep the trust of others. In his attention to interpersonal relations, Hume's analysis of social cooperation starts with the cooperation of the family. The most indissoluble bond in nature, he claims, is the love of parents for their children: it is intimate, it is unchosen, and it is between unequals.

Although Hume did not specifically renounce bias among the philosophers of his time, he has been considered by some as the "woman's moral theorist," specifically because his theory supports Gilligan's research. Baier (1987) suggests that "to Hume, moral theory is not a matter of obedience to universal law, but of cultivating proper character traits" (p. 37). Those traits he considered most important were those concerning relations with others; family, sentiment, sympathy, and the recognition of others are all elements of his theory of moral development. For Hume and for Gilligan, moral development must occur through actual activity and correction of the sentiments.

After Hume, other thinkers also advocated rights and freedom for women as well as men. Mill, in the eighteenth century, argued that equal rights and equal opportunities should be extended to women and that women should be able to own property, to vote, to be educated, and to enter the professions (Hunter College Women's Studies Collective, 1983). But Mill's views ran counter to those of Comte, who reasserted the biological inferiority of women to men. As the "father of sociology," Comte asserted that the female sex was formed for a state of essential childhood (Okin, 1979).

MORAL PHILOSOPHY AND PSYCHOLOGY: IN A DIFFERENT VOICE

In modern philosophy, psychology, and the law, the theory of moral development is the heir to the ongoing dichotomy of opinions and research concerning women and men. Modern theorists are still very interested in morality and virtues. Erikson (1950), Gilligan (1982), Kohlberg (1971), Perry (1970), Piaget (1965), and Rawls (1971) are all interested in the development of morality in humans. But it is from the theories of Kohlberg and Gilligan that the most controversial modern debate stems. Kohlberg (1981) maintains that moral development (as a premise from the justice tradition of Locke, Kant, and Rawls in which social contract theory and personal liberty are linked so that an individual has personal and moral autonomy) involves a six-stage process divided into three two-stage levels. At the preconventional level (stage one), people defer to authority; but as they learn to satisfy their own needs and consider the needs of others, they enter stage two. At this point individuals move to the conventional level, in which they seek others' approval by conforming to stereotypical roles (stage three). Later, this stage is augmented by a sense of the value of maintaining the social order and of the contribution of dutiful conduct to that order (stage four). Finally, individuals obtain the postconventional level: Here they associate morality with rights and standards endorsed by society as a whole (stage five), but ultimately, they go on to think in terms of self-chosen, yet universal, principles of justice (stage six). Kohlberg argues that women are unable to advance much past the fourth stage of moral development, advancing the idea that moral progress relates to the justice tradition of the ideal, rational person.

Gilligan (1982, 1987) takes issue with this single-track conception of moral development and argues that the perspective of caring that many women possess provides an alternative course of development leading to equally adequate moral reflection. Gilligan, in several studies, provides empirical data concerning the moral decision-making strategies of women. Her results led her to conclude that the justice perspective fails to capture the import of concerns expressed by women, the decision-making strategies used by women, and the course of women's distinctive moral development.

Instead of the hierarchical ordering of values characteristic of the justice perspective, Gilligan's female respondents describe a "network of connection, a web of relationships that is sustained by a process of communication" (1982, p. 33). For these women, moral problems do not result from a conflict of rights to be adjudicated by ranking values. Rather, moral problems are embedded in a contextual frame that eludes abstract, deductive reasoning. The traditional perspective Kohlberg adopts portrays the responses of women as deficiencies in moral capabilities. Against this view, Gilligan argues that the morality of many women is distinct from that of men but, nevertheless, is of commensurate worth. The process of moral development that Gilligan has discovered comprises a six-stage series marked by three levels of development. At the preconventional level, the orientation is toward personal survival. The first stage is marked by a focus on caring for the self to ensure survival. In the transitional second stage, the concern of the first stage is judged to be selfish. This allows the move from selfishness to responsibility. At the conventional level, the focus is on care and conformity, and there is a concomitant desire to please others. What is good is caring for others, and goodness is frequently associated with self-sacrifice. This self-sacrifice causes disequilibrium that initiates the transition from the concern with goodness to the concern with "truth." At the postconventional level (a morality of nonviolence), stage five is dominated by a dynamics of relationship that leads to dissipation of tension between self and others, leading to stage six. At the final stage, relationships are understood to require participation and interaction of integral selves rather than self-sacrifice. Care becomes a self-chosen principle that recognizes the interdependence of self and others and is accompanied by a universal condemnation of exploitation. Gilligan claims that this developmental structure is as morally adequate as Kohlberg's. Her maturational account of the care perspective follows the same sequence as Kohlberg's; moreover, Gilligan has explained that subjects who spontaneously adopt the justice perspective often agree that the solution suggested by the exponents of the care perspective is the better solution (Kittay and Meyers, 1987).

Gilligan's approach also provides a holistic perspective on moral development (q.v. Gestalt psychology). *In a Different Voice* (1982) is Gilligan's criticism of Kohlberg's theory of moral development. Gilligan points out that Kohlberg's analysis of the stages of development of man's moral or ethical values is just that—man's development. In his studies that traced students' lives over a generation, Kohlberg included only male respondents, and yet claimed universality of the theories developed from his studies. Gilligan's point is this: If Kohlberg's (or Piaget's) study began with women and derived developmental constructs from their lives, a different moral conception would emerge. In this conception, moral problems arise from conflicting responsibilities rather than competing rights. This is the view of morality as being concerned with care and with an emphasis on connection and relationships, as opposed to the concept of morality as fairness of rights and rules with an emphasis on separation. But Gilligan, too, is cognizant of the complementary nature between responsibilities and rights; she states:

> To understand how the tension between responsibilities and rights sustains the dialectic of human development is to see the integrity of two disparate modes of experience that are in the end connected. While an ethic of justice proceeds from the premise of equality—that everyone should be treated the same—an ethic of care rests on the premise of nonviolence that no one should be hurt. In the representation of maturity, both perspectives converge in the realization that just as inequality adversely affects both parties in an unequal relationship, so too violence is destructive for everyone involved. This dialogue between fairness and care can not only provide a better understanding of relations between the sexes, but also gives rise to a more comprehensive portrayal of adult work and family relationships (1982, p. 174).

Since the publication of Gilligan's work, there has been an outpouring of material on the issues she raised and criticisms of her original work. Much of the research that supports and elevates Gilligan's work is "feminist" in nature; it values women as human beings, and it concentrates on adding to knowledge and scholarship about women.

Issues about method, methodology, and epistemology have been interwoven with discussions of how best to correct the partial and distorted accounts in traditional analyses. Harding (1987) speaks of reasons for feminist studies, including the fact that scholars have begun to recover and reappreciate the work of women researchers and theorists. Much of women's work has been ignored, trivialized, or appropriated without due credit, and feminist social research can and should examine women's contributions to activities that are important and worth studying.

Some feminist material is radical and adopts a Marxist view or approaches the study of women in much the same way that men have been accused of studying women—from a view of man as deficient. Radical feminist studies tend to be discredited more often than other feminist studies. However, the vast majority of feminist studies seek to diminish masculine bias, give attention to the experiences of women, and facilitate women's development. As Harding and Hintikka (1983) explain, "We cannot understand women and their lives by adding facts about them to bodies of knowledge which take men, their lives, and their beliefs as norms. Furthermore, it is now evident that if women's lives cannot be understood within the inherent inquiry frameworks, then neither can men's lives" (p. ix).

AFTER GILLIGAN

Gilligan's work represents a milestone in the current literature and research about women. The quarterly journal *Social Research* devoted the entire Autumn 1983 issue to responses to Gilligan's work. Many books have discussed women and moral theory (Kittay and Meyers, 1987), have validated the Gilligan thesis of the ethics of care and connection as the basis of their own research (Belenky, et al., 1986; Noddings, 1984), and have discussed women's leadership styles on the basis of a Gilligan model (Gillett-Karam, 1988; Desjardins, 1989a and 1989b; Helgesen, 1990).

Miller's book *Toward a New Psychology of Women* (1976) is a precursor to Gilligan's research. In this work, Miller celebrates the value of the differences of women in our society and points out the psychological strengths of women. Gilligan draws heavily on the works of Miller (1976), Dinnerstein (1976), and Chodorow (1978).

Ruddick (1987) assesses whether gender accounts for distinctive cognitive style and mode of reasoning and reports that any claim to difference is not epistemological but political. It is Ruddick's contention that women's reasoning yields a morality of love and that traditional women's work gives rise to maternal thinking. Since maternal work can be distinguished, for example, from military work, it yields a different perspective on violence and nonviolent action. The maternal view understands the fragility of strengths and weaknesses and emphasizes the importance of giving and receiving while remaining in connection with the other actors in the drama. It emphasizes peace instead of war. Eisler (1988), in *The Chalice and the Blade*, refers to the gender-holistic perspective of cultural transformation theory, which includes the dominator model (or the life-taking model) and the partnership model (or life-giving model). Her message is that in a partnership model, diversity is not equated with inferiority or superiority—rather, diversity is valued in this life-generative, nurturing model for behavior.

Evans (1985) points out the influences of Perry (1970) and others on the works of Gilligan. It was Perry's work on intellectual and ethical development that accommodated a more relativistic approach to the intellectual and ethical development of morality in women and in people who could not make distinctions between right and wrong in moral dilemmas. Gilligan (1982) discovered that principles of justice were irreducibly tied to contextual, psychological, and historical interpretation (p. 154).

Belenky (1986) used both Gilligan's and Perry's ideas in her book, *Women's Ways of Knowing*. She describes five different perspectives from which women view reality and draw conclusions. Her work discusses how women's conceptions of the nature and origins of knowledge evolve and how their understanding of themselves as "knowers" changes over time. Using Perry's scheme for interviewing, but not his language, Belenky grouped women's perspectives on knowing into five major epistemological categories: silence, in which women think of themselves as mindless, voiceless, and not in control of themselves; received knowledge, in which women conceive of themselves as capable of receiving knowledge but not creating it; subjective knowledge, in which truth and knowledge are conceived of as personal, private, and subjectively known or intuited; procedural knowledge, in which women are invested in learning and applying objective procedures for obtaining and communicating knowledge; and constructed knowledge, in which women view knowledge as contextual, experience themselves as creators of knowledge, and value both subjective and objective strategies for knowing. Regarding goals in the education of women, Belenky states:

> We argue that educators can help women develop their own authentic voices if they emphasize connection over separation, understanding and acceptance over assessment, and collaboration over debate; if they accord respect to and allow time for the knowledge that emerges from first-hand experience; if instead of imposing their own expectations and arbitrary requirements, they encourage students to evolve their own patterns of work based on the problems they are pursuing. These are the lessons we have learned in listening to women's voices (p. 15).

WOMEN AND EDUCATION

Plato, Locke, and Mill stressed the importance of education for both women and men (Okin, 1979), but achieving full educational opportunity for women has been difficult. Solomon (1985) reveals how pressure for higher education for women has come at critical periods in American history; for example, rapid growth of women's education in America occurred between 1870 and 1900, when the percentage of women attending institutions of higher education rose to 35 percent. Problems and turmoil ensued as women began attending colleges in greater numbers. Solomon reports:

> Within one decade of the opening of the doors of the University of Chicago to women, the percentage of women

rose from 24 to 52 percent, and between 1892 and 1902 women received a majority (56.3 percent) of the Phi Beta Kappa awards. An alarmed President Harper began to segregate undergraduate classes and cut back on full coeducation for women. Although faculty liberals, including John Dewey, fought for the reinstatement of full coeducation for women, they lost their fight, as separate classes for freshmen and sophomores in the so-called junior college were established in Chicago in 1902 (pp. 58-59).

Martin (1982), in her article "Excluding Women from the Educational Realm," eloquently demonstrates the biases toward women as they fought to achieve higher education. Agreeing with Bluestone (1987) that society abused women's educational privileges, Martin offers Pestalozzi's Gertrude (rather than Rousseau's Sophie) to depict women as models for good educators. Gertrude is a wise and capable teacher; her behavior is worthy of emulation. Martin also mentions the valuable contributions of Maria Montessori as a modern theorist of education. She holds up both Gertrude, as a fictional character, and Montessori, as a preeminent teacher, as excellent role models for women in education.

Rosenberg (1982) tells the fascinating story of the rebellion of women against the Victorian scientific, medical, and social dogmas concerning the separate spheres of men and women in education in the first part of the twentieth century. She highlights the careers of Marion Talbot who, along with John Dewey, opposed the awkward and demeaning view that the education of women interfered with their reproductive abilities. Another of the brilliant educational leaders Rosenberg discusses is Helen Thompson Wooley, whose tests of the intelligence of college men and women showed no important or consistent differences between the sexes. Keller (1985) also discusses further examples of the ways in which the ideologies of science and gender inform each other and produce "male standards" of rationality that omit and delete the contributions of women. The woman whose work most helped change the opinions traditionally opposed to feminist scholarship was Margaret Mead. Mead's studies (beginning in the 1930s) not only challenged the social and sexual norms of the period, they demonstrated that stereotypically "masculine" and "feminine" traits were the products of Western mores and custom, not the irreversible results of iron-clad biological and psychological evolution. Mead seemed to provide a beacon for other women; by the 1930s and 1940s, more women than ever before were "breaking into" higher education.

The number of women in colleges and universities continued to grow throughout the twentieth century, reaching 53 percent of the total enrollment in 1987 (Andersen, 1989). Although the number of women in colleges surpasses that of men overall, men predominate in enrollments in four-year liberal arts colleges and in graduate and professional schools (Solomon, 1985). Women are well represented in graduate education (at the Master's degree level) in the following fields: education (where they outnumber men two to one), health sciences (three to one), and public affairs and services (two to one). At the doctoral level, degrees are awarded to men at twice the rate they are awarded to women, and there are no fields in which women outnumber men, according to the U.S. Department of Education. But even more bleak is the fact that over the last two decades, there has been little growth in overall representation of women within faculty ranks; women now hold 27.5 percent of all faculty positions (Simeone, 1987). Women, to the present day, remain the "second sex in most of academia" (Solomon, 1985). Although Gillett-Karam (1988) has attempted to explain the differential (attributing the gap to women's tendency to take time off for child-rearing), others suggest that uninterrupted participation would not be enough to offset the negative effects of bias against women .

On the other hand, over the last two decades, female scholarship has grown in size and recognition. One manifestation of the emphasis on female scholarship has been the continuing growth of women's studies programs all over the nation (Farnham, 1987), although one goal of many women's studies practitioners is mainstreaming, meaning that feminist scholarship would be incorporated into the entire curriculum (Deglar, 1982). Simeone (1987) and others, however, argue that women in such programs should strive for recognition of their role as "women of knowledge" because of issues of equity, status, and scholarship. Whether in women's studies courses or mainstreamed into departmental curriculum, inclusion of the new scholarship on women offers "more women a new intellectual grasp on their lives, new understanding of our history, a fresh vision of the human experience, and also a critical basis for evaluating what they hear and read in other courses and in the society at large" (Rich, 1979, p. 233).

Komarovsky (1985) studied college women to determine the impact of sex differences and attitudes in contemporary society. Her study points out that graduates of women's colleges are higher achievers and are encouraged to develop their leadership qualities more than are women graduates of coeducational institutions (see also, Tidball and Kistiakowsky, 1976; Oates and Williamson, 1978; Brown, 1982). The conclusion reached by Brown (1982) is that if women in selective women's colleges, regardless of their initial career plans, seem more likely than others to aspire and obtain higher degrees, then research should focus on identifying the characteristics of those colleges that facilitate women's leadership.

WOMEN AS LEADERS

Most of the research on women in leadership roles is new. This is not to say that women have not been leaders in history. Many histories and biographies have been written about great women in history, but few about the process of leadership and the characteristics of women leaders. Most of the contemporary research (Kanter, 1977; Heller, 1982; Hennig and Jardim, 1976; Loden, 1985; Helgesen, 1990) on women as leaders looks at women as business leaders; the literature has been scant on women as leaders in educational institutions (Eaton, 1981; Berry, 1979; Evans, 1985; Shakeshaft, 1987).

While some researchers make a point of the difficulties women encounter in positions of authority (Horner, 1971; Miller, 1982; Jacobson, 1985), others focus on how authority is created in women (Young-Eisendrath and Wiedemann, 1987), and still others examine the relationship of women to power (French, 1985; Messinger, 1980; Janeway, 1980; Ruddick, 1987). Josefowitz's (1985) concept of power incorporates two points of view: power as perceived in others and power as perceived in self. She sums up these two types of power with the statement, "I am both the recipient of power others have over me and the wielder of power over others" (p. 200).

Women have power of which they are not aware; hence, they are unaware when they give away their power. Women are now learning that their power is increased through networking, intuition, and providing leadership. Josefowitz (1985) concludes that power is a tool used to obtain a desired outcome and that women need to identify that outcome:

> Women may be better equipped than men to adjust to the new requirements of effective leadership. The prototype of tough, authoritative leader is no longer advocated as effective. The traits that women have been criticized for in the past, sensitivity and role of catalyst, appear to be the attributes of the future. Incorporating the ideas and contributions of others to encourage teamwork, she is used to and able to tolerate more informality and to function in a less authoritarian manner (p. 121).

A study by Loden (1985), *Female Leadership: How to Succeed in Business Without Being One of the Boys*, examines the idea that women may succeed with their own type of power. This work looks at styles of management based on the research of Maccoby (1980), Burns (1978), and Rosener and Schwartz (1980). As part of research she conducted with 4,000 managers of the Bell Telephone Company over a period of seven years, Loden directed a program titled the Male-Female Awareness Workshop. The program was designed to heighten awareness of sexism in the workplace and to help integrate women into management and other nontraditional jobs. The question Loden chose to examine centered on why competent women were prevented from succeeding in middle- and upper-level management positions. Her study found a unique management style for women, supporting the idea that women have a different style of leadership. She noted that "feminine leaders see the world through two different lenses concurrently, and as a result, respond to situations on both the thinking and the feeling levels" (p. 61). Loden agrees with Josefowitz that the use of power for women relates to outcomes and sees women as favoring personal power (McClelland, 1978).

Heller (1982) compared women's and men's leadership styles in *Women and Men as Leaders*. She examined a small group of matched pairs of women and men who perceived themselves as successful leaders in business, social institutions, and education. Both the leaders and their co-worker groups were interviewed (one-half of the women and one-half of the men were interviewed by a female interviewer). Heller asserts that the "inclusion of women in the study of leadership might challenge and redefine basic assumptions about the way people in positions of authority behave" (1982, p. xv). What emerged from the Heller study was a list of stereotypes of subordinates' attitudes toward male and female leadership. People saw men as too focused on procedures, remote, authoritarian, and sexist, but relaxed, with separate work and social roles, and the abilities to think categorically and work independently. Women were seen as too focused on people, emotionally demonstrative, but more humane, open, friendly, egalitarian, efficient, and organized. Heller also found that leadership itself could spring from a more androgynous perspective (although as Dinnerstein [1976] and others warn, it is the androgyny of humanity). The innovations of female leadership are also of interest. Heller (1982) lists three innovations in research on female leadership:

- Innovation in topic (this includes efforts by researchers, such as Dinnerstein [1976], Kanter [1977], and Hennig and Jardim [1977], to relate family life and leadership in the family to leadership in public and private organizations)
- Innovation in the attitude of the researcher toward the subjects of the study (Smircich [1983] suggests an empathetic approach, rather than a neutral one)
- Innovations in reporting research (Schreibner [1979] contends that methodological and procedural snags and doubts should

be included in research to lessen the predominance of "machoistic research" [pp. 165-166])

In a new work, *The Female Advantage,* Helgesen (1990) looks at the leadership styles and practices of American women who are presently CEOs. Using Mintzberg's work on managerial style (1973), Helgesen compares men to women and rejects the "nature of managerial work" posited by Mintzberg. Women's leadership is seen not as pyramidal but circular; not in terms of vision but in terms of voice; not as the warrior's conquest but as the magician's quest. Helgesen's work is a seminal study of women's "way of leadership."

WOMEN AS EDUCATIONAL LEADERS

Although only a limited number of studies look specifically at the role of women as educational leaders, that emphasis is also growing, especially among current dissertations (Mulder, 1983; Miller, 1987) and in texts about women leaders in educational administration (Shakeshaft, 1987; Taylor, 1981; Berry, 1979). Miller (1987) studied 55 women presidents of two- and four-year educational institutions and compared them to male counterparts according to leadership and organizational style. She found a significant difference between men and women in three areas: salaries, leadership, and communication. Moreover, she found that women believe they are different from men because they speak out on controversial topics, they stress employee relationships over task accomplishment, they recognize employee achievement, they talk and listen to students, and they use trusted staff and faculty to help manage their institution.

Taylor (1981) studied women community college presidents who were in office in 1979. The elements of the study included the factors that influenced women to become college presidents, the attitudes and beliefs of women about their positions, their advice to future leaders, and their future plans. Most of the women interviewed cited power, financial advantage, support from colleagues, and a desire to influence education as the reasons they wanted to become a college president. Each woman credited a single mentor, always a woman, with having special influence or having offered support in the course of her professional career. Most of the presidents had earned doctorates in education or educational administration. Almost all of the presidents arrived at their position with significant experience in community colleges. When asked what they saw as obstacles to the advancement of women administrators, they indicated the following: marital responsibilities; maternal responsibilities; inadequate networks for women; women's views of themselves as assistants or helpers rather than as managers or executives; and men's preferences for men as appointees to top posts. The advice they gave to help other women shore up their leadership abilities included: gaining the necessary knowledge and professional preparation; developing personal attributes, such as good judgment, recognition of the importance of a sense of humor, inner strength and emotional stability, a high energy level, and intelligence; and maintaining professional attitudes that require a positive belief in self and others. Finally, women presidents reported that their future plans included possibly moving to another institution for reasons of salary, location, or institutional prestige.

Shakeshaft (1987) studied women in public school administration. She documents from research the current status of women in educational administration and posits "stages of research on women" (p. 13). Much of Shakeshaft's book is a discussion of the barriers to women in educational administration, but it also provides rich resources from current research that may guide and inform others. In the following table, Shakeshaft's discussion of the stages of research about women provides a model for examining the issues of women in educational administration. Research questions are combined with appropriate and requisite questions about women in educational administration, the approaches that should be used, and the outcomes that can be expected.

Shakeshaft's Stages of Research on Women in Administration

Stage	Questions	Approach	Outcome
1. Absence of women in studies	Number of women in Educational Administration? In what positions?	New surveys	Documentation
2. Search women as administrators	Characteristics and history of women?	Studies of present and past administrators and descriptions	Demographic & attitudinal experimental studies
3. Disadvantaged, subordinate status	Why so few women leaders in Educational Administration?	Attitudes toward women; experiences	Identification of barriers to advancement
4. Women studied as women	How do women describe themselves?	Interviews/ observational studies	Female perspective
5. Women challenging theory	How must theory change to include women's experiences?	Analysis of current theories/methods	Reality that theories don't work for women
6. Transformation of theory	What are theories of human behavior?	Range of approaches	Reconceptualization of theory

Source: Shakeshaft, 1987

Shakeshaft asks that research on women in education include the voice of women and suggests that current theories devaluing women's contributions to educational administration be exposed so that a reconceptualization of the theory of human behavior, one that applies to both women and men, can be posited.

CONCLUSION

Pearson, Shavlik, and Touchton in *Educating the Majority* (1989) and Green in *Leaders for a New Era* (1988) have provided compelling notions for the serious student on the current issues and direction of women in higher education. Pearson, Shavlik, and Touchton examine how women's diversity and commonalities can be understood, discuss learning environments that are shaped by women, emphasize "reconceptualizing" the way we think and teach, and advocate transforming institutions and changing environments and societal demands. Green is a strategist; she speaks to the need to use strategies for women and minority groups in higher education and provides models for doing so.

Desjardins (1989a) contributes a chapter on how Gilligan's work can be applied to the learning environment to Pearson, Shavlik, and Touchton's volume. Interviewing 72 community college presidents, Desjardins demonstrates that patterns emerge along gender lines with strong implications for leadership styles. Specifically, she found that a majority of the women she interviewed exhibited a belief system built on a concept of morality concerned with the ethics of care and centering around the understanding of responsibility and relationships; a majority of the men interviewed exhibited a belief system built on the concepts of justice as fairness and centered around the understanding of rights and rules. Desjardins (1989b) emphasizes that men and women are fully capable of using both their voices to solve moral problems and dilemmas; she reports that men excel in self-esteem, self-confidence, enjoying a challenge, self-control, involvement in change, and commitment to community service, whereas women excel in presence (projecting enthusiasm or strength), optimism, initiative, decisiveness, persuasiveness, and interest in developing people.

Josefowitz (1980, p. 208) would agree with Desjardins; she emphasizes that women in positions of power tend to:

- place a greater emphasis on collaboration as opposed to competition
- pay attention to process and not just to task

- trust people
- share power
- be authentic as opposed to playing games
- appropriately express feelings rather than shutting them off
- view people as whole persons and not just in terms of their job descriptions
- accept and utilize individual differences instead of resisting or fearing them
- show many personality facets rather than only those related to work

Gillett-Karam's research (1988) also examined the role of gender differences in leadership. Twenty-one female CEOs and 21 male CEOs of community colleges were interviewed and compared according to the concept of transformational leadership posited in *Shared Vision* (Roueche, Baker, and Rose, 1989). All interviewed CEOs had been identified as excellent leaders. These college presidents/CEOs were asked to respond to research questions focusing on five leadership concepts— vision, influence and empowerment, orientation toward followers, values orientation, and motivation orientation. Specific competencies that defined the leadership concepts emerged from their written and oral statements. For example, under the concept of vision, the competencies that defined excellent leaders included: is able to conceptualize a specific future; believes that he/she can shape the future; takes appropriate risks to bring about change; is committed to specific courses of action; articulates a sense of mission; is able to cause followers to share vision of the future; and is committed to student access and success.

Gender differences *did* emerge among the 34 competencies that defined the concepts of leadership; behavioral characteristics denoting "feminine strengths" included four of the five categories, including vision, influence and empowerment, orientation toward followers, and values. Male strengths were found in the categories of influence and empowerment and orientation toward followers. Women tended to be greater risk takers and change agents in demonstrating their leadership vision, more team-oriented and dedicated to shared governance, and more caring in their orientation toward followers; finally, they regarded "openness and trust" as essential leadership values. Men were characterized by a bias for action as they exhibited their leadership style and were interested in rewarding behavior in their orientation toward followers. Finally, women reported spending more hours at work (75 hours a week compared to 60 hours a week reported by the men); and they began their ascent to or became a CEO six to seven years later than did the men.

Although the Gillett-Karam and Desjardins studies of leadership in American community colleges both focused on leadership competencies and gender differences, they used different methodologies for analyzing their interview data and for reporting distinctions between male and female leadership. However, both researchers concluded that the framework posited by Gilligan is critical for examining gender and leadership and that the care and connection mode of moral development is associated with female characteristics or attributes of leadership, whereas the justice-rights mode of morality is connected to male attributes of leadership.

Furthermore, critical to studies of leadership is the reality that both women and men exhibit excellence and mediocrity. Women cannot be denied positions of leadership on the grounds that they do not have the "right stuff," for researchers conclude that it is the very integration of male and female leadership characteristics that makes for the best leaders, and that it is those who are most "prosperous" in heart who offer the most to others. De Tocqueville (1945) spoke of this prosperity in 1835:

> If I were asked to what the singular prosperity and growing
> strength of the Americans ought to be attributed, I should
> reply, "To the superiority of their women."

CHAPTER FOUR

❧

MINORITIES: EXPRESSION AND EXPERIENCE IN ACADEMIC LITERATURE

❧

Research and writing about women and research and writing about minorities have a common link: controversy surrounds both. Women and members of ethnic minorities challenge much of the knowledge and information that has traditionally been used to explain and describe them. Much of this knowledge and information treats these two groups as inferior, deficient, or deviant. Much of the literature about these groups refers to the concepts of discrimination and prejudice, which are critical issues. And finally, much of this literature and information documents the treatment of these groups as unequal under the law—a serious concern in a democratic system. The literature about women is challenged by the women's movement and modern philosophical theory concerning moral development. The literature about minorities has found a parallel challenge from political and sociological theory, philosophical inquiry, civil rights legislation, social revolution, and legal action.

What is different about the expression and experience of women and the expression and experience of minorities in academic literature is their unique historical antecedents; what is similar about them is their common struggle to break away from the restrictions of those histories. In the case of women and Blacks, for example, each group has been associated with a peculiar institution—women with the family and Blacks with slavery. But although different institutions tried to define them, women and Blacks in the past shared a common status: they were "property." And in the case of Black women, that condition was doubled. For both groups, integration and participation in society meant facing and overcoming political, social, and economic obstacles.

In addition, these obstacles and barriers have not always been obvious; they have been embedded in the American way of life. The

Constitution of the United States, from its origin, denied citizenship to women, Blacks, and Native Americans, and later took away citizenship from Asian Americans. As the nation began to determine its manifest destiny, it regularly excluded, in the form of immigration quotas, peoples from Eastern and Southern Europe and the Far East. And even in periods in which conscientious democratic theory prevailed, it did not take long for "sanity" to return as exclusionary policies and programs for certain groups were renewed or newly invented.

BASIC CONCEPTS: TERMS, ISSUES, AND POLICIES

A plethora of terms and concepts have been used to represent the different groups of heterogeneous America. In the following discussion, we review commonly used terms, issues around immigration, migration, culture, and institutional policies affecting ethnic minorities. In most instances, attitudes about racial and ethnic groups are expressed in language; the very manner in which we talk and write connotes differences and separation among groups. Moreover, those differences are exacerbated by the use of a single, impoverished yardstick for behavior. For the most part, our expectations for behavior are drawn out of an Anglo-Saxon core culture that "sets the norm" for expected outcomes in society, government, law, decision making, and education. Social scientists see this as an impediment to a pluralistic, democratic society where the espoused framework for existence is egalitarian (Dahl, 1989). Much debate and social upheaval have grown out of this paradox in which we espouse one value and demonstrate another.

Defining key terms helps point out prevailing racial and ethnic relations. These definitions arise out of social usage and are not derived from concepts of biological determinism that see groups as self-evident or genetically fixed with unchanging physical or mental characteristics. Social definitions are derived from agreed-upon determinations centering around physical and cultural characteristics that are deemed critical to singling out a group for social interest.

An ethnic group can be defined as a group socially distinguished or set apart, by others or by itself, primarily on the basis of cultural or national characteristics. This term should not be confused with racial group, which refers to real or alleged physical characteristics of groups that can be subjectively selected (Feagin, 1989).

A minority group is a group of people who, because of their physical or cultural characteristics, are singled out from others in a society for differential and unequal treatment and who therefore regard themselves as objects of collective discrimination (Feagin, 1989). The term implies a corresponding "majority group," or a dominant group with superior rights and advantages; these concepts imply a racial-ethnic hierarchy or stratification system. Dominant and subordinate are sometimes preferable terms for such groups inasmuch as a "majority" group is sometimes numerically a minority.

Ethnic minorities are social groups who are distinguished on the basis of their "ethnos," or immigrant "nation" status, and on their attachment to the concept of "ethnoi," or people other than the dominant White cultural group. Both this term and the term racial-ethnic minorities are used in this book to refer to ethnic and racial groups; occasionally we also use the term "minorities." In each case, we are referring to the predominant ethnic and racial groups in America (but not to White, or European, Americans). These include African Americans, Asians and Pacific Islanders, Hispanic and Spanish-speaking Americans, and Native Americans.

One enormous difficulty in addressing the barriers and obstacles confronting ethnic minorities is associated with the term prejudice, which usually has negative connotations. Prejudice is defined as an antipathy based on a faulty and inflexible generalization. It may be felt or expressed. It may be directed toward a group as a whole or toward an individual because he or she is a member of that group (Feagin, 1989). Much of the concept of prejudice is best understood by the idea of ethnocentrism, in which one's own group is seen as the "center of everything" and all other groups are scaled and rated with reference to it (Sumner, 1960). Although positive ethnocentrism is the natural outcome of a social group's loyalty to their values and beliefs, this ethnocentrism invariably becomes linked with negative views of outgroups, often manifested in prejudice and stereotypes. Research on prejudice has been based on many theories, ranging from psychological to situational. For example, prejudice may be seen as a function of externalization in which individuals vent their own psychological problems onto external objects; this is an example of intentional prejudice (Allport, 1958).

Other branches of research conclude that conformity accounts for prejudice (Williams, 1964; Pettigrew, 1971). People accept their own social and community situation as standard and hold to the prejudices they have been taught; they are conforming to prevailing beliefs. Schermerhorn (1970) believes that prejudices are the products of variable situations and thus are unintentional. His view addresses the social-adjustment function of prejudice, in which attitudes are not individually determined preferences, but rather shared social definitions of racial and ethnic groups, as evidenced by Northerners and Southerners "adjusting" to new racial beliefs as they move from region to region.

Finally, prejudices, and more importantly, stereotypes (more recent prejudices that may not be embedded), help the dominant group rationalize a subordinate group's position. Stereotyping becomes the prevailing attitude that alienates dominant group sympathy from "inferior" or "incompetent" groups. Social scientists use words like exploitation, manipulation, colonialism, and imperialism to combat prejudice and stereotyping. Indeed, ideological racism may be viewed as a complex set of stereotypes aimed at rationalizing the actions of certain nations, groups, or individuals who believe that the physical characteristics of other groups are linked in a direct, causal way to inferior psychological or intellectual characteristics and who thus, on that basis, lay claim to a "natural superiority." This is racist mythology and pseudoscience; to think or believe that physical differences, such as skin color, are intrinsically tied to meaningful differentials in intelligence or culture is dangerous. With ideological racism in mind, the United Nations Educational, Scientific, and Cultural Organization (UNESCO) declared that "inherited genetic factors are not the major forces shaping cultural or intellectual differences among human groups—environment is far more important" (1950, p. 174). But, although we may confront rhetoric about racial or ethnic groups, it is not easy to confront discrimination.

Discussions of discrimination and of government programs that attempt to eradicate it are often confusing, in part because the different dimensions of discrimination are not distinguished. Feagin (1989) sees discrimination dimensions (motivation, actions, effects, and their various interdependent relationships) as they affect institutional and social contexts. As an example, Feagin discusses the discriminatory acts of legalized exclusion of Black children from White schools that endured through the 1960s. If one uses the various dimensions of discrimination, questions that might be raised include: What was the motivation for exclusionary school practices? What forms did the exclusionary actions take? What were the effects of these practices? Were these practices typical of an institutionalized pattern of segregated education? Have these patterns been part of a larger social context of general racial subordination of Black Americans across many institutional areas? Thus, Feagin sees discrimination as a multidimensional problem encompassing schools, the economy, and politics. Feagin depicts the dimensions of discrimination in the following manner:

The Dimensions of Discrimination

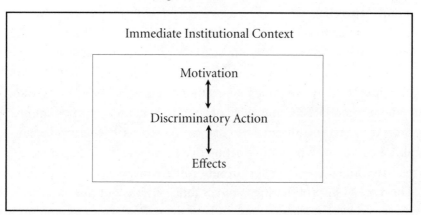

Larger Societal Context

Immediate Institutional Context

Motivation

Discriminatory Action

Effects

Source: Feagin, 1989.

Social scientists have wrestled with the notion that one form of motivation—prejudice—is usually seen as the single cause of discrimination, virtually excluding all other dimensions of discrimination. In a classic study, Myrdal (1944) saw racial prejudice as "the whole complex of valuations and beliefs which are behind discriminatory behavior on the part of the majority group" (p. 52). Thus, privilege theories and institutional discrimination may account for people's actions: The intent to harm lying behind much discrimination may not reflect prejudice at all, but may be simply a desire to protect one's own social and economic privileges. In the historical struggle over resources, where politics is seen as the struggle over the values of a society (Dye and Ziegler, 1989), systems of racial or ethnic stratification rest on the economic and psychological benefits, or privileges, given to the dominant group. Their struggle to maintain privilege—and thus discrimination—becomes a rational response to struggles over scarce resources (Wellman, 1977).

The "institutionalization of privilege," a phrase used by Hamilton and Carmichael (1967), is another definition of discriminatory practice. Hamilton and Carmichael used terms such as individual and institutional racism and analyzed discrimination separately from prejudice or "intent to harm." Feagin (1989) distinguishes between intentional and unintentional discrimination and defines discrimination as "actions carried out by members of dominant groups, or their representatives, that have a differential and harmful impact on members of subordinate groups" (p. 14).

According to Feagin, discrimination can be isolated or small-group discrimination, in which harmful action is taken intentionally by a single member of a dominant group or by a small number of dominant-group individuals against members of a subordinate racial or ethnic group, without being socially embedded or supported in the larger community context. Direct institutionalized discrimination refers to organizationally or community-prescribed action that by intent has a differential and negative impact on members of subordinate races and ethnic groups. This type of discrimination can be subtle (visible, but not blatant) or covert (hidden, malicious, and difficult to document). Common types of covert discrimination include manipulation, tokenism, and sabotage. Indirect institutionalized discrimination consists of practices having a differential and negative impact on members of subordinate races and ethnic groups, even though the organizationally or community-prescribed norms or regulations guiding those actions have been established and are carried out with no intent to harm the members of those groups.

These concepts extend our understanding of institutionalized discrimination in that they force us to think about subtle and covert forms of racial discrimination embedded deeply in the institutions of U.S. society. Moreover, subtle and covert discrimination is much more difficult to eliminate with civil rights legislation than is traditional overt discrimination. Various combinations of discrimination can coexist in organizations or communities. Members of subordinate groups can suffer from both institutionalized regulations intended to have harmful effects and from those not so intended. As Feagin notes, "From a broader perspective, the patterns of discrimination interlocking political, economic, and social organizations may comprise systematic discrimination. For a victimized group, oppression can be interlocking and cumulative, involving many institutional sectors" (p. 17).

In 1980 the National Urban League hired a polling firm to interview 3,000 Black American households. Two-thirds of those surveyed felt there was "a great deal" of discrimination in this country (Feagin, 1989). Contrary to some views, then, discrimination is not rapidly disappearing from U.S. society. Diversity seems invariably linked to racial and ethnic hierarchy and to stratification. Social organizations, whether they exist for religious rituals or for governing, involve ranking systems. Obviously, class systems are ranking systems, but so too are ascriptive rankings, in which attributed, not achieved, group characteristics such as race or ethnicity are major criteria for social position and rewards. The American experience reveals the presence of racial-ethnic, class, and gender hierarchies from its very beginnings.

IMMIGRANT AND ETHNIC TRADITIONS IN AMERICA

Since America was and is a nation of immigrants, the history of America flows around the settlement of immigrants and their acquisition of and contributions to a uniquely American culture. The origin of racial and ethnic relations lies in intergroup contact. Contact can be between an established or native people and a migrating people or between migrating groups moving into a previously uninhabited area. When different groups, often with no common ancestry, come into one another's spheres of influence as a result of migration, a variety of outcomes can occur: exclusion, egalitarian symbiosis, and ethnic stratification (Feagin, 1989).

Exclusion and genocidal destruction (the killing off of one group by another) was a common outcome of contacts between American settlers and the Native American population in the first century of the United States as a nation. This kind of destruction continued until the early twentieth century. Egalitarian symbiosis involves peaceful coexistence and a relatively equal economic and political status between groups. Symbiosis may also occur when stratification is displaced by full assimilation of incoming groups within the core culture. This assimilation can take two forms: cultural conformity or cultural pluralism. When the incoming group demonstrates conformity to the dominant group and rough equality is attained by surrendering much of one's cultural heritage, then cultural conformity occurs. Northern European immigrant groups, such as Scottish and Scandinavian Americans, gained equality in this way. Stratification or separation of groups can also be replaced by egalitarian inclusion through cultural pluralism; for example, certain White immigrant groups (such as Irish Catholic and Jewish Americans) have found socioeconomic and political assimilation while retaining substantial cultural and primary-group distinctiveness.

A more common result of migration and contact is hierarchy or stratification. Two hierarchies that can result from intergroup contact are based on migration and immigration (Lieberson, 1961). Migrant superordination occurs when the migrating group imposes its will on indigenous groups, usually through superior weapons and organization, as with the Native American populations that were not completely destroyed by White settlers. Indigenous superordination occurs when groups immigrating into a new society become subordinate to groups already there, as in early Chinese immigration to the West Coast. Continuous stratification with some acculturation and exploitation, ranging from moderate to extreme, of the subordinate race or ethnic group is the most common form of modern intergroup contact. In persisting racial or ethnic stratification, the extent and inequality of the stratification can vary; but for many non-White groups in America, political and economic inequality have remained so great that these groups' conditions have been described accurately as "internal colonialism." Even among such groups, however, partial assimilation usually occurs in terms of adaptation to the core culture (for instance, to the English language).

THEORIES OF RACIAL AND ETHNIC RELATIONS

In the United States, explanatory theories of racial and ethnic relations have been concerned with migration, adaptation, and stratification. Such theories can be roughly classified as order theories or power-conflict theories. Order theories tend to promote assimilation, either as cultural conformity or cultural pluralism, concentrating on progressive adaptation to the dominant culture and stability in intergroup relations. Power-conflict theories give more attention to hierarchies and stratification of racial and ethnic groups; they include the internal colonialism theory and class-oriented theories.

ASSIMILATION THEORIES

Assimilation is the orderly adaptation of a migrating group to the ways and institutions of an established host group. An early theorist, Park (Park and Burgess, 1924; Park, 1950) saw this process as involving contact, competition, accommodation, and, finally, assimilation. After people are

83

brought together in a contact stage, conflict and competition occur over economic resources; then accommodation—a forced adjustment of a migrating group to a new, albeit better, social situation—occurs. Assimilation occurs when groups acquire and share patterns, experiences, and history, and live a common cultural life. This is the famous "melting pot" concept in which a new amalgamated group appears: out of heterogeneity comes homogeneity.

Gordon (1964) viewed intergroup contact from the perspective of assimilation to the dominant Anglo-Saxon Protestant culture and society. For Gordon, immigrant adaptation typically is (and should be) directed toward conformity to the dominant Anglo culture. He believes that this conformity has been substantially achieved by generational adaptation or acculturation, at least in regard to cultural assimilation. Gordon distinguishes several processes of adaptation leading to assimilation: cultural (change of cultural patterns to those of the core society); structural (penetration of cliques and associations of the core society at the primary-group level); marital (significant intermarriage); identification (development of a sense of identity linked to the core society); attitude-receptional (the absence of prejudice and stereotyping); behavior-receptional (the absence of intentional discrimination); and civic (absence of value and power conflict). In more recent writings, Gordon (1978, 1981) examines to a limited extent the role of power and conflict issues around assimilation, and he views optimistically the assimilation of Black Americans into the core culture and society. He argues in favor of traditional liberalism and its emphasis on individual rights, thus rejecting affirmative action as a manifestation of corporate liberalism that recognizes group rights only along racial lines. (We will address this dilemma further in our discussion of racial and ethnic groups in America and their access to education.)

Some assimilation theorists do not accept the argument that most European American groups have become substantially assimilated to the Anglo-Saxon way of life. A few social scientists have begun to explore models that depart from Anglo conformity in the direction of cultural pluralism. Most analysts of pluralism accept a substantial amount of

Anglo conformity as inevitable, if not desirable. In *Beyond the Melting Pot*, Glazer and Moynihan (1963) agree that the original customs and ways of European immigrants have been typically lost by the third-generation American, but they argue that this does not reflect the decline of ethnicity: European immigrant groups often remain culturally distinct in terms of name, identity, and other cultural attributes. This theme of ethnic group persistence in later generations as part of the adaptive process has been further discussed under the conceptual term ethnogenesis. Greeley (1974) and Parenti (1980) posit that the traditional assimilation model does not explain the persistence of ethnicity in the United States or the emphasis among immigrants on ethnicity as a way of creating identity.

A critical examination of assimilation theories demonstrates that their concept of ethnic adaptation depends on White European groups and virtually ignores non-European groups. In Myrdal's (1944) view, a fundamental ethical dilemma exists in the United States, seen clearly in the contradiction between the democratic principles of the Declaration of Independence and the institutionalized subordination of Black Americans. For Myrdal, this represents a "lag of public morals," a problem solved in principle but still being worked out in an assimilation process that may or may not be completed. More optimistic analysts have emphasized the concept of progressive inclusion, which will eventually provide Black Americans and other non-White Americans with the full rights and privileges of citizenship. Assimilationists, then, believe full equality for Black Americans is inevitable (Parsons, 1966) as egalitarian, universalistic societal forces are forged by collective action to overcome less tolerant value systems. They reason that as Europeans have desired assimilation and absorption, so too will non-European and non-White groups. Assimilation theorists are criticized for having an "establishment" bias, for not distinguishing carefully enough between what has actually happened and what the establishment felt should have happened. Many Asian scholars, for example, reject the assimilation theory as applicable to themselves, particularly because they postulate that it originated in a period of intense attacks on Asians by White

Americans (Wong, 1985). As Geschwender (1978) points out, most assimilationists have forgotten important historical facts that emphasize racial and ethnic conflict and exploitation. Missing from most assimilation theories is a concern with the inequality, power, exploitation, and discrimination issues emphasized by power-conflict theories.

POWER-CONFLICT THEORIES

Power-conflict theories emphasize economic stratification and power issues. Internal colonialism theories and a variety of class-based theories are representative of power-conflict theories of race and ethnic relations. Power-conflict theories stress the following recurring themes in the writings of such scholars as Cox (1948), Bonacich (1980), Blauner (1972), and Omi and Winant (1986):

- A central concern for racial and ethnic inequalities in economic position, power, and resources
- An emphasis on the roots of racial inequalities and hierarchies in the economic institutions of capitalism
- A major concern with the class structure of capitalism and its impact on racial relations
- An emphasis on the role of the state in legalizing racial exploitation and segregation and thus in defining racial and ethnic relations
- An emphasis on intergroup relations and conflict in a broad historical perspective

At the heart of the intercolonialism model is an emphasis on power and resource inequalities, especially White/non-White inequalities. The framework for internal colonialism is derived from the concept of colonialism and imperialism, or the running of another country's economy and government by an outside power, a common historical phenomenon inflicted by European countries on less technologically developed countries from the fifteenth century until the present time (Balandier, 1966). In cases where continuing dependency results even after formal independence has been granted (neocolonialism) or where a large population of White settlers remains in the colonialized nation, control and exploitation of subordinate groups often passes from Whites in the home country to Whites, or Europeans, in the newly independent country. This concept is critical to internal colonialism theorists, who posit similar patterns in the American experience: White American businessmen and entrepreneurs saw non-White laborers—such as Black slaves, Chinese railroad workers, or Mexican farm workers—as a cheap, easily controlled labor market (Blauner, 1972).

The historical origin and stabilization of internal colonialism in North America began curiously during the colonial period. The process of systematic subordination of non-Europeans began with the Native Americans who were killed or driven off desirable lands and continued as slaves brought from Africa provided a cheap source of labor for Southern agriculture and as Asian and Pacific peoples were imported as indentured workers. Mexican agricultural development was forcibly taken over by Anglo settlers, who then became economically dependent on cheap Mexican labor (Blauner, 1972). It was this process of exploiting the labor of non-White people, whether as slaves or low-wage employees, that brought substantial growth to the American capitalist economy. From the internal colonial perspective, contemporary racial and ethnic inequality and stratification are based in the economic interests of Whites in cheap labor. Internal colonialists have also recognized the role of government in supporting the exploitation of non-White minorities; examples include the legitimization of slavery and the provision of military troops to subordinate Native Americans and Mexican Americans throughout the United States. Internal colonial theories focus mainly on non-White immigrant groups, analyzing the establishment of racial stratification and control processes that maintain White dominance. Carmichael and Hamilton (1967) used the term internal colonialism to describe discrimination of the White community against Blacks as a group; they view Blacks as a "colony" in White America in regard to education, economics, and politics.

Other scholars combine an internal colonialism perspective with an emphasis on class stratification. Barrera (1979) suggests that within

American internal colonialism there is an interactive structure dividing society along class lines, including a small group of capitalist elites who buy the labor of others (including their managers) and who have administrative control over workers; a small group of independent merchants who are self-sufficient and need little outside labor; and a huge group of blue-collar and white-collar workers who sell their labor for wages. Within each of these classes, racial segmentation separates out those suffering institutionalized discrimination. Minority workers share a class position but suffer from a subordinate economic position because of structural discrimination along racial lines, such as lower wages and concentration in lower-status occupations. Bonacich (1980) claims that the majority group of White workers does not share the interests of the dominant political and economic class, but does share in the attitudes of discrimination against non-Whites. What White workers try to do, she says, is protect their own privileges, regardless of the limitations of those privileges. Organized White workers in the last century have been successful in protecting both their jobs and their wages by restricting the access of Black workers to many jobs, thus splitting the general labor market, reducing Black incomes, and increasing Black unemployment problems. This split labor market view is another of the class-based theories (Greenberg, 1980). Even when racial and ethnic groups find their economic niches as middlemen or in ethnic enclaves and fill jobs that the dominant group does not want, they may retain an excluded status. However, Cubans in Miami and Koreans in Los Angeles, according to Portes and Manning (1986), have demonstrated through their ethnic enclaves and economic participation that they may overcome the relegation of immigrants to positions of inferiority and exploitation.

Power-conflict theories are not without their critics. Moore (1976) and Omi and Winant (1986) see the relationship between Third World nations and the colonial powers that previously dominated them as a model not easily transferred to experiences between Whites and non-Whites in America. They conclude that such a model cannot be superimposed on subordinate non-White groups in America because they neither represent a geographic entity nor have a superior, integrated

White elite within their communities. Theorists of internal colonialism counter-argue that these views represent a neocolonial interdependence in which views are restricted to territorial colonization. Moreover, they argue that in America non-Whites are residentially segregated, are exploited in employment, are deficient in almost all comparisons with White immigrants, are culturally stigmatized, and feel that many of their own leaders have been co-opted or absorbed.

Omi and Winant (1986) have developed a theory of racial formation. The most innovative aspect of this perspective on race relations is a central emphasis on the role of government in the social and political definition of racial and ethnic relations. Racial and ethnic relations are substantially defined by the actions of governments, ranging from the passing of legislation (such as restrictive immigration laws) to the imprisonment of immigrants defined as a threat (such as Japanese Americans in World War II). Omi and Winant re-examine and reject economically determinist positions, which state that the economic base determines cultural and political structures, and they also go beyond class reductionism. Their work focuses on politics and the state, on ideology and culture, and on the ways class, gender, and race are interconnected; they also address the contemporary politics of right-wing and neoconservative ideologies that "promote the resuscitation of economic and imperial power, and the restoration of traditional cultural and social values" (1986, p. ix).

Omi and Winant see the goals of the political right as having an underlying racial tone, although race is reduced to a "mere manifestation of other supposedly more fundamental social and political relationships such as ethnicity and class" (1986, p. ix). Three themes guide their analysis: (1) the way new social movements have emerged that rearticulate important political and cultural themes and thus can mobilize mass adherents; (2) the location of race at the center of American history and their interpretation of race as a co-determinate with class and gender; and (3) their analysis of the manner in which the state (government and policy) shapes and is shaped by the racial contours of society and the demands that emanate from those racial realities.

Omi and Winant note that from the beginning the United States government has been concerned with and actually shaped the politics of race; a lengthy series of laws have defined racial groups and interracial relationships. Politics and culture play a significant role in the creation, recreation, and destabilization of hegemonic relations. This analysis, which recognizes the efficacy of political and cultural action, does not reduce action to mere economic exigencies. Relations between racial and social movements, and social movements and the state, can be analyzed to discover current realities about race. By tracing our history and social movements, we can make sense of policy and policy challenges as they relate to racial, ethnic, and gender issues. Moreover, such deliberation illustrates that failure to consolidate challenges around majoritarian aspirations through cultural change fuels opposing reactions, and new opposing agendas emerge.

LEGAL HISTORY AND MINORITIES

Ethnic groups' or ethnic minorities' relationships to the dominant culture and their respective positions and situations *vis-à-vis* the institutions that have grown and developed out of the dominant culture deserve consideration. Just as cultural integration eludes these groups, so do justice and equality, economic and social advancement, educational development, and full inclusion in the basic American institutions.

The literature and research around "minority" groups have found focus in the current era. For, with the exception of a few early works (such as those from abolitionists like Frederick Douglass or from academics such as W.E.B. Du Bois and Booker T. Washington), it is government action, and not academic research, that has explained the role and the experiences of racial and minority groups in America. Thus, the ebb and flow pattern of research on minorities is reflective of societal and historical patterns.

BLACK AMERICANS

Until 1620, America had no legislative attitude regarding minorities. At that time, Virginia decided that people of color were different and were to be treated differently from others; they were restricted from land ownership, from being educated, from voting, and from participation in local or territorial government. Thus, a colonial act set a pattern that would continue through the twentieth century; issues concerning Blacks would be controlled, by and large, through legislation enacted by the individual colonies or individual states. By the 1700s, one of the few things that Americans in the North and South agreed on was the slave trade: The South profited from slave labor, and the North profited from the mechanics of the slave trade—ship building, commerce, and sales transactions.

Then, during the Constitutional Convention in 1787, slavery was implicitly acknowledged by the American Constitution; the Three-Fifths Compromise, for purposes of taxation and representation, counted Blacks as three-fifths of their actual number. The continuing debate over slavery reached a critical point in 1857, when both abolitionists and states rights advocates battled over the status of Dred Scott. Supreme Court Justice Taney determined that, at the writing of the Constitution, slaves were not viewed as citizens and, therefore, Dred Scott's slave status denied him citizenship and the legal right to sue, and the courts had no jurisdiction to render any decision. The decision is important; statements in judicial opinions, not always necessary to the decision, have the force of forming opinion. In effect, it destroyed Blacks' pursuit of rights and removed the protection of the legal system for their rights, regardless of residence.

By 1860 the issue of slavery had become the impetus for a war; and even the declaration of freedom for Blacks, the Emancipation Proclamation, had no effect on Blacks who were still considered slaves by the Confederacy. It would take constitutional reform of civil rights to redress the ills of slavery and to abolish it. The Thirteenth Amendment prohibited slavery anywhere in the United States of America; the

Fourteenth Amendment granted state and national citizenship to former slaves and prohibited states from making laws that would abridge the rights of their citizens; and the Fifteenth Amendment extended voting privileges to Blacks. But federal law enforcement after Reconstruction was virtually nonexistent, as previously granted rights were ignored and denigrated. "Jim Crow" policies reigned.

Although post-Civil War laws had unequivocally established the patterns of American legal thought and action toward American Blacks, in reality the enforcement of these decisions was constantly challenged. The reaffirmation of Southern hegemony around the ubiquitous states rights issue reappeared quickly as the evangelism and fervor of Northern abolitionists began to subside. By 1900 the initial thrust for civil rights was relinquished by interpretation and treatment from individual states. Although Black leadership endeavored to battle this trend, neither the executive nor the legislative branch of government was helpful. Rather, it was the judiciary, especially the Supreme Court, to whom the vain hopes of Black leadership were turned. But until the 1930s, the Supreme Court upheld the rulings of state judiciaries unsympathetic to civil rights causes.

In 1869 the Supreme Court entrenched racial discrimination by instituting the concept of separate facilities for the Black population and the White population. This idea, originally attached to railroad facilities, was later extended by inference to cover everything from bathroom facilities to education. *Plessy v. Ferguson* was actually the first court case specifically articulating the doctrine that facilities could be separate but equal. When Congress passed the Civil Rights Act of 1875, which made it a federal crime for any owner or operator of a hotel or public conveyance or theater to "deny the full enjoyments of the accommodations thereof" because of race or color (Abraham, 1988, p. 408), five court cases, known as the Civil Rights Cases of 1883, declared the 1875 Civil Rights Act unconstitutional. At this time, the courts insisted that the Fourteenth Amendment applied to state action only and that it did not give Congress authority to forbid discrimination by private individuals. The court sharply limited the "privileges or immunities" concept of national citizenship to the actions of state government officials. One judge commented that "Blacks should cease endeavoring to obtain special treatment" and "there had to be a time when Blacks stopped being the special favorite of the law" (Abraham, 1988, p. 409).

In 1900 almost 90 percent of America's Blacks lived in the South. The South was the residing hall of racial discrimination on both a public and private level. Public segregation of buses, streetcars, taxis, waiting rooms, drinking fountains, schools, colleges, universities, hospitals, jails, cemeteries, parks, libraries, and theaters was commonplace. Private citizens acted to deny access to Blacks and other non-Whites. As the twentieth century progressed, many Black leaders and other civil rights advocates began to challenge segregation. In 1941, in an executive order, Franklin Roosevelt established the first Committee on Fair Employment Practices (CFEP), which made some progress toward racial equality in government-related workplaces, but by 1946 Congress abolished the CFEP by consolidating Southern and Northern conservative congressional forces. Attempts to outlaw Jim Crow practices like the poll tax and lynching were consistently ignored by Congress. Congressional reluctance to enforce civil rights challenged President Truman; he appointed the Committee on Civil Rights and the Committee on Government Contract Compliance, issued executive orders to ban "separate but equal" armed forces, and established a Fair Employment Board. Truman's actions shook Southern Democrats, who immediately seceded from the party to form the new Dixiecrat party.

Then in the 1950s, two watershed events took place: the Public School Segregation Case of 1954 and the Civil Rights Act of 1957. The school cases, a consolidation of cases in four states—Kansas, South Carolina, Virginia, and Delaware—were decided under the umbrella of the *Brown* decision, which demanded remedial action by government officials everywhere. It pointedly accused Congress for its failure to act. The *Brown* decision rejected the doctrine of separate but equal, saying it "no longer had validity, was improper, incorrect, and would not be utilized in looking at education in the United States" (Abraham, 1988, pp. 424-425). The cases were remanded to district courts "to take such preceding and enter such orders and decrees consistent with this opinion as are necessary and proper to admit to the public schools on a racially, nondiscriminatory basis, with all deliberate speed, the parties in these cases" (Kluger, 1976, p. 678).

The Civil Rights Act of 1957, the first major legislation of its kind since Reconstruction, created the United States Commission on Civil Rights, an assertive unit in the government's struggle against discrimination. It transformed and strengthened the Department of Justice and its civil rights section (the Civil Rights Division), and assigned an assistant attorney general to this government body. This act developed a process to challenge actual or threatened interference with the right to vote. Meanwhile, as a result of the "March on Washington," civil rights access moved into the hands of the people. In the 1960s addressing discrimination became a federal imperative.

The Civil Rights Act of 1964 mandated the end of discriminatory practices based on race, ethnicity, and gender. Title VI specifically prohibited discrimination on the basis of race, color, or national origin in any program receiving federal funds. Title VII prohibited discrimination in employment by institutions with 15 or more employees. The Equal Employment Opportunity Commission was created to enforce the 1964 act. Executive Order 11246, signed by President Lyndon Johnson in 1965, prohibited discrimination in any agency receiving federal contracts of over $10,000 and in institutions with more than 50 employees; programs receiving federal contracts of over $50,000 were required to write an affirmative action plan to demonstrate inclusion for women and minorities. This affirmative action plan has invoked criticism and opposition since its inception (more discussion of affirmative action follows in Chapter Five).

Education for Black children was another aspect of post-Reconstruction America in which Blacks were denied full equality. Federal aid, private organizations, religious organizations, and philanthropists were the first promoters of public education for Blacks. But from early on, education for Black children meant separate facilities, especially in the South, where almost all Blacks lived until the 1950s.

Bullock (1967) reminds us that schools were anything but equal; as much as 10 times more money was spent on White schools than on Black schools. In the 1930s, for example, the average yearly expenditure for White children in 10 Southern states was about $50; for Blacks, it was $17.

Despite institutionalized discrimination and differential school expenditures, by the early twentieth century over 1.5 million Blacks were in schools, and 34 Black colleges had been established (Franklin, 1974). Two great voices speaking up for education for Blacks were Booker T. Washington, founder of Tuskeegee Institute, and W.E.B. Du Bois—both extraordinary visionaries for their time.

The end of enforcement of the *Plessy* decision began with the enforced desegregation of four university law schools—University of Missouri, The University of Texas, University of Oklahoma, and University of Maryland—in the 1930s and 1940s. A suit against the University of Oklahoma forced the dismantling of a segregated graduate school program (Bullock, 1967). By 1954, desegregation was extended to public education, although the ruling was largely ignored in the South. In 1956 President Eisenhower had to send the National Guard to desegregate a Little Rock, Arkansas, high school. Over the next three decades, the courts expanded their attack on segregation through busing (the *Swann v. Charlotte-Mecklenburg* decision in 1971), selective attendance zones (the *Keyes v. Denver* decision in 1973), and through gerrymandering. Although the majority of desegregation took place in the South, Northern school systems were also forced to desegregate. In Boston, a court order to desegregate met with widespread opposition and violence (Glazer, 1975; 1987).

Liberal social scientists began to reconsider court-ordered desegregation and argued that it accelerated the suburbanization of Whites (Coleman, 1966). Although this argument proved somewhat faulty, today local Black leaders in large, predominantly Black cities and many Whites everywhere have given up on comprehensive desegregation (Feagin and Feagin, 1978), and new standards for both employment and school desegregation have been sought. The presidential action for this turnaround was instigated by the Milliken decision in 1974, which overturned a lower-court order to desegregate Detroit urban and surrounding schools. This precedent paved the way for limited desegregation in metropolitan areas.

The issue of forced integration in education, and its mixed blessings, is nowhere more confusing than in the case of higher education. When Oberlin College opened its doors to women and Blacks in the 1830s, it was an unprecedented action. But by the next century, higher education was common for Blacks, whether they attended traditionally Black colleges and universities or predominantly White institutions. By the 1950s, Black students were encouraged to attend college, through outreach programs, affirmative action programs, and financial assistance. By the 1970s and 1980s, three-quarters of Black college students were in predominantly White institutions. In 1980, 11 percent of all undergraduates were Black, but by 1988 that number dropped to 8.8 percent, graduate participation had decreased by 12 percent, and the number of Black faculty and administrators had also decreased as the progress of the previous decade came into question (*Newsweek*, 1987). In the late 1980s and in 1990, civil unrest returned to college campuses.

NATIVE AMERICANS

Although America is now primarily a land of immigrants, it did and does have an indigenous population—that of Native Americans. Originally, the British and French treated the Native Americans as allies for purposes of war. But that treatment was short-lived, as the natives thwarted European expansion and settlement. The British viewed all Native American tribes as dependent nations and their individual members as aliens. This viewpoint was adopted by the United States government. Although treaties established relationships between the United States and the various "Indian nations," gradually those treaties constrained the autonomous stature of Indian nations. As treaties were signed with these Indian nations and then broken, the United States sought its Manifest Destiny, what it believed was its God-ordained imperative to extend its borders from the Atlantic to the Pacific. The removal of Indian tribes from the lands east of the Mississippi was ordered, and further westward expansion continued the segregation of Native Americans, accomplished by the policy of reservations, or reserving lands for Native Americans. Population data reveal the effects of these policies: Of the original 10 million Native Americans in North America, by 1850 only about 200,000 survived. This population figure remained between 200,000 and 300,000 until the 1930s (Feagin, 1989).

Since the commerce clause controlled all aspects of trade with foreign nations, it also provided the United States with a constitutional basis for dealing with Native Americans. A 1790 law extended federal criminal jurisdiction over Native American lands; it established the process for dealing with criminal violations that occurred on Native American lands. This act also required that anyone trading with Native Americans must be licensed by the federal government. As the "Indian problem" became more and more an issue over land ownership, this act was extended in the 1830s. Then Supreme Court Justice John Marshall issued a dictum establishing the guardian-ward relation between "weak Indian tribes" and the strong United States government; this relationship gave official license for governmental actions beyond regulating commerce.

Land ownership and the pursuit of land ownership was a fundamental demand of both the United States government and its peoples. Johnson and Graham's court case *Leasee v. MacIntosh* in 1823 gave title to all land in the continental United States that was neither a state nor a territory of the United States to the United States on the basis of the North American colonists' claim to it. According to this decision, the Native Americans had the right only to occupy the land, not to own it. Prior to this decision, persons could appropriate such land only if they paid a fair price for it and only if Native Americans were willing to sell it; thus, ownership was implied. This decision, however, changed people's perceptions: ownership by Native Americans was not possible, payment was not necessary, and Native Americans were occupying land that rightfully belonged to the United States government and its citizens.

Native Americans were not considered citizens. They were conquered people and thus were barred from the protection of the Thirteenth, Fourteenth, and Fifteenth Amendments. Native Americans became citizens primarily by naturalization; that citizenship was very limited. In 1888 a law allowed a Native American woman citizenship upon marriage to a White man. In 1901 the Dawes Act set criteria for citizenship: to become a citizen, Native Americans had to divorce themselves from their heritage, their residency, and their people. Finally, in 1924, the Citizenship Act made all Native Americans citizens.

The formal educational experience of Native Americans under the White educational system began in the reservation period. In 1887 over 14,000 Native American children were enrolled in 227 schools operated by the Bureau of Indian affairs, religious groups, or with government aid (U.S. Bureau of Indian Affairs, 1975). By 1900 a small percentage of Native American children were receiving U.S. government-sponsored schooling; for the remainder, schooling took place within tribal circles. In the Southwest, approximately one-fourth of all Native American children from the 1890s to the 1930s attended boarding schools; a small percentage attended public schools. Then day schools within commuting distance and public schools began to replace boarding schools. The Johnson-O'Malley Act (1930) provided federal aid for those states developing public schools for Native American children. Pressure from Native Americans between 1960 and 1980 extended primary, adult, and vocational education. With President Johnson's "War on Poverty" funds, the first reservation community college opened its doors on the Navajo reservation (Olson and Wilson, 1984). From 1970 to 1980, the Native American population in public schools grew to about 200,000 students; several thousand were in college. But these changes in educational attainment have been snail-paced; drop-out rates are high (40 percent), and school attendance on reservations remains low. Much of the criticism of Native American schooling focuses on boarding schools, which institutionalized the concept of colonialism and enforced acculturation for Native American people (Cahn, 1969).

HISPANIC AMERICANS

Stereotypes including popular images of Texans' glory at the Alamo, Zootsuiters, lawlessness and border raids, and illegal "wetback" immigrants are part and parcel of Hispanic people's history in the United States. In many ways, the history of Spanish-Mexican influence in the American Southwest is a history of conflict between two dominant cultures: the Spanish Catholic *ranchero*-mining culture and the White Protestant plantation-farming culture. The Spanish actually came to North America long before Anglo settlement and claimed Florida, Texas, Arizona, New Mexico, Colorado, Utah, Nevada, and California as colonies. Spaniards' contact with the Native Americans was integrative; intermarriage produced the *mestizo*, the individual of mixed Spanish and Native American blood. The mestizo people calling themselves Mexican won independence from Spain in 1820 and claimed the southwestern lands of North America. When Mexico sought to settle its provinces, it gave vast areas of land to Anglo *impresarios*, who colonized the land in exchange for Mexican citizenship. In just over a decade, the incoming White population outnumbered the Mexican population.

In Texas, that population had more in common with the American South than with Mexico. Soon another revolution took place, and Texas became an independent republic. Much of the resentment and violence in battles such as the Alamo, Goliad, and San Jacinto stemmed from the clash of Spanish-Mexican and Anglo cultures. Obviously, it was the aim of Sam Houston, a hero of the Texas Revolution and a friend of Andrew Jackson, to annex Texas, and after much debate in Congress around the acceptance of Texas as a "slave" state, Texas entered the Union. But the bitter antagonism between Texas and Mexico continued as war broke out between Mexico and the United States; in the resulting treaty, Guadalupe Hidalgo ceded almost the entire Southwest to the United States. Mexican nationals were promised citizenship if they remained on these lands, but by 1850 their lands were seized or occupied by incoming White settlers (Acuna, 1972).

In California both land and land resources proved invaluable—by

1849 gold was discovered and land ownership was contested violently. Thus, by the mid-nineteenth century the Mexican system of communal land holdings and land grants was replaced by the North American system of private land ownership. To White Americans, this period was seen as a time of liberation in which "unused" land was distributed to citizens. Lynchings and acts of terrorism were common, and oppression was a familar tool of law enforcement. The Texas Rangers were one group documented for their use of belligerence and aggression against Mexican landowners (Paredes, 1958). Mexican Americans lost an estimated two million acres of private lands and another two million acres of communal lands between 1854 and 1930 (Rubio, 1986).

Although Mexican nationals numbered about 120,000 in the 1850s, millions of Mexican, Puerto Rican, and Cuban immigrants came, legally or illegally, to the United States. With the exclusion of Asian immigrants and the rapidly increasing industrialized economy, there was a sharp decline in agricultural workers. Mexican workers were deliberately drawn into the Southwest because of the demand for cheap labor; this demand was met with local criticism and opposition, and soon immigration restrictions (the Immigration Act of 1924) and temporary work permits replaced earlier access. In the 1920s the Border Patrol of the Immigration and Naturalization Service was created, and by 1929 legislation made it a felony to enter the United States illegally. The Border Patrol conducted exclusion and deportation campaigns during the Great Depression (Samora, 1971), as well as the recession of the early 1980s. During the Depression, pressure was exerted to demand deportation of undocumented workers, and social agencies established organized caravans to expel Mexican workers (Cardenas, 1975).

The demands of World War II altered the situation. In 1942 the Bracero Agreement (the Emergency Farm Labor Agreement) between the United States and Mexico provided a much-needed agricultural work force. For 20 years, nearly five million *braceros* worked the land, and it is estimated that between four million and seven million undocumented migrants entered the United States during this time (Samora, 1971). But unions and other business and working groups condemned the programs, and eventually their voice found legislation. The 1965 and 1976 Immigration Acts placed restrictive quotas on Mexican immigration. Amnesty for some illegal and undocumented workers finally came in the 1986 Immigration Reform and Control Act; by 1988 almost two million Mexican nationals had responded (Keeley, 1988). But this welcome-and-embrace, nonwelcome-and-exclude rollercoaster ride between the United States and Mexicans had other manifestations besides those of worker and immigration laws.

In 1900 Mexican labor camps were raided by the Ku Klux Klan; in 1911 the federal Dillingham Commission on Immigration declared that Mexicans formed an unskilled, and therefore undesirable, population; and in the 1920s Congressional inquiry deemed Mexicans a "mongrelized" race, as testimony given to the House Immigration Commission reported the racial inferiority of Mexicans (Garcia, 1974).

Researchers documented the Mexican American culture as one of passivity and fatalism, primarily family-oriented and overly prolific (Stoddard, 1973). Moreover, as with other immigrants, I.Q. testing and scores were used to claim intellectual inferiority (Sheldon, 1972). By the 1940s and 1950s, the Zoot Suit Riots in Los Angeles and Chicago once again drew attention to Mexican Americans—this time as crime-oriented villains. The famous Miranda case of 1966 reflected this attitude. Although the court's decision sought to remedy arrest injustices, and would eventually safeguard the rights of the accused in criminal law, it nevertheless focused on the infamy of the Mexican American.

Moreover, skill levels fell as *rancheros*, who once owned land, were reduced to hired farm workers. Job discrimination occurred in differential wages and differential treatment. In California the Foreign Miners Act placed a license tax on foreigners to exclude them from work, while Mexican laborers worked for a few dollars a day in stoop-labor positions. The California Federation of Labor worked in the 1920s and 1930s to exclude Mexican laborers (McWilliams, 1968; Grebler, Moore, and Guzman, 1970). From the 1920s to the 1980s, Mexican American workers predominated in fields such as farm workers, urban laborers, or service workers in the Southwest. Runaway industries set up shop in the

Southwest to take advantage of low-wage regions; food processing plants and the garment industry are examples (U. S. Department of Health, Education, and Welfare, 1984). Poorly paid jobs meant inferior housing and segregated urban ghettos, or *barrios*. In the Southwest, restrictive covenants kept Mexican Americans out of certain housing areas (U. S. Commission on Civil Rights, 1970). Poverty, the prevailing economic reality of the majority of Mexican Americans, and discrimination have had a monumental effect on their education.

Sanchez (1966) and Carter (1970) speak to the issue of education and Mexican Americans. Segregation was the rule for schools from California to Texas, when there was any schooling at all for Mexican American children. Segregation of Hispanics was mainly accomplished through gerrymandering or local law discrimination. Segregated housing patterns contributed to *de facto* school segregation; even today, Hispanic children in the Southwest attend schools (approximately 1,000 of them) that are predominantly segregated. In Texas and California, Mexican American children have been overrepresented in classes for the mentally retarded; placement usually reflects pigeonholing more than accurate testing procedures (Mercer, 1973).

Three Supreme Court decisions have addressed the discrimination of Hispanics in America. The 1974 decision in *Lau v. Nichols* ruled that school systems could not ignore the English language problems of national origin minority groups. The "Lau Remedies" established bilingual programs, a highly controversial and much opposed remedy in education, especially in the Southwest. In 1966 and 1988, in the famous Edgewood cases, attention was focused on unequal education based on differing *ad valorem* tax structures within the city of San Antonio, Texas. These cases, which reflect *de facto* segregation in Texas schools, have also been controversial. The Texas legislature continues to debate and defer public school funding and parity (Brey and Gillett-Karam, 1988).

Puerto Ricans are a large immigrant group in America; between World War I and the present, approximately one million Puerto Ricans have migrated to "the mainland." Puerto Rico became a Spanish colony in 1493, and by the end of the nineteenth century it sought autonomy from Spain. The United States went to war with Spain in 1898 and was ceded Puerto Rico in the resulting peace treaty. A United States governor was appointed, English became the mandatory school language, and by 1917 Puerto Ricans were made U.S. citizens under the Jones Act (Maldonado-Denis, 1972). By 1948, Puerto Rico became a commonwealth with its own constitution, its own elected officials, and control over its legal system and schools, and Spanish once again became the official language. When the United States took Puerto Rico in 1899, it profited by acquiring a maritime station and a lucrative agricultural state. At that time, 93 percent of the land belonged to the local population. By 1930, 60 percent of the land was in the hands of large sugar, tobacco, and shipping companies. Eventually, even the independent farmers growing coffee were driven out. With no land and no jobs, Puerto Ricans became cheap labor for international corporations, or they began to migrate to the United States. After World War II, the United States implemented "Operation Bootstrap" to provide Puerto Ricans access to American investment capital. Government programs provided electricity, tax breaks, land, and roads. But modernization brought an abrupt end to an agricultural economy and labor base, and massive unemployment ensued: 20 percent of all Puerto Ricans left Puerto Rico. A 1950s boom in the U.S. economy in textiles and sweat shops provided jobs for many Puerto Ricans but did not last; by the 1970s there were few employment opportunities left. Thus, even on the mainland, Puerto Ricans were unemployed and their poverty increased. Puerto Ricans are the second-poorest minority group in America, with only Native Americans being poorer.

Cuban Americans represent about 6 percent of Hispanics in the United States. Mexican Americans make up 60 percent, Puerto Ricans about 14 percent, and the remaining 20 percent are Central Americans who are recent political refugees. Most of the Cuban immigration to the United States took place in the 1960s as middle- and upper-income Cubans fled the Cuban socialist revolution led by Fidel Castro. Many settled in Florida. Another influx of Cubans occurred in the late 1960s and early 1970s; this group was not as affluent, and the last group of

Cuban immigrants, who came in the 1980s, were poor. Their economic status became a causal factor in their relations with the U.S. government; the poorer Cubans were placed in detention camps for years after their arrival because the government feared many were criminals. In the early 1980s, Miami, now a majority Cuban city, began to experience riots among the Black, White, and Cuban communities. Blacks particularly argued that Cubans were taking their jobs (Hispanic Policy Development Project, 1984). Tensions were exacerbated by the fact that educational levels, job skills, and income were different among the three groups— Cuban immigrants, Blacks native to the United States, and White Anglos. Cuban Americans are seen as an enclave community (Portes and Bach, 1985) with substantial resources, access to important social networks, and support from governmental programs. Entrepreneurial strength makes the Cuban Americans a strong economic group.

ASIAN AMERICANS

Chinese immigration to the United States occurred in two time frames: from 1850 to 1882 and not again until 1965. Between 1850 and 1880, 250,000 Chinese immigrants came to the United States. Most entered as low-wage earners for mining, railroad, and service occupations along the West Coast. The Chinese were recruited mainly to remedy labor shortages and to fill menial positions that European American miners and settlers did not want. Almost from their initial immigration, the Chinese were targeted for discrimination. In California in the early 1850s, the Tingley Bill enforced Chinese labor commitments through the courts through the "coolie process," which brought Chinese people to California solely for their labor, or through the "credit ticket," a process much like the indentured servant experience. Then in 1854, in *People v. Hall*, the California Supreme Court, acting on the same law that prohibited Blacks, mulattos, and Native Americans from testifying in court, determined that the Chinese could not testify in court either.

By 1882 great concern was growing in California about the increasing numbers and influence of Chinese people. Unions were beginning to grow and organize during this period; they feared Chinese laborers would work for lower wages and would accept poorer working conditions than their union members. Thus, the first Chinese Exclusionary Act was passed. This act excluded skilled and semi-skilled Chinese laborers from entering this country for 10 years. In 1884, the Act was amended to extend exclusion to merchants; it also limited travel by legitimate residents who had come to America prior to 1882—if they left the U.S. to visit China, they could not return.

In 1888 the Scott Act further limited travel by declaring that a laborer who visited China could get back into the United States only by proving that he had a family here or by owning property valued in excess of $1,000. The Gary Act extended exclusion for another 10 years. In 1902 the act was extended again and then further amended in 1904 to include the territory of Hawaii. Not only could the Chinese not enter Hawaii, but those Chinese who were in Hawaii could no longer enter the United States.

From the 1890s to the 1960s, then, Chinese immigration was virtually halted. After 1960 immigration legislation finally eased up on restrictive quotas. Between 1961 and 1985, over half a million Chinese people, especially from Taiwan, immigrated to America.

With Chinese exclusion, immigration opened up for the Japanese. Of all the ethnic minorities in the United States, the Japanese were the strongest and most protected. The Japanese government strictly limited the number of Japanese who were given passports and allowed to leave their country. Japan, therefore, was able to furnish its emigrants with money and passage and even set up dormitories and hotels for them in the port cities on the West Coast. Unlike the Chinese, Japanese people entering the United States were, for a short period, self-sufficient. Those who immigrated to Hawaii usually came under contract labor agreements; when those agreements expired in 1894, many of the original 30,000 immigrants stayed on to form the large present-day Japanese American community.

But by 1908 the influence of the Japanese community in California also became problematic. Japanese immigration was regulated by the

"Gentlemen's Agreement," which reasoned at the time that Japanese military strength and preparedness superseded American strength and preparedness. Thus, under the Gentlemen's Agreement, Japan limited the number of passports to skilled and unskilled Japanese workers, and in exchange the United States agreed to prevent restrictive laws relating to Japanese people in California. But journalists and laborers became more and more vociferous against the Japanese labor force. In 1905 California newspapers warned of the "yellow peril" as a threat to American institutions and social practices. President Roosevelt interceded and arranged for government prohibition of Japanese immigrants. The Gentlemen's Agreement took on new meaning as no passports were handed out to Japanese people except those already in the United States or their close relatives (Manchester-Boddy, 1970; Kitano, 1976). By 1924 Japanese immigration was halted, based on an earlier Supreme Court decision, *Ozawa v. U.S.*, which said only immigrants of White or African origin could become citizens of the United States (tenBroek, Barnhart, and Matson, 1968).

Then the Pearl Harbor attack on Hawaii in 1941 precipitated governmental action against Japanese Americans. Executive Order 9066 withdrew the protection of citizenship from Japanese Americans, placed them in internment camps, and seized their property and money. Military districts were established in California, Washington, Oregon, and Arizona, in which Japanese, Italians, and Germans were considered suspect aliens; but only the Japanese were forced to resettle and transported to concentration camps (Spicer, 1969).

Anti-Asian restrictions continued until 1965. Asians were non-White and non-European, and as such they were not allowed access to educational institutions. In 1863 the California State Board of Education mandated separate schools for Chinese and White children, but then did not build many schools for minority children; thus, minority children were largely uneducated in the state of California until 1885. Then a San Francisco court held that the Fourteenth Amendment gave a Chinese girl the right to attend public school, and she attended public school until a Chinese school was built. The new school was to be for all

Asians—Chinese, Japanese, and Korean (the 1895 treaty with Japan had required that Japanese children be educated in the United States, but separate schools were preferred). Between 1920 and 1928 over 100 Japanese-language schools with 4,000 students sprang up in California; these schools focused on preserving traditional Japanese values and strengthening community bonds. Reactions to these schools, from the California legislature and exclusionists, led to their demise. The Japanese also made great strides in public education through the college level for both men and women. During the 1940s Japanese Americans got their schooling in camps; later, they reintegrated into the public school system. By the 1980s the median level of education for Japanese Americans was 12.9 years of schooling, and for Chinese Americans, 13.4 years, compared to 12.5 years for all adult Americans (U.S. Bureau of the Census, 1983). At the nation's top universities, Asian Americans, who make up 2 percent of the college-age population, accounted for 11 percent of the entering freshman class in 1986. Now the greatest problem Asian American students have is cutbacks by higher education for their admission.

CONCLUSION

In examining the histories of racial and ethnic groups in America, we have become more aware of how unique each group is and how difficult it is to present all minorities as a unified group. We have noted the special circumstances and the identity of each immigrant group and attempted to zero in on each history. We have examined the obstacles each group has encountered in becoming citizens of the United States and the struggles of each group to become educated and to achieve the promises and prospects of American democracy and opportunity. In almost every instance, the path to citizenship and to education has been difficult. In almost every case, formidable obstacles and barriers have met each group as it has attempted to overcome or transcend its assigned "place" in social, economic, political, and educational institutions. An important part of these struggles to gain full representation in American institutions has been learning how to use the American system and the promises of equality to engender social movements that call for change in the status quo. Many times these achievements are short-lived, and most of the time there is great controversy and debate over these challenges to the system.

The impetus for protest—and yet sometimes the downfall of particular goals—is contained in the social movements that have called for expanding rights and liberties to all Americans. In some instances, policies and programs have been wrong-minded, and bad guesses about how changes should be incorporated into policy have caused additional burdens. Unless new goals are culturally embedded, real change will not occur. This process takes time.

Community colleges are the recipients of nontraditional students. They promise not to discriminate on the basis of race, ethnicity, gender, class, or handicap. They are being challenged to face a "mission impossible" and to confront the needs of an intensive care unit. And almost everybody believes they can do it!

CHAPTER FIVE

❧

AFFIRMATIVE ACTION: THEN AND NOW

❧

How Did We Get There and When Did We Get Back?

The Challenges of Affirmative Action

Ambiguities of Affirmative Action

Confronting the Tiger and the Beautiful Lady: The Courts

Community Colleges and Affirmative Action: California

   David Mertes: Guiding the State

   Marjorie Blaha: Implementing an Internship Program

   Donald Phelps: It's Déjà Vu, All Over Again!

   Tom Fryer: Achieving Cultural Pluralism

Conclusion

Lessons from the past reveal the problems surrounding alternately exclusionary and inclusionary policies aimed at women and racial-ethnic minorities in the United States. These practices result from prevailing attitudes and values embedded in the political, economic, and societal cultures. Transformation of gender and racial order occurs by means of alternately balanced and disrupted relationships between the formation of ideology and the positing of reform policy.

The goals of underrepresented groups in America may be understood as a process, or movement, which allows for rearticulation of ideology and cultural values. Movements that begin as social, political, or educational projects both build on and break away from their cultural and political predecessors; they take shape in the interaction between society and the development of new policy. For example, groups may begin by simply questioning the meanings of identities—such as minority/majority status—and segregation. Meanwhile, policy initiatives seek to reinforce or transform what such movements point out as an unstable equilibrium of gender or racial politics. Such "projects" challenge ideas, ideology, and policy. They are efforts to rearticulate the meanings of gender, race, and ethnicity, and as such they involve a dual process of disorganization of the dominant cultural framework and ideology and construction of an alternative, oppositional framework.

The dominant ideology can be disorganized in various ways. An insurgent movement, arising in opposition to civil authority or "the establishment" and led by "intellectuals," may question whether the dominant gender and racial-ethnic ideology properly applies to the collective experience of its members. Examples of this interrogation of the pre-existing system of racial categories and beliefs may be found not only in militant movement rhetoric, but also in popular and intellectual discourse. During the 1960s and 1970s, minority economists, political scientists, sociologists, and psychologists rejected dominant social science perspectives on racial grounds:

> For years, traditional social science research—especially on political life and organization—told us how politically workable and healthy the society was, how all the groups in society were getting pretty much their fair share, or moving certainly in that direction. There was a social scientific myth of consensus and progress that developed (Gutierrez, 1974, p. 231).

Insurgent racial minority movements also try to redefine the essential aspects of group identity. Militants in the 1960s attacked the political accommodations and compromises of organizations such as the NAACP, the Urban League, the GI Forum, and LULAC for succumbing to "co-optation" (Meier and Rivera, 1972). This concept of co-optation, which is sometimes called absorption or assimilation by other thinkers, became a rallying point for the more radical elements of the racial-ethnic minority movements. But those movements and their insurgency were not without reaction. During the 1970s, conservative movements, such as those of the "new right" or the "unmeltable" ethnics (Novak, 1973), developed counter-egalitarian challenges to the reforms that minority movements had achieved in the previous decade. In this way, the overarching ideology—in which racial minorities and the white majority alike recognize themselves—was called into question.

Philosophy and philosophical inquiry also pose challenges to dominant belief systems. The school of thought of postmodernism offers deep and far-reaching criticisms of the institution of philosophy and perspectives on the relation of philosophy to the larger culture; it seeks to develop new paradigms of social criticism that do not rely on traditional philosophical underpinnings. Postmodernists are skeptical of the strides taken by modern feminists whom they say are essentialists (replicating universalizing tendencies of academic scholarship and extending even faulty generalizations, thus perpetuating the failure of academic scholarship to recognize the embeddedness of its own assumptions within a specific historical context), while feminists respond that postmodernists are androcentric and politically naive (Nicholson, 1990).

For disorganization of existing paradigms to take place, the construction of a new set of assumptions, values, and artifacts must occur. The transition from "old" to "new" projects is marked by considerable instability and tension. The construction of an oppositional movement may involve a wide variety of themes, identities, and meanings. The idea of rearticulation of beliefs and ideologies involves the recombination of pre-existent meanings, as well as new perspectives and sources. For the individual, challenging dominant ideologies inherently involves not only reconceptualizing individual identity, but also reformulating the meaning of the changed idea or belief as the individual interacts within society. Gender and racial-ethnic movements that build on the terrain of civil society necessarily confront the ideological and legal system of government as they begin to upset the equilibrium of accepted and tried order.

Once an oppositional ideology has been articulated, and once the dominant ideology has been confronted, it becomes possible to demand reform of national, state, and local institutions and their policies. By the same token, once such challenges have been posed and become part of the established discourse, they, in turn, become subject to rearticulation. The state reforms won by women's and minority movements of the 1960s, and the new definitions and meanings embodied in these reforms, provided a formidable range of targets for counter-reformers in the 1970s. Countervailing ideological currents, armed with the still-dominant social scientific paradigm of gender or racial-ethnic theory, are able to carry out their own projects. In the 1970s and 1980s, they were able to rearticulate gender and racial-ethnic ideology and thus to restructure gender and racial-ethnic politics once again.

HOW DID WE GET THERE AND WHEN DID WE GET BACK?

In March of 1985, 2,500 people gathered in Alabama to commemorate Martin Luther King's Selma-to-Montgomery march, considered a turning point in the struggle to attain voting rights for Blacks. In 1985 the message of the Southern Christian Leadership Conference was this:

"We have kept the faith, but the nation has not kept its promise" (Omi and Winant, 1986, p. 109). The condition of Black America is worsening when measured by indicators such as employment rates, numbers of families falling below the poverty line, and higher educational attainment. Yet despite these continuing problems, many Americans retain a certain callousness about the situations of Blacks and other minorities; many feel that far from being the victims of deprivation, racial and ethnic minorities are unfairly receiving preferential treatment with respect to jobs and educational opportunities. How did we get to this point?

Some would say we got there from George Wallace's 1968 presidential bid, which encouraged White Southerners to defect from the Democratic party, leaving it weak and ineffective. Others would say we got there from Richard Nixon's policies, which gave lip service to Black capitalism but real economic support only to large, established corporations. And there are those who would say we got there through social and cultural alarmism, which has blamed radical democratic policies of the 1960s for changing family values, increased crime, high unemployment, loss of American international military and economic hegemony, inflation and stagflation, and humiliation over Vietnam, Nicaragua, Iran, and OPEC. These events of the 1970s called into question the scope and capacities of the so-called "welfare state."

President Johnson's Great Society program promised the elimination of poverty and racism in the United States. But problems only increased. Public opinion and political beliefs that had been sympathetic and supportive of social change began to turn against government policies they had previously sanctioned. A new political ideology began to emerge. Neoconservatives, previously liberal in their political ideology, now vehemently rejected government interference and the policy of pouring money into social programs. Part of their attack was a popular backlash movement tied to affirmative action. The argument of this backlash runs something like this: Through reckless intervention, the state committed "reverse discrimination," making Whites the victims of racial discrimination in both the job market and education.

For a short period, racial, ethnic, and gender movements had dramatically reshaped the political and cultural landscape of this nation. They imparted new meanings to established traditions, artifacts, values, and beliefs. Equality, group and individual rights, and the legitimate scope of government action were reinterpreted and rearticulated by these movements in democratic discourse. Ironically, by challenging the verities of the past and arranging the political terrain, these movements invited reaction: The expected transformation to egalitarian ideals, framed by minority movements, could not sustain itself. True, society acknowledged the women's movement, but issues of pregnancy, divorce, female heads of households, and women's place in the labor force remain controversial. True, society acknowledged the need for racial equality, but it did so by viewing it as colorblindness. And in this vision, racial considerations must never be entertained in the selection of leaders, in hiring, or in educational pursuits. True, society acknowledged the discrepancies of standardized admissions or hiring processes that discriminated against women and racial-ethnic groups, but soon thereafter affirmative action was seen as a new injustice, granting a new form of privilege—preferential treatment—for racial-ethnic minorities and women and against White men.

THE CHALLENGES OF AFFIRMATIVE ACTION

In what would become viewed as a break with tradition—albeit a fundamental premise of pluralism—racial-ethnic minorities in the United States began to question the legitimacy of reforms based on the principle of equality of individuals, seeking instead a radical collective equality, or "group rights." True, the Great Society theorists had hinted at the necessary equality of results; Lyndon Johnson had said, "We seek not just freedom, but opportunity—not just legal equity, but human ability—not just equality as a right and a theory, but equality as a fact and as a result" (Rainwater and Yancey, 1967, p. 126). But those same theorists quickly drew back from the implications of this position.

By the early 1970s, opposition to minority demands for group rights had become the centerpiece of an intellectual, neoconservative rhetoric.

These writers minimized references to "reverse discrimination" or "reverse racism," preferring to center their critique on the illegitimacy of governmental policies that invited thinking along "racial" lines. Thus, Glazer's (1987) objections to affirmative action policies centered on their ineffectiveness and their challenge to the fundamental civil ideals that had made the American ethnic pattern possible: individualism, market-based opportunity, and the curtailment of excessive state intervention. To Glazer, affirmative action meant that

> ... we abandon the first principle of a liberal society, that the individual's interests and good and welfare are the test of a good society, for we now attach benefits and penalties to individuals simply on the basis of their race, color, and national origins. The implications of this new course are increasing consciousness of the significance of group membership, an increasing divisiveness on the basis of race, color, and national origin, and a spreading resentment among the disfavored groups against the favored ones (p. 220).

Glazer and others (Bell, 1976; Novak, 1973; Nisbet, 1977) argued, therefore, for public concern for the individual and the ability of the individual to work out his or her own fate by means of education, work, and self-realization. Glazer's argument is that resentment against such programs was inevitable; there is, in Glazer's pronouncement, fear of the politics of ressentiment (individuals' sense that they exist in an indifferent society and that it is futile to try to improve their status) as an unwanted consequence of state overinvolvement. Opposition to affirmative action can be seen as consistent with the goals of the civil rights movement; it is a challenge to thinking based on race, ethnicity, or gender. According to the logic of this opposition, only individual rights exist, only individual opportunity can be guaranteed by law, and only merit justifies the granting of privilege. Neoconservative criticism and critique of affirmative action expose both discrimination and antidiscrimination measures as being based on group rights principles and seek to refocus debate on the question of what means are best for achieving equality.

The equation of racial-ethnic polarization to the issue of "classical liberalism" elicits a unique kind of polarization—that of confrontation over the meaning of individual versus group rights. An emphasis on group rights over individual merit is acceptable in some situations, such as labor unions and the institutionalization of allocation of benefits within schools and state agencies. Thus, the attack on affirmative action is not only about "fairness," but also about the maintenance of existing social position and political stability.

The current unpopularity of affirmative action extends far beyond the neoconservative "reverse discrimination" critique; public opinion demonstrates the defeat of affirmative action. People in this country have trivialized the meaning of equality. Discrimination never derived its main strength from individual actions or prejudices, however great they were or are. Rather, discrimination's most fundamental characteristic was always its roots in the racially organized social order. It was to this order that the minority movements of the 1950s and 1960s addressed themselves; but this questioning of the social assignments of identities and racial meanings is turned on its head by the assault on affirmative action. Limiting the meaning of racial discrimination to the curtailment of individual rights, whether the rights of Whites or non-Whites, eliminates any recourse to address explicit prejudice or institutionalized inequality.

Attacks on affirmative action have also grown to include other threatening social issues, such as those addressing certain traditional values of family, the work ethic, feminism, and welfare rights. What came out of this alliance against various social issues was a new intellectual and policy-oriented realignment. Republicans opposed every major civil rights measure considered by Congress, and Democrats began to suffer defeat as a party because their party was seen as having "lost touch with a majoritarian constituency" and as needing "to shed its image as the vehicle for special interests" (Omi and Winant, 1986, p. 132).

AMBIGUITIES OF AFFIRMATIVE ACTION

Affirmative action polemics provide an excellent example of the cycle of oppositional-counteroppositional movements and their foray into ambiguity. Glazer, for example, warns of "affirmative action and preferential hiring as an abandonment of the first principle of a liberal society—that public policy should take account of individual rights and welfare without consideration of group membership," and he alternately states that "no consideration of principle—such as that merit should be rewarded, or that governmental programs should not discriminate on grounds of race or ethnic group—would stand in the way of a program of preferential hiring if it made some substantial progress in reducing the severe problems of the low-income Black population and of the inner cities" (Glazer, 1987, p. 220). Thus, Glazer reaches a negative judgment by balancing various principles and factual assessments against one another, but then holds to no absolute rejection of affirmative action.

Others declare themselves in favor of "genuine" affirmative action— that is, the attempt to search out qualified minority candidates for job openings, thereby widening the pool of applicants as much as possible. But they have been militantly opposed to most of the steps devised to institutionalize and bring about such an effort on a large scale once discrimination has been found—steps such as the gathering of racial information about job holders and applicants, the establishment of goals and timetables that, if not met, place the burden of proving a good-faith effort on employers, a systematic skepticism toward job tests that disproportionately disqualify minority applicants, and the prescription of definite remedial measures such as the hiring of a given number of minority candidates or the transfer or promotion of employees identified by race or sex (Steinfels, 1979).

Neoconservative and liberal views of affirmative action are summarized in the following table.

Neoconservative View

1. In the mid-1960s the nation reached an effective consensus that racial, religious, and ethnic distinctions had no place in the provision of public services, access to public facilities, public education, employment, and housing.

2. By the end of the 1960s, discrimination was no longer a major obstacle to minority progress in employment, and minorities were in fact making considerable gains before affirmative action programs were instituted.

3. Lack of skills and ambition, cultural differences, and an understandable hesitance of Whites remain obstacles to Black and Hispanic progress in employment, education, and housing; there is no clear way to deal with these problems.

4. Affirmative action programs promise no benefits for the inner-city poor who need assistance the most; instead, they boost segments of the minority population that are already rapidly improving their status.

5. Once caught up in the machinery of courts, federal commissions, and other enforcement agencies, affirmative action is transformed into a rigid, costly, and unjust exercise in which statistical compliance drives out any remaining concern for individual qualifications (Steinfels, 1979).

Liberal View

1. Racial discrimination is still deeply embedded in American society, not only in overt prejudice, but also in inherited patterns of association, culture, and residence that work to perpetuate inequities even after racial prejudice has been eliminated.

2. The progress of Blacks and other minorities in the 1970s was facilitated by a happy economic situation and a vociferous civil rights movement; neither of these ' has maintained itself, and the continued economic gains of minorities have become correspondingly uncertain.

3. It is precisely the goal of any movement, like that for civil rights in the 1960s, to institutionalize its demands so that they do not fade with the inevitable loss of the movement's momentum; one form of that institutionalization is government requirements for affirmative action.

4. The dangers of allowing bureaucracies to traffic in racial classifications are quite real, and they can lead to absurdities and injustices, but it is possible to oversee this process and, allowing for trial and error, to establish distinctions that answer both the need to overcome a long-standing division in our society and the obligation to respect individual rights.

Neoconservative View	Liberal View

Neoconservative View

6. Affirmative action programs, as they have evolved, threaten to make identification and distinctive treatment by racial (or social) category a pervasive and permanent aspect of American life, reversing the nation's traditional recognition of the individual's rights and abilities, regardless of race, color, sex, or creed.

7. At least one form of educational affirmative action, busing, has proved to be educationally meaningless at the same time that it has been politically and socially disruptive.

8. Affirmative action fuels the resentment of Whites, especially "ethnics" and lower-to-middle-income groups, who feel that, after having had to "make it on their own," they are being forced to pay an undue proportion of the cost of preferential treatment, not only in taxes, but also in pressures on their schools, jobs, and neighborhoods.

9. While accomplishing few positive results, affirmative action undermines the efforts of successful minority-group members by creating a climate in which it will be assumed that their achievements do not reflect individual worth as much as special consideration (Sowell, 1983 and 1984).

Liberal View

5. The resentment of Whites should be attended to, but not by the abandonment of affirmative action and certainly not by misrepresentation or exaggeration of the advantages it grants minorities.

Both the neoconservative and the dominant liberal positions have been criticized for their "strategic naiveté" (Maguire, 1977). For the liberals, this criticism has to do with the potential drawbacks of courts and bureaucratic agencies implementing policy—this is the liberals' blindspot. Conservatives' optimism over the decline of discrimination in America is their blindspot; they vastly overestimate the degree to which meritocratic standards already operate in institutions such as universities. Studies document the importance of personal associations, informal networks, and stereotypes of all sorts in the hiring and selection procedures, no less so in higher education than elsewhere. To some extent, affirmative action has forced institutions to be more meritocratic by challenging these habitual practices. What is clear, Steinfels notes, "is not that neoconservatives are mistaken in their detailed criticism of affirmative action, but that they are mistaken in interpreting this debate as a drastic revision of our notions of equality" (1979, p. 230). Opinion in the courts and elsewhere continues to swing back and forth; no point of equilibrium has been established.

Even more perplexing in neoconservative-liberal debate is the two groups' attitudes on equality and egalitarianism. Much of the concern of neoconservativism involves the use of the term equality by egalitarians or neoliberals. Examples of neoconservativism can be found in the writings of Glazer, Bell, and Nisbet. Glazer fears the awesome potential of the revolution of equality in which "there is no point at which the equality revolution can come to an end" (as quoted in Steinfels, 1979, p. 214). Bell (1976) warns of wholesale egalitarianism that insists on complete levelling. Nisbet (1977) proclaims that demands for equality carry a sense of religious zeal that threatens liberty and social initiative. One wonders why neoconservatives are in so much turmoil over the concept of equality. Shouldn't minorities and women have an equal chance of achieving the patterns of inequality existing among Whites and males? There seems to be very little in the debate over affirmative action that suggests that we are approaching an egalitarian precipice, but neoconservatives continue to chafe over the supposed incompatibility of equality, liberty, and meritocracy.

The Moynihan report addressed the democratic ideals of liberty and equality. For Moynihan and others, liberty and equality are not the same thing: While some might argue that the distribution of success and failure within one group may be roughly comparable to that within other groups, equality of opportunity is not coequal with liberty. Equality of opportunity, rather, ensures inequality of results; thus, the demand for economic equality is not the demand for equal opportunities for the equally qualified, but rather the demand for equality of economic results. Programs to aid minorities make opportunities available; they cannot ensure the outcome. Moynihan points to the shifts in the meaning of equality that neoconservatives find so menacing: "the shift from equality of opportunity to equality of results" and "the shift from equality between individuals to equality between groups" (as quoted in Rainwater and Yancey, 1967, p. 126).

Thus, what had begun as a reformulation of the principles of the "intellectual rigor" of the neoconservatives became an intense re-examination of the relation between education and equality. This relationship seems to be a particularly tangled topic because the "result" of education, especially early education, was and is believed to determine "opportunity" for the rest of one's life, especially in a credential-conscious society. After Coleman (1966) completed the massive study *Equality of Educational Opportunity*, Moynihan reanalyzed the study's data and denounced with great skepticism the idea that public education is a lever for change. Furious debates broke out over compensatory education programs like Head Start, community control of inner-city schools, and theories linking I.Q. differences and race. Jencks (1972) tied the debates together as he simultaneously rejected both hereditarian theories of intelligence and liberal confidence in schooling as a remedy for inequality (Steinfels, 1979, p. 218).

Conservative attacks on America's community colleges, seen as society's safety valve for upward mobility (Clark, 1960; Karabel, 1972; Corcoran, 1972; Zwerling, 1976; Orfield, 1984), continue until the present day. As successful products of existing educational systems, as teachers and scholars within them, and as defenders of the liberal university's legitimacy against the criticism and sometimes disruption of the left, neoconservatives might easily have felt that "equality" was a key that had opened the door to the tiger and not to the beautiful lady. Rather than gaining access and opportunity through the door to the beautiful lady, they had to confront the tiger of anger, obstacles, and possible attacks. Perhaps the choice of doors was better left to the courts.

CONFRONTING THE TIGER AND THE BEAUTIFUL LADY: THE COURTS

Beginning with Chief Justice Warren (1953-1969), continuing with Burger (1969-1986), and now with Rehnquist as Chief Justice, Supreme Court decisions have been a reflection of the debates around discrimination and civil liberties. And although the Warren Court was the most judicially active and liberally egalitarian in its decrees, the Burger court did not move to greater conservative stands on the issues of civil liberties. For example, the Burger Court was the first court to uphold busing, the first to require desegregation in the North, and the first to overturn laws on the grounds of sexual discrimination (Baum, 1989). But membership on the court has been directly affected by the presidents who have nominated justices; court members in the Reagan and Bush years are more conservative, and their opinions reflect a movement away from liberal egalitarian philosophies.

Compensatory treatment for past injustices and preferential treatment to bring about increased employment opportunities, promotions, and admissions to colleges for minorities and women became more and more controversial in the 1970s. Quotas, goals, guidelines, and set-asides utilized to compensate for the ravages of the past—preferential treatment through affirmative action that all but guaranteed numerically targeted slots or posts based on membership in racial and sexual groups—became the targets for "reverse discrimination" decisions such as the Bakke decision (1978), the Weber decision (1979), and the Fullilove decision (1980). In each of these decisions the court debate centered on whether attention to race represents justifiable, compensatory action to redress past wrongs or whether any racial quota system is a violation of the explicit language of the Civil Rights Act of 1964 (Abraham, 1988). But, although the debate has been heated, the courts have not backed away from affirmative action. The Bakke decision, although it held for the defendant, did not abrogate affirmative action programs based on racial preference. The Weber and Fullilove decisions confirmed affirmative action programs (racial quotas were found to be neither illegal nor unconstitutional), although the dissenters on the court saw this action as judicial legislation. In subsequent cases the courts ruled that:

- Racially based hiring and promotion programs may be applied to minority groups generally and not confined to individually identified victims of discrimination
- Federal trial judges may set goals and timetables that employers must meet to remedy past discrimination
- States and cities have broad discretion to agree to adopt affirmative action plans that go well beyond what courts may order (1986 Cleveland and New York cases)
- Judges may order strict racial promotion quotas to overcome "long-term, open and pervasive discrimination" (*U.S. v. Paradise*, 1987)
- It is permissible to take sex and race into account in employ- ment hiring and promotion decisions and to bring the work force in line with the local population, even without any proof of past discrimination (*Johnson v. Transportation Agency*, Santa Clara County, 1987)

Affirmative action/reverse discrimination rulings underscore differ- ences in society and demonstrate ideological variances. People see the Court's role as a restraining or an active one, as a body that finds the law or a body that makes it. The Court in the 1990s is more oriented toward judicial restraint and conservativism. Marshall is the very last of the liberal egalitarians on the court.

COMMUNITY COLLEGES AND
AFFIRMATIVE ACTION: CALIFORNIA

California community colleges enroll approximately 1.25 million students annually. Replicating that number is not easy; only by adding the totals of the next four highest-enrolling states—Texas, Illinois, New York, and Florida—do we get comparable populations of students enrolled in community colleges. Approximately 22 percent of all community college students and 12 percent of all higher education students in the nation are enrolled in California community colleges. With these data in mind, the California legislature, in a bill sponsored by John Vasconcellos, wrote:

> The California Community Colleges face an unprecedented challenge in the coming two decades, as California undergoes a major demographic, social, and economic transformation. The community colleges are at the center of this change, and the state's future as a healthy and free, diverse, and creative society depends in major part upon the commitments expressed through and in the community colleges (AB 1725, California Legislature).

California's population is expected to increase from its present 27 million to 33 million by the turn of the century. It will have a diverse cultural and ethnic pluralism: 51 percent of the school-age children in 1989 were minorities, and the majority of the population will be non-White in the following decade. There is no one "minority community" in California. Moreover, by the year 2000 California will have more elderly citizens than any other state in the nation; 20 percent of its population will be senior citizens. In an economy of rapid change and intense international competition, there will be much job displacement, and workers of the future will need new literacy skills and more ability to communicate and learn on their own. In the labor shortage analysts predict for California by 2000, the real issue will not be numbers, but quality. The important questions will be whether working men and women will have the skills required for jobs characterized by rapid transformation and whether California will be able to compete economically with other states now making massive investment in their educational systems. As the California legislature noted:

> The convergence of these tendencies, both demographic and economic, lead to the possibility of an increasingly stratified society. This can include what has been called a "permanent underclass," mostly minority, and a semipermanent, semi-employable stratum of low-skilled workers. The consequences of this development would be dire: the permanent underutilization of the energies and talents of our people, the deepening of racial resentments and fears, and the constant anxiety among more and more of us that the future has no place for us (AB 1725).

California's Assembly Bill 1725 predicts that more minorities, immigrants, elderly people, and working men and women will come to community colleges to achieve their goals. Community colleges will be called on to retrain workers, to teach English to immigrants, to provide skills and opportunities for the elderly, to provide opportunities for secondary school drop-outs, and to continue to provide lower-division transfer education. The California legislature states that it is

> committed to an alternative vision in which California remains a place of opportunity and hope, where innovation and creativity mark our economy and our culture, and where the minds and spirits of all our communities contribute to our common future. The community colleges will be at the heart of whatever effort we make to insure that the future is equitable and open, that California's economy remains healthy and growing, and that both rural towns and rapidly expanding urban centers have educational resources close at hand.

> The majority of people in California welcome this new epoch as a challenge of unprecedented opportunity. The legislature shares this view and expresses the intent that sufficient funding and resources of this state be provided to forge into

a new range of educational engagements for our people. It is important in this regard to honor those who teach basic skills and literacy, as well as those who teach Shakespeare and Plato, to facilitate effective communication between "vocational" and "liberal arts" departments in an epoch where all vocations will require deeper and more subtle forms of literacy, and to build a new and diverse curriculum which engages all our diverse students and demands the best of their minds and spirits.

The people of California should have the opportunity to be proud of a system of community colleges which instills pride among its students and faculty, where rigor and standards are an assumed part of a shared effort to educate, where the hugely diverse needs of students are a challenge rather than a threat, where the community colleges serve as models for the new curricula and innovative teaching, where learning is what we care about most.

AB 1725 was intended to be a blueprint for the future, providing direction and support for the community colleges. Its contents are summarized here:

1. The mission of the community colleges is clarified; priorities for transfer and vocational education are designated as the primary mission of California community colleges. Remedial instruction, English as a Second Language, adult noncredit instruction, and student support services are designated as "important and essential;" community services are designated as "authorized." And in new language (September 1990: AB 462, Hayden), community colleges "may conduct institutional research concerning student learning and retention to facilitate their educational missions."

2. A Board of Governors of the California Community Colleges is created to administer and govern a statewide postsecondary system of education, the California Community Colleges. The regulations of the Board of Governors must be responsive to concerns raised from within the community colleges: a two-thirds vote of the 71 local governing

boards can stop state board regulations. The board is required to strengthen the role of local academic senates regarding determination and administration of academic and professional standards, course approval and curricula, and other academic matters; this is the "Shared Governance in the California Community Colleges" policy statement. Minimum standards also ensure the participation of staff and students in district and college governance.

3. Each community college district is required to establish an affirmative action employment program. Technical assistance teams from the chancellor's office are established to review the affirmative action plan for each district that fails to comply. The goal: that the system's work force reflect proportionately the adult population of the state by the year 2005.

4. New programs and services are authorized for districts, including the following programs: Career Resource and Placement Centers, Programs for Staff Development and Improvement, Faculty and Staff Diversity Fund (Affirmative Action Initiative), Board of Governors (assistance in identifying, locating and recruiting), and qualified Members of Underrepresented Groups.

5. A transfer core curriculum is planned for fall 1991.

6. Remedial limits are set: 30 semester units or 45 quarter units as of July 1990, with ESL and learning-disabled students exempted.

7. A severe hiring crisis will occur in the next 15 years—55 percent of current full-time faculty will retire—creating a window of opportunity to significantly change the ethnic mix of faculty and to ensure that faculty will be culturally balanced and more representative of the state's diversity. The bill takes note of the following realities:

- Retiring faculty positions cannot become part-time faculty positions
- Recruitment and maintaining morale and enthusiasm among faculty is dependent on the intellectual and personal environment within each campus; that environment is created by faculty authority over the substantive direction of the programs and courses in which they work, through the quality of their rela-

tionship with college administration, and in the quality of their interactions with students

- Faculty and administrators must be hired and retained
- A goal is set that represents 75 percent of the total faculty population
- A plan for new faculty qualifications is in place, with transition provisions for meeting qualifications, considering projected demographics and affirmative action policies and programs
- New critieria for hiring are determined, with emphasis on faculty responsibility to ensure the quality of their peers, on clear and complete job descriptions, and on appropriate training in affirmative action procedures and goals
- Evaluations should include a peer review process addressing affirmative action concerns

8. These student-directed concerns will be addressed:

- Articulation of vocational and academic programs: initiation and expansion of 2+2 programs
- Academic assessment and counseling on enrollment
- Determining the extent to which students are underrepresented on the basis of ethnic origin or gender in vocational education programs
- Increasing the number of students entering the teaching profession at the community college
- Adult literacy training, citizenship training, and basic skills education

DAVID MERTES: GUIDING THE STATE

David Mertes, chancellor of California Community Colleges, said of AB 1725 and its relationship to issues of population diversity and economic complexity in his state:

> The legislature focuses on ethnicity, economic complexity and the distribution of wealth, and the role of community colleges and their effectiveness. Reflecting the needs of a diverse popu-

lation, the legislature seeks to mainstream and better support minority populations that have been discriminated against on the basis of the economic and social structure. Particularly, their focus is on the ways that the community college role can be effective in aiding that process—especially in the work force—so that it will reflect the existing population. The first phase of AB 1725 is an attempt to present the community college and education in a positive way and an attempt to find links connecting the hiring process to the issue of population representation. The second phase asks critical questions, including: How do we increase people in the pipeline? Have conferences on staff diversity been held? What can we do to recognize the efforts of individuals and groups, and their programs in community colleges, who provide exemplary leadership directed at cultural diversity?

A recognition and awards program of the California Community College System recognized two affirmative action officers—one from Southern California and one from the North. Two districts have been recognized as implementing the best team approach to the situation—San Diego Community College District and the Los Rios Community College District, where a mentor program for minority students has been established. Mertes has also honored colleges establishing state fairs for employment.

Mertes defines and describes his role as one of accomplishing attitudinal change. For example, when asked "How do you get more people to think about becoming community college teachers?" Mertes answers "Making the high school, community college, and senior college connection." For example, at the University of Southern California-Edison, 100 students were identified as scholarship recipients, and each has been assigned two mentors—one from the community college in which they will eventually be employed and one from the senior institution who guides the student's undergraduate and graduate program. USC-Edison uses mentors that serve in the student-mentors group as well.

Mertes's leadership role is discussed in terms of challenges. He constantly challenges himself to reach out, to be the best or to try to be the best, and he makes a similar challenge to community colleges. Mertes believes the future depends on an educated citizenry and an educated work force. He feels that community colleges are on the cutting edge of causing both attitudinal and institutional changes. His intent is to play a leadership role in defining and designing for diversity the society we will become:

> We're not just thinking of a way to add something to the already established procedure, and we're not just being nice guys. We're saying that the state would be better off by bringing diversity into the mainstream—that we want to mainstream the community college. This is not a fad or a trend or a report to put on a shelf. To get involved you have to push up your sleeves and work. My role is not a regular or complacent one; if California community colleges want to be perceived as being out in front, as nurturing, as rewarding, as building change aimed at institutional change, then I must actively pursue those goals. Almost every college is developing some attachment to the statewide goal; and you really have to look at these colleges and identify the best ideas that they have for working with their everyday problems.

The California Community College System likes to identify and nurture colleges that work toward these goals, and also asks colleges to present what they have done so that it can be replicated. The challenge of hiring 30 percent ethnic minority faculty reflects Chairman Vasconcellos's idea that there is, and has been, discrimination in the California state system. Mertes deliberately does not use the term "affirmative action." He says that California is looking for staff diversity, and a 30 percent hiring goal is neither a set aside nor a quota—it is a goal. Mertes's language is positive. He says, "We are going to make changes!"—and he believes that present efforts are working well.

In conjunction with the Intersegmental Coordinating Council and the California State University (CSU) Teacher Diversity Program, an effort is underway in California community colleges to develop strategies for encouraging more students from underrepresented groups to prepare for careers in teaching; intersegmental partnerships have been established to examine the issues of underrepresentation and teachers. Currently, although half of the K-12 students are from ethnic minority groups, 80 percent of the state's teachers are White. The CSU Teacher Diversity Program addresses the racial imbalance between students and teachers and guides individuals through the system to earn teaching credentials. At CSU-Fullerton, for example, the "Teacher Track" program, a project to increase teacher diversity, includes a class for high school students, taught by a university professor, who describes the rewards and challenges of teaching. At Hayward, the Urban Teacher Academy is a partnership between junior and senior high schools, the South County Community College District, and business and community organizations.

MARJORIE BLAHA: IMPLEMENTING AN INTERNSHIP PROGRAM

Marjorie Blaha, chancellor, Los Rios Community College District in California says:

> This is a different time from the past. People seem to understand that California does represent a nontraditional majority; and therefore less stereotyping is going on, and attitudes are changing. Our immediate problem is not forcing change in attitudes but in finding people in the pipeline who can work in the community colleges. The district has a strong attitude toward affirmative action, and that is the reason I came to the district.

Every year the Los Rios district sets goals for increasing staff diversity. They analyze the needs of the various campuses and focus on recruitment, participating in staff review fairs. Blaha is interested in diversity and in people who represent nontraditional roles. She is interested in programs that mentor the underrepresented, and she uses state staff diversity funds to set up intern programs in her colleges in these nontraditional programs. The Los Rios Community College District's Internship Program for Ethnic Minorities and Women is designed around the following concept:

> To better reflect California's increasing cultural diversity and the characteristics of students, more ethnic minorities and women will be needed to teach in the state's community colleges. AB 1725, mandating affirmative action in community college districts statewide, identifies the following ethnic minority groups: American Indian/Alaskan Nation, Asian or Pacific Islander, Black, and Hispanic (Los Rios Community College District, 1990).

The District's Internship Program is in place to assist members of these underrepresented groups to become community college instructors. The program assumes that potential interns already have subject matter expertise in the course(s) they will teach, but that they need an opportunity to learn and to practice the teaching techniques appropriate for community college students. The interns are assigned to a Los Rios instructor for one class for one semester; day, evening, and weekend opportunities may be available, and interns are paid $1,000 to teach one class with a mentor instructor. Eligibility includes graduate students nearing completion of master's degrees, master's or doctoral degree holders who have not had postgraduate teaching experience, and bachelor's degree holders with a minimum of two years' full-time occupational experience in a vocational-technical area.

The Los Rios District is focusing on the concept of "growing your own" in a 2+2+2 system. At American River College, Queen Randall, college president, has begun visiting high schools and senior colleges to promote a new program, Teachers of Tomorrow, designed to encourage minority students to become teachers. She is raising money for program support and raising consciousness in her college service area.

One can best understand the California reality by looking at the state's demography; one need not look any further than grades K-12 to understand the impact of demographics and the resulting new majority in California. The state is very attractive to migrants and to immigrant populations. Blaha speaks of California as a frontier state—people come there for opportunity, they come with an attitude of being able to succeed, and they come because there is open-door education. The community college system in California is the largest educational system in the world. Moreover, the legislature has made it possible for everyone to attend college, and there is a strong social and monetary commitment to higher education in California. Blaha believes that for California to move with the times, the staff and faculty at all colleges must reflect the populations they serve. The term "affirmative action" may still trigger negative feelings; she prefers the idea of and the term "staff diversity." She believes that our future depends on elevating the importance of teaching as a career and enticing many from our underrepresented populations to consider becoming teachers themselves.

DONALD PHELPS: IT'S DÉJÀ VU, ALL OVER AGAIN!

Don Phelps is chancellor of the Los Angeles Community College District, the largest community college district in the nation. Phelps provides a humorous view on what is happening in terms of minority rights and implications for change, cultural pluralism, and diversity by quoting Yogi Berra, who once remarked, "It's *déjà vu,* all over again!" Phelps finds it fascinating that people look at the strategies and address the issues surrounding diversity as though they were some new phenomena. Whatever has happened in the past, he says, has been forgotten. But the paradoxes that surround the issues of diversity are related to what happened prior to this decade and what happened prior to the Reagan Administration.

In Phelps's view, North Americans have trouble with the word "minority." We have trouble with it because it implies statistics, it implies a number, it implies a quota system, and it implies the concept of affirmative action. Phelps believes that there is a distinct difference between the old-style Civil Rights concept of equal opportunity employment and the new-style values and emphasis on diversity and cultural pluralism. He calls it the "then and now difference." The "then" was government, and laws were sympathetic to the issues of minorities and seemed to be on the side of minorities. "Now," he says, "is defined by new utterances with contradictions galore from the national administration. What are the issues? How have the issues of civil rights been treated? The Justice Department and the Supreme Court, for example, have not rendered opinions for minorities for some time. And we find that neither Mr. Reagan nor Mr. Bush has funded issues that they claim to support." He adds, "From where should the benefits be derived?— from a national leader who recognizes the problem!"

As these issues relate to education, Phelps sees few substantive programs in the ranks for faculty and administration. In his opinion, "The same people get cycled and recycled." It is not enough to acknowledge himself as the first Black man to head up the largest community college in the nation; it is important to ask where he came from, to ask who placed him there, and to acknowledge the truth that when a Black man is replaced, there is one less Black leader. He questions, "What are my chances at being replaced by another person of color?" and answers, "Recycling from the same pool means numbers of minorities do not grow. I truly believe faculty should play a key role in the selection of peers and administrators, but I firmly believe these groups should be made aware of the importance of addressing current hiring issues."

Phelps is well aware of the significance of environment and climate in his district, and he integrates that understanding into his own "culture of change:"

> Is the act of "sensitizing" them to their moral obligations enough to cause change? No! Thus, I'd rather appeal to the instinct of survival. There are 70,000 members of ethnic gangs in L.A.; death is as frequent as weather reports. People live behind gates and iron bars—we are literally imprisoned in our homes or wherever we are. We are not safe because of what we've allowed society to become. If there is potential for safety, health, and welfare, that potential has a stronger pull than moral sensitivity. Self-survival is the first law of nature; we must make certain that all people have the opportunity to

compete in the marketplace. If you don't believe this, you are in danger.

Finally, Phelps is most eloquent when he recites the *déjà vu* theme. For him, civil rights must be worked at and must be developed for future generations, starting now:

> How long has it been since the Revolution? Do you think you made a difference? Civil rights is like fitness, you have to work at it all the time. I think I'd better make a difference—part of the reason I was hired in Los Angeles was because I am a member of a minority group, and I need to make a distinctive difference above and beyond others' abilities. My position as chancellor is to keep human dignity right on the table, to talk about it often, to implement it, and to make myself the model for that behavior. If every president in the district was an ethnic minority, I'd never apologize for it—my challenge here is to provide a vehicle for change, while at the same time to never compromise quality or principles of providing quality education.
>
> I should be able to see in young people of color and gender that they have potential, I should demonstrate that I have confidence in their potential, and then I should bring them along. I see value in developing that potential. I believe that along with affirmative action, diversity, and equal opportunity, we ought to deal with the concept of freedom. I like to think of myself as free. An analogy might be found in busing—I like to ride in the safest part of the bus, which is in the back, but I like to think I have the freedom to choose whether I ride in the front, middle, or back. I then have freedom. I safeguard freedom for others and for myself.

TOM FRYER: ACHIEVING CULTURAL PLURALISM

In 1988 Tom Fryer, chancellor, Foothill-DeAnza Community College District in California, addressed his faculty on the issues of cultural pluralism:

> For many of us, especially those of us who are not people of color, it is hard to remember the times in which Dr. King's speech was given. The White and Colored waiting rooms and water fountains that I grew up with in the South are gone. Black people are not required to ride in the back of buses, and they're not prohibited from eating at lunch counters or swimming in public swimming pools. These and other details of what some might call an American version of apartheid are, as I say, easy for some of us to forget. But they are vivid and deeply painful personal memories for others. They seem so foreign to some of us today, so almost South African. But they are not foreign at all.
>
> Prejudice is a subject that arouses strong feelings in all of us, so strong in some cases that the feelings drive out our capacity to examine issues rationally. But I am deeply troubled by the permission that an increasing number of people give themselves these days to express such mean-spirited feelings about fellow human beings and to do so merely on the basis of the person's color, or culture, or religion, or sex, or sexual preference, or age. Please try to think with me on this subject for a few moments. I take it on directly for several reasons. First, I am troubled. Second, I share Dr. King's dream, as I'm sure many of you do, of a society in which people "will not be judged by the color of their skin but by the content of their character." Third, in my opinion, we are not discussing these issues either in our country or in our colleges openly and constructively. Fourth, the very existence of our institution, the community college, rests fundamentally on the social value of democratizing opportunity. If we

betray that value, we lose the moral authority that empowers us. And lastly, we in community colleges must not fall victim to the accusation that has been made of us, namely, that we perpetuate an economic underclass by providing the illusion of education in what is in reality an educational and economic cul-de-sac (Fryer, 1988).

Fryer believes that colleges must "summon the will, create the ideas, and allocate the resources to achieve the kind of genuine pluralism in our institutions that is characterized by fundamental respect and hard-won understanding for the differences among us." At Foothill-DeAnza, extensive discussions concerning its affirmative action program led to the creation of the position of a high-level district officer whose sole duty is affirmative action and who sought first-quality minority candidates. Moreover, faculty positions were created on each campus—affirmative action leadership chairs. These positions are linked directly to the college presidents, the academic divisions, and the district director of human resources and affirmative action. These leadership chairs will work closely with faculty, staff, and students to build a climate that enhances achievement, mutual understanding, and respect among all groups.

Following are the proposed changes in the district's affirmative action structure:

- The purpose of these changes is to represent visually Foothill-De Anza's commitment to affirmative action at the highest levels and to fix responsibility for the achievement of our affirmative action goals
- The duties and responsibilities of affirmative action officers will be to be responsible for programs in achieving affirmative action goals and timetables; to provide leadership in achieving the objectives of staff diversity and creating a climate of genuine cultural pluralism; to monitor indicators that provide information on the effectiveness of our efforts and to suggest changes when appropriate

Carolyn Fountenberry, affirmative action chair of DeAnza College, is actively recruiting members of racial and ethnic minorities by traveling to the Southwest and interviewing graduate students, thereby establishing a network for potential teaching candidates for the Foothill-DeAnza District. She and the regional affirmative action director, Geraldine Kaspar, are guided in their concerns about mandated hiring goals by written standards contained in the "Cultural Diversity/Affirmative Action Standards Plan," organized under four areas: institutional policies; institutional structures; institutional climate; and implementation standards. Institutional policies beginning with the Board of Trustees' Cultural Diversity/Affirmative Action Policy define the board's commitment to student and staff diversity and affirmative action, and communicate the board's support for a positive institutional environment in which cultural diversity is valued. Structures are in place to support the accomplishment of the identified goals. Implementation standards specify the performance factors used to achieve diversification of faculty, staff, students, and administrators, with particular attention given to recruitment and retention, hiring, institutional research and evaluation, special programs, curriculum, publications and media, and professional development.

Conscientious efforts are made in the district to create the conditions, policies, and programs to attract, recruit, and retain women, underrepresented groups, and the disabled; timelines are monitored. Hiring is a critical goal for the district and the search committee (which includes an affirmative action representative), and a "hypothetical test" is a standard for invoking affirmative action considerations. According to the Cultural Diversity/Affirmative Action Policy:

> If enough positions were available to offer a position to more
> than one finalist, then would more that one finalist be offered
> a position? If so, from those that would be offered a position,
> the decisive factor in the selection of the finalist shall be the
> district's affirmative action policy as expressed in the division's
> goals and timetables as long as parity as reflected in those
> goals and timetables has not been reached.

The Foothill-DeAnza Community College District is actively working to increase the conditions necessary to achieve cultural pluralism in its community. The district has defined the concept of cultural pluralism, and it has explored several areas that build a culturally pluralistic environment, including raising sensitivity levels, providing support for the affirmative action leadership chair positions, and developing cultural pluralism across the curriculum. And, along with Stanford University, the district cosponsors a Minority Fellowship Program designed to benefit minority doctoral students and to increase the number of minority faculty. The program offers five fellowships to doctoral students who commit to teach in the district, to contribute to the recruitment and retention of underrepresented people and the improvement of campus climate, and to participate in both departmental business and the teaching resource center to improve teacher effectiveness.

CONCLUSION

There are no easy answers to the debate over affirmative action policies. That community colleges are able to look beyond the obvious pitfalls of the debate and recognize the urgent need to include diversity as a commitment to representativeness and as an answer to the realities of demographic changes means that they are preparing for everyone's future. Most certainly, it will be community colleges with whom business and industry will continue to cooperate, because it is community college students whom business and industry will most likely hire. It will be community colleges to whom state legislatures will turn for positive reforms in higher education to help emerging groups, because these colleges offer access to all groups. And it will be community colleges who will provide the standards for democracy and egalitarianism in education that emerging democratic nations of Eastern Europe and the world will want to emulate.

CHAPTER SIX

֍

INCLUSIONARY PRACTICES: HIGHLIGHTING EXEMPLARY PROGRAMS

֍

Inclusionary Practices: Programs that Work

    Kellogg Leadership Fellows

    National Institute for Leadership Development

    AACJC: Networks and Mentoring

    The American Association of Women in Community and Junior Colleges

    National Council on Black American Affairs and Presidents' Roundtable

    National Community College Hispanic Council

    The Hispanic Association of Colleges and Universities

    Texas Association for Chicanos in Higher Education

Showcasing College Programs That Promote and Support Diversity

    Miami-Dade Community College

    Midlands Technical College

    Greenville Technical College

    Palomar College

    Santa Fe Community College

    Prince George's Community College

    East Los Angeles College

    Madison Area Technical College

    City College of San Francisco

    Clovis Community College District

    Fond du Lac Community College

    Valencia Community College

Conclusion

Underrepresentation and underutilization of women and minorities is a topic that arouses the attention of many community college leaders who call for egalitarian and equalitarian education and for education as a principle that promotes human development and change. Their efforts and responses to exclusionary practices underscore the philosophy that exclusionary practices—and underutilization and underrepresentation of women and racial-ethnic minorities—are antithetical to the stated purpose and goals of community college education. Their courage needs to be celebrated; it is the courage of the risk-taker, the reformer, and the change agent. Their leadership and programs are a vanguard for representational and inclusionary reform, and they offer programs worthy of emulation. As researchers who have examined exemplary programs, we consider the following points relevant:

We see the leaders and their state and college programs as critical to the continuing development of the community college in America, and we believe their voice is indispensable.

We see these leaders and their state and college programs as being consistent with the mission and purpose of the community college, an open-access institution that demands quality and excellence while at the same time opening doors of opportunity.

We see the leaders and their state and college programs as an achievement, a social movement that rearticulates policy and programs aimed at gender, racial, and minority group integration and inclusion in the community college.

Finally, we see the leaders and their state and college programs as the hope for future generations of Americans who will be ready to contribute to the economic, political, and educational needs of a multicultural society and nation.

Looking specifically at key leaders and state and college programs draws attention to essential characteristics of leaders and their responses to gender and racial-ethnic issues. Effective leaders challenge current and dominant cultural artifacts, values, and assumptions, and they rearticulate new political-cultural themes to mobilize a basis and a base for adherence. Yet, while leaders and programs challenge existing exclusionary policies and consolidate their new perspectives, retention of the dominant cultural values and nonconsolidation of "new perspectives" promote reactions to these challenges that may destroy them. This is the theme of Gillett-Karam's challenge-rechallenge framework that, building on the notion of cultural embedding factors, identifies the difficulty of "bucking the system" unless alternative cultural embedding mechanisms are in place.

The Challenge-Rechallenge Framework

→ challenge and changing values → maintaining status quo values

↑↓   ↑↓

challenging existing policy → reacting to new perspective(s)

↑↓   ↑↓

determining new policy → rejecting and nonconsolidating

↑↓   or   ↑↓

embedding policy in culture → finding value in new policy →

Gillett-Karam, 1991

For gender and racial-ethnic minority groups, the role of the community college in this challenge-rechallenge framework merits attention. The avowed purpose of the community college is to extend the basis of egalitarian educational privilege. This doctrine imposes a culture of pluralism and of diversity on the community college. Although there are certainly those who view this culture in the same light as "social welfare" and social engineering, we maintain that the community college exists in order to allow access without regard to privilege or handicap. It frames itself in the hope of a democratic state that promises equal opportunity to all its citizens. This perspective motivates the greater attention community colleges pay to teaching principles as opposed to research orientations; it motivates the recognition community colleges give to developmental skill preparation for their students; and it motivates the spirit of service that community colleges demonstrate and promote for the public good, the community, and the individual.

Are community colleges the intensive care units and the emergency rooms of educational services? Yes, they are! As such, they have to be more attuned to the emergencies and critical care needs of the populations that visit them; they must be attuned to the services that make their patients healthy and newly able to attend to their jobs, their positions, and their future responsibilities.

Community colleges today are facing another of the many crises and emergencies of an increasingly technological workplace and an increasingly global view. In many ways, the community college defines itself by listening to the pulse of its society: It reflects and is quickest to respond to changes in the economy and society. While our demographics clearly demonstrate the rapid growth of racial-ethnic minorities and a decline in the growth of the White population, it is also clear that community colleges will reflect these changes and must respond to them for the benefit of future generations. Many Americans wonder about the condition of future society if our present population is undereducated and unskilled. Philosophers Sikora and Barry (1978) have questioned at length our obligation to future generations; specifically, they have examined the question of whether we have an obligation to make sacrifices when there is a threat to human survival. Although these threats usually involve such issues as population explosion, nuclear destruction, and lethal pollution, considerable attention is now being paid to the moral obligation we have to the welfare (the creation of happiness) of future generations. Will we leave the world a better place for them?

Some scholars also question the injustice of acts of neglect toward future generations (Sikora and Barry, 1978). Although the virtue of humanity requires us to respond to others' needs, justice requires that we give them their due—if something is due you, you do not have to show that you need it or that you will make better use of it than other possible claimants (Rawls, 1971). If this precept is applied to the current debate over affirmative action, it would follow that if people are suffering because of inadequate education and training, then the case for helping them based on humanitarian need is clear. A case can probably be made for the proposition that members of the current generation have a duty of justice and a passion for justice (Solomon, 1990) to contribute to the public good constituted by the welfare of the next generation. And whether we act on the basis of mutual advantage, fairness, or compassion, future generations are the beneficiaries of justice.

The community college is much like our symbolic image of the Statue of Liberty. Just as that statue has become the image attached to immigrants' journeys to freedom, the community college has become the image attached to the journey toward another freedom: the freedom provided by educational opportunity. The Statue of Liberty symbolizes open arms to all immigrants; the community college symbolizes open access to all those who seek higher education. Where opportunity has been denied, both the statue and the community college symbolize hope for a new beginning. As America has accommodated the stages of growth of its own expansionism and embraced a large diversity of people and cultures, so too has the community college learned to accommodate this expansionism. Another opportunity has been presented to the community college—the opportunity to expand its bases for leadership to greater numbers of women and members of minority groups. As pathfinders and inclusionary institutions, community colleges have demonstrated again and again that they can develop leadership and programs that pave the way for greater participation and productivity of citizens.

The practices of our colleges are crucial to leadership growth and revitalization for the twenty-first century. Higher education has the obligation to develop new leadership models—to identify, develop, and select leaders who will lead in different capacities, who will have different backgrounds, different styles, and different skills (Green, 1988). If the model of transformational leadership predicts that leaders envision and act out plans and practices based on their followers' motives and values, then the immediate beneficiaries of diversifying leadership will be women and minorities.

In many community colleges, leadership is currently being developed among these populations. Learning to lead as a part of one's current assignment or job role is not uncommon. In the Dallas County Community College District (Texas), administrators are making efforts to recognize internal talent and resources among students and faculty; candidates recognized as having potential are trained to assume leadership positions within the district. Metropolitan Community College in Nebraska, under the leadership of J. Richard Gilliland, organized a one-year lecture series devoted to leadership development and the value of diversity. Gilliland explains:

> In general systems theory, diversity is a natural property that
> allows for creativity and for new ideas to be tested. Pathways
> for program development and institutional innovation exist
> so that experiments can be evaluated against desired results,
> with the results being an even more diverse system. I suggest
> the same logic for including culturally different people in a
> leadership team that would be richly diverse and truly representative,
> including minorities. The more points of view and
> the more references of experience there are, the more options
> appear and the more diverse the leadership team becomes.

INCLUSIONARY PRACTICES: PROGRAMS THAT WORK

KELLOGG LEADERSHIP FELLOWS

With grant funds provided by the W.K. Kellogg Foundation in Michigan to the League for Innovation in the Community College (Terry O'Banion, executive director) and the Community College Leadership Program at The University of Texas at Austin (John Roueche, professor and director), over 100 community college rising stars who are presently "in the pipeline" will be trained to assume positions of leadership at the dean, vice president, or vice chancellor levels. Twenty Fellows, each nominated by his or her CEO, will be selected annually to enter the program between 1990 and 1995. The Expanding Leadership Opportunities for Minorities in Community Colleges Program's objectives and outcome orientation for its Fellows include:

- An increased understanding of leadership skills and abilities
- An increased knowledge of critical issues facing community colleges
- An increased ability to act as a change agent
- An increased development of selected leadership skills
- Membership in a national network of peers and community college leaders.

Program activities were designed after careful analysis of a one-year pilot program. During the 12-month program, each Fellow:

- Designs a professional development plan—a roadmap to the year-long process of introspection, activity, and learning
- Works with one mentor (or more) who is an established community college leader (usually from his or her own home institution) to develop special areas of expertise
- Participates in an internship (at the home institution or another college or agency) of three to 12 months
- Identifies one critical issue, analyzes its status and parameters at the national level, reviews how the issue is addressed on his or her own campus, and develops a project to address the issue

- Attends intensive two-week seminars to be held on the campuses of League members
- Attends the final week-long seminar, held in conjunction with the annual international conference on leadership, Leadership 2000

Perhaps the most important component of the program is the mentor relationship with an established community college leader. Each Fellow selects a mentor with whom to work in clarifying professional goals, developing leadership skills, and acquiring knowledge of critical issues facing community colleges. The Fellow and the mentor meet regularly throughout the year to assess progress in accomplishing the professional development plan and to adapt the plan to circumstances and opportunities that might arise. A national advisory committee of leading community college educators, currently chaired by Nolen Ellison, president of Cuyahoga Community College, Ohio, assists in reviewing the program components, identifying potential applicants, securing mentors, and helping to develop networks.

NATIONAL INSTITUTE FOR LEADERSHIP DEVELOPMENT

In the Leaders Project (formally known as the National Institute for Leadership Development) at Rio Salado Community College in Arizona (Maricopa County Community College District), Mildred Bulpitt and Carolyn Desjardins have provided for a decade leadership institutes and training for nearly 1,800 women, who have then been successful in filling leadership positions in community colleges around the nation. Desjardins (1989b), in her postdoctoral study at Harvard, used the Gilligan-Kohlberg concepts of moral development theory to study gender differences among community college CEOs. Her findings underscore Gilligan's conclusion that moral "voice" is gender-related but not gender-determined. Desjardins concludes that there is a "movement toward a more horizontal model of leadership that values people (both female and male) within the organization," and that the "movement of women into leadership positions in community colleges may well be influencing this new, more humane style of leadership" (1989b, p. 9). In

149

the summer of 1990, the National Institute for Leadership Development was honored at the Leadership 2000 conference; the document developed by the Maricopa County Community College District, *Those Who Dare to Lead… A New Look at Leadership*, provides the basis for the following description.

Throughout the 1980s, the National Institute for Leadership Development sought to identify and cultivate female leadership in both community colleges and universities in America. Originally, the idea of the program was a vision of a few women, including Mildred Bulpitt, Marjorie Blaha, Eileen Rossi, Muriel Kay Heimer, and Betty Steege. The American Association of Women in Community and Junior Colleges (AAWCJC) and the League for Innovation in the Community College also saw the need for a professional program to prepare women for the next generation of leadership and helped support the program's development. The Maricopa County Community College District and specifically the Rio Salado campus became the home of the project. Here, Mildred Bulpitt guided the project, which came to be known as "Leaders for the Eighties" or the Leaders Project. Paul A. Elsner, chancellor of Maricopa County Community College District, states:

> Maricopa is pleased to be the genesis of the largest training and preparation program for women executives in the United States. Hundreds of women have achieved upper-level management and CEO positions as a result of the Leaders Project.

Originally a three-year project funded by the Fund for the Improvement of Postsecondary Education (FIPSE), the project exceeded all expectations. In its first three years, over 300 women attended the workshops and developed a project specifically tailored to their institution. Carolyn Desjardins became the co-director. By 1983, 40 percent of the first-year class and 22 percent of the second were promoted. FIPSE grant officials cited the project as one of their most successful programs and provided funding for another two years. With a second FIPSE grant, the Leaders Project was charged with creating a self-supporting national institute.

Candidates for leadership training, or "Leaders," must have a master's degree or the equivalent and full-time employment in a two-year institution. In the application process, the potential Leader must express a strong interest in career advancement, must seek out a college mentor (often the CEO), and must submit a project designed to benefit the college and involve the participant in new leadership roles. The success of the Leaders Project, which has approximately 200 participants per year, is based on a three-phase structure:

- An innovative campus project—"learning by doing." These projects offer the opportunity for the Leader to gain skill-building experience within the context of real-world organizational dynamics. The mentor is invaluable, often serving as coach and guide through the administrative maelstrom to help ensure the success of the college project.

- An intensive week-long workshop—"achieving by believing." The workshop begins the energizing process of change within the individual by emphasizing vision and confidence. The participants are exposed to exemplary role models—powerful, multicultural, supportive people from colleges across the country. This group creates new frames of reference based on leadership styles and administrative issues. Skill-building exercises are designed to promote individual growth.

- A supportive nationwide network of contacts—"succeeding by cooperating." A support and information network is in place to help women access data and tap into a strong circle of knowledge. A newsletter also keeps participants in touch.

Max Castillo, president of San Antonio College in Texas, says of the Leadership Project:

> This program exposes faculty and mid-management women to a broader set of leadership skills. Like a diamond in the rough, the Leader begins to shine as various talents are revealed. The college reaps great benefits from the projects, and I feel very confident in recommending these women for advancement.

Nationally recognized for its finely tuned leadership learning dynamics, the National Institute for Leadership Development now offers three additional leadership programs. Leaders for Change is devoted to the special challenges facing women whose next step up the career ladder is the CEO position. New Issues in Community College Leadership is a lively forum designed to keep women community college presidents and CEO-level administrators at the cutting edge of community college issues. Leadership for a New Century is a program tailored for the leadership challenges facing women administrators in four-year colleges and universities.

Marjorie Blaha, chancellor of Los Rios Community College District in California, has spoken about the effect of the Leaders Project and the instrumental role of its founding director:

> California community colleges are reaping the benefits from the National Institute for Leadership Development. I have seen firsthand how women return from the Institute with renewed enthusiasm for the community college mission. Their increased knowledge and growth in self-confidence very often result in promotions to leadership positions. Our students and institutions are the ultimate beneficiaries as the Leaders generate new direction, programs, and management styles. Mildred Bulpitt, who has spent 38 years in education, gave 10 years to the Leaders Project; she is the person who made the project happen! She was in a unique position to reach out—to get women in the pipeline and to reach for opportunities for women in leadership roles. In 1975 there were 12 women presidents/CEOs; today there are 165.

Leadership projects are remarkable for their diversity and, more important, for the benefits they provide to the participants' campuses. Projects have focused on many topics. Several are included here:

- Special populations (issues of diversity, special populations, minorities, women, and disabled students)
- Teaching/learning (faculty issues, staff development, renewal, professional grants, teaching improvement centers, and evaluations of faculty)

- Administration (administrative issues, trustee relations, staff development, evaluation, facilities, administrative searches, legislative issues, policy manuals, and human resources)
- Cross-curriculum (developing dialogue about writing, math, decision-making ethics, public speaking, and even the elimination of war, across the curriculum)
- Leadership (developing leadership skills through classes, seminars, and internships for staff, students, and minority groups)
- International (developing resources, feasibility studies, networks, cross-cultural mentoring and exchange programs, international business, and international fundraising)
- Technologies (developing technologies such as computers, teleconferencing, and on-line services for students and faculty)
- Student services (improving services to students, such as career centers, tutoring, mentoring/advising programs, financial aid, counseling, work/life centers, and academic intervention)

Sharon Yaap, president of the American Association of Women in Community and Junior Colleges, notes:

> Graduates of the program can count on having a strong base of information that provides a global view of leadership. Colleges can be assured that they are supporting a program that trains the best and brightest for their future. The AAWCJC is proud to be part of this endeavor.

AACJC: NETWORKS AND MENTORING

The American Association of Community and Junior Colleges (AACJC) has been responsible for several internal organizations or affiliated councils that encourage and facilitate groups in their development in community and junior colleges. We will discuss several of these organizations: the American Association of Women in Community and Junior Colleges; the National Council on Black American Affairs; the Presidents' Roundtable; and the National Community College Hispanic Council.

Mentoring and networks are also important vehicles for inclusionary practices and are responsible for turning national attention to the under-representation of women and members of minorities in positions of leadership. Mentoring involves the care and concern of a visionary or a decision maker who breaks away from the mold of self-preservation and seeks to help others demonstrate their unique competencies. Moreover, in early 1990 the AACJC, responding to the recommendations of several constituent groups, established the Commission to Improve Minority Education to study the needs, wants, and demands of the growing racial-ethnic minority cohort in community colleges and the importance of education addressed specifically to minorities.

The charge of this group, headed by Texas legislator Wilhelmina Delco, is to offer solutions and make recommendations to address critical issues such as retention and recruitment, hiring, and improving success rates for minority students. "Recognition of colleges who are making a difference is a part of the Commission's task," according to AACJC President Dale Parnell. "Awards and money will be given in recognition of exemplary programs in community colleges. AACJC's number-one priority is its minority education initiative." This task force of national community college leaders will meet biannually for three years to examine issues, establish goals, and make recommendations to guide community college education into the twenty-first century.

Clyde Sakamoto, acting provost of Maui Community College in Hawaii, is a representative member of the commission and reminds us:

> If we are to address issues of specific groups and if we are suggesting that outcomes are critical, we must also be aware that we are in danger of being called "exclusionary." Our role is not only to uncover the needs of nontraditional groups, but also to celebrate the diversity of all groups who make up the community college constituency.

THE AMERICAN ASSOCIATION OF WOMEN IN COMMUNITY AND JUNIOR COLLEGES

The American Association of Women in Community and Junior Colleges began in 1973 with an EDPA grant for a six-week summer project for women; from that initial effort the AAWCJC has become an important voice for women. Organized on both a state and regional basis, the AAWCJC offers a variety of professional development activities for women in community colleges at local, state, regional, and national levels. In addition, the association publishes a newsletter and a national journal, and it provides a job bank for women. AAWCJC has a membership of 2,000 women nationwide and is the largest council of AACJC. Its mission includes maintaining visibility, developing leadership at all levels (trustees, faculty, and administration), providing diversity of leadership and promoting women of color, developing research documents focusing on women, and monitoring and acting on federal legislation to make changes through the political system. The Stellar Program recognizes important programs for women, such as the Leaders Project.

AAWCJC recognizes "Innovative Programs for Community College Women." The first recipient of this award was the Steps to Success program at Mt. Hood Community College in Oregon, funded by a state grant and helping over 800 women annually make the transition from welfare to the labor force.

In summary, the major purposes of the AAWCJC are:
- Fostering the development of comprehensive educational career opportunities for all persons
- Providing information, assistance, and support for all educators as they serve students through education and services that are sensitive to the needs of women students
- Encouraging and supporting professional development and advancement of all women employed or enrolled in community colleges

- Collecting and disseminating data and research relating to women's professional development issues

Although all these purposes are critical to the AAWCJC, perhaps the association's professional development workshops provide the greatest benefits to women. In meetings offered throughout the year and in each of the 10 geographic regions, officers and regional directors offer guidance and coaching to women who recognize their own need for professional development.

Pam Fisher, vice president of professional development at AAWCJC and vice chancellor of Yosemite Community College District in California, points to the politics of leadership and "the value of knowing and appreciating what's going on around us. Politics," she says, "are formidable: To effect change we must understand these politics and work from there to make a difference. We have to think about what makes us respond to issues, to weigh carefully our reactions, and to take time to acquire political savviness." She offers the following tips for women leaders:

- Fit the image of how a leader looks, sounds, and behaves
- Gain confidence in presentations and speaking; be "deliberate"
- Make eye contact with people as you interact with them
- Know and understand how to deal directly with conflict
- Understand dysfunctional people—who they are and what to expect
- Find friends outside of work
- Get involved in professional organizations such as AAWCJC

AAWCJC President Sharon Yaap, dean of communications and fine arts at Grossmont College in California, advises that women must create their own niche in the 1990s. This is the identifying aspect of women's leadership behaviors, the area of expertise that each woman brings to her setting and college environment. To Yapp, visibility and success are linked, and the path to success lies in a future leader's ability to create a space for herself in the organization or system. She suggests:

- Be visible: volunteer, obtain a knowledge base, accept and request new tasks, use persuasive communications, be in charge and have control, make presentations from department level to board level, and write articles

- Promote your program and your division with supervisors, with the press, and in professional organizations
- Market yourself: videotape your résumé
- Gain support from others (such as supervisors, your institution, colleagues, and through networking) and work "above and beyond" your call of duty
- Be creative and memorable: Be persistent (think BIG), ask "what if" questions, identify key data and actions, carry ideas to realization, search for facts to support what you do, take calculated risks, and have no guilt or fear about success
- Develop knowledge in support areas (such as print media or marketing research)
- Have vision: keep your finger on the pulse, read as much as you can about issues, know the trends, and move into the vacuum as the first authority
- Value autonomy

AAWCJC Board members Leila Gonzales Sullivan, president of Middlesex Community College in Connecticut, and Jacquelyn Belcher, president of Minneapolis Community College, both speak to the personal side of their presidencies. Both women represent an exceptionally small group of presidents—presidents who are women and members of racial-ethnic minority groups. Both note that although there are more women graduate students who are also members of racial-ethnic minority groups, they lag far behind men from racial-ethnic minorities as chief executive officers (although the number of ethnic minority men in CEO positions is also very small). Gonzales Sullivan asserts:

> The reality is that tokenism is still around. There are only 10 women Hispanic presidents; we are still unusual, we get watched, we get called on to speak more than others, and we are always on call and on view.

Belcher discusses three main issues—women's kinship with diversity, the campus climate's response to diversity, and a presidential model for addressing diversity—when she notes:

> The entire society is grappling with diversity—this is an especially important issue for higher education. Community colleges represent opportunity; they are the open-door access station for nontraditional students. We should be "feeling the press," but we are not; we have not developed the expertise necessary to confront the barriers to diversity. Women, however, know because we have been discriminated against and disempowered. Our charge is to raise the level of cultural consciousness to others.

Belcher raises the question: Can we function in a pluralistic environment? and replies, "Not if we don't understand other cultures, not if we as teachers and leaders have low expectations and inappropriate rewards for our culturally diverse students whom we praise less frequently, call on less frequently, seat farther away from us, and believe to have lower achievement levels." She believes we are all teachers and that as such we must address classroom issues that adversely affect pluralism. "We must focus on current symbols and practices, including the homophobic and ethnic slurs, hate mail, and denigrating slogans—in other words, we must be sensitive to campus bigotry and increasing racist practices on campuses," she says.

One example of Belcher's ability to sensitize others and alleviate fears is an innovative idea of her own. Staff members visit campuses, committing people to the "Racial Free Zone" pledge, which states, "We believe in all of us; everybody here is good, worthwhile; we will not allow any discrimination in our school." People write their own commitments and declare themselves a Racial Free Zone. Belcher says, "Although this vaccination doesn't take the first time, we keep on building ties. We do so in different ways; we give feedback, and we establish teaching and learning principles for the classroom."

NATIONAL COUNCIL ON BLACK AMERICAN AFFAIRS AND PRESIDENTS' ROUNDTABLE

The goal of diverse representation in leadership, according to the National Council on Black American Affairs, presently under the leadership of Carolyn Williams, demands commitment from contemporary community colleges to a philosophy that specifically supports the growth and development of leadership positions for members of ethnic minority groups and women. This philosophical premise should become the foundation for developmental programs, hiring and recruitment practices, and policies that reward innovation and creativity. Nolen Ellison, president of Cuyahoga Community College in Ohio and a council member, states:

> I recommend that graduate programs, foundations, and other leadership programs throughout the nation, including leadership development programs, work in concert to develop the means to stimulate change; we need a collaborative effort. Doctoral programs must be aggressive in reaching out to minorities and nurturing them. Foundations and other leadership development programs must recruit minorities for leadership training.

The Presidents' Roundtable is a nationwide network of Black expertise and an affiliate of the National Council on Black American Affairs. Its mission is to provide Black community college presidents with an operational network to identify and respond to issues affecting Blacks in community colleges; provide mentoring opportunities for Blacks; share professional resources; provide other national and international professional opportunities for Black CEOs; and support the goals and objectives of the National Council on Black American Affairs.

In pursuit of its mission, the Presidents' Roundtable:

- Monitors and reviews inequity in the delivery of educational and other services provided to Blacks in community college education
- Promotes the professional development and advancement of Black CEOs

- Provides mentoring opportunities for Blacks within member institutions
- Establishes internships among member institutions to provide opportunities for Blacks to have practical administrative experiences
- Shares published and unpublished speeches, research findings, and other items to assist members in their professional responsibilities
- Develops an updated list of Black CEOs with information about each president's availability as a resource person to universities and other institutions or other countries
- Develops a Third World nation support package that emphasizes current and emerging technology for appropriate nations as requested
- Plans and holds two meetings annually
- Seeks funds for special projects

Earl Bowman, president of the Presidents' Roundtable, is a seven-year member. He states:

> There are only 60 to 70 Black presidents, chancellors, and campus directors in the country. Therefore, it is important and vital to confer, discuss, and compare experiences with them. Considering that many first- or second-year presidents have enough operational activity to deal with their colleges and campuses, their contact with ethnic peers becomes more valuable. This potential contact and exchange will continue to be significant for all.

NATIONAL COMMUNITY COLLEGE HISPANIC COUNCIL

Michael Saenz, president of Tarrant County Junior College, Northwest Campus in Texas and president of the National Community College Hispanic Council (NCCHC), talks about the need for Hispanics to enter the work force in greater numbers, but he specifically looks to leadership to focus on our total human resources and to examine the relationships among business, industry, politics, and education. He places special emphasis on a pluralistic society that sees all its people as assets:

> We must prepare all persons, understand where they are in terms of their background, in terms of their skills, in terms of their productivity. If we are falling behind in our training, then we must look at minority participation; we must look at the fact that America has not been forward-thinking, but rather backward-thinking about its minority citizens; and we must achieve opportunities in higher education for minorities.

Saenz raises serious questions: Can and will higher education provide leaders who understand pluralism? Can higher education allow women and ethnic groups access to leadership? One avenue of response comes through the NCCHC, which is dedicated to quality education for Hispanic Americans, the enhancement of a pluralistic society, and the development of the nation's total human resources. Program emphases include leadership development, curriculum reform, and affirmative action policies that promote Hispanics in American community colleges.

THE HISPANIC ASSOCIATION OF COLLEGES AND UNIVERSITIES

The Hispanic Association of Colleges and Universities (HACU) was established in 1986 in support of the Center for Hispanic Higher Education, an institution formed to make potential resource providers aware of predominantly Hispanic institutions and their needs. At the time of HACU's formation, institutional membership was limited to nonprofit accredited institutions of higher education in the continental United States with at least 25 percent Hispanic student enrollment. The association identified 58 such institutions, or 2 percent of the total number of U.S. institutions of higher education, that enrolled almost one-third of all Hispanic students in the continental United States.

As part of its activities, HACU conducts special projects that address the importance of education in the economic progress of the U.S. Hispanic population. The first such major project was the Hispanic

Student Success Program (HSSP). In the summer of 1987, the Ford Foundation awarded a six-month planning grant to HACU for a Hispanic Student Success Program to address the low college attendance rate of Hispanic high school graduates and the high attrition rate of Hispanic students who enrolled at community colleges. The planning process resulted in a proposal for a pilot project focusing on attracting and retaining large numbers of Hispanic college students to two- and four-year institutions. The staff studied the institutions' individual approaches to the problem and efforts at cooperation between community colleges and four-year institutions and looked at how colleges and universities could help Hispanic middle and high school students better prepare themselves for college.

To qualify for institutional membership in HACU, a college's enrollment must be at least 25 percent Hispanic; 113 nonprofit colleges and universities in the United States are members. These institutions are located in 10 states (Arizona, California, Colorado, Florida, Illinois, New Jersey, New Mexico, New York, Texas, and Washington) and Puerto Rico. For the purposes of this report, the colleges and universities eligible for HACU membership are called HSIs—Hispanic-serving institutions.

The HSIs enroll about 45 percent of all postsecondary Hispanic students in the United States. Hispanic student enrollment at these institutions ranges from 25 to 99 percent of their student bodies. National demographic changes will result in more institutions achieving the minimum 25 percent Hispanic enrollment criterion; early in the next century, some 150 colleges and universities should be eligible for HACU institutional membership. The top five states in terms of number of HSIs are Texas (21), California (19), New Mexico and New York (10), and Florida (7).

TEXAS ASSOCIATION FOR CHICANOS IN HIGHER EDUCATION

In 1974 several Hispanic educational leaders in Texas, including Ramon Dovalina, vice president of continuing education and community services at Austin Community College, Max Castillo, president of

San Antonio College, Baltazar Acevedo of the Dallas County Community College District, Ann Lopez, program director, Community Colleges and Technical Institutes of the Texas Higher Education Coordinating Board, and Leonardo Valverde, vice president of instruction of the University of Texas at San Antonio, coordinated a number of organizations specifically designed to promote educational opportunity for Hispanics or persons of Mexican ancestry in Texas. The Texas Association for Chicanos in Higher Education (TACHE) is the higher education component of those original organizations and the only one to survive for almost two decades. Currently the organization, under the leadership of Adriana Barrera, assistant to the president at Austin Community College, has worked to build networks within colleges and universities and with non-Hispanic networks to cooperate "within the establishment" as a means of providing for and increasing the numbers of Hispanics in higher education. Leadership training workshops are also part of their new agenda. TACHE has 40 institutional members and over 400 members in Texas.

SHOWCASING COLLEGE PROGRAMS THAT PROMOTE AND SUPPORT DIVERSITY

MIAMI-DADE COMMUNITY COLLEGE

At Miami-Dade Community College (M-DCC) in Florida, diversity and cultural pluralism have been successfully integrated into programs and policies. When college president Bob McCabe came to M-DCC in 1960, 82 percent of the students were White; now only 20 percent are non-Hispanic, White students. Obviously, the college has changed considerably. Demographic data are extremely important for Miami-Dade Community College as well as for the students. Now a critically acclaimed formula for success, the Miami-Dade model—described in *Access and Excellence* (Roueche and Baker, 1987)—has become a model for revitalizing and reorienting community colleges as they face both internal and external demands.

Mardee Jenrette is the director of M-DCC's Teaching-Learning Project, a new project aimed at changing the institutional climate to accommodate the needs of nontraditional students and to recognize the implications of impending faculty shortages in the coming years. Faculty are fortunate at Miami-Dade Community College—they are able to take courses that focus on classroom research and effective teaching and learning (emphasizing diversity and learning styles). One of the focal points of this new project is that the issue of diversity is not a cellular structure where only Black teachers teach Black students, only Hispanic teachers teach Hispanics, and so on. Jenrette says:

> We are asking people to learn new skills; therefore, the institution has to recognize the needs of faculty, and there has to be a reward system that recognizes the change and the commitment to change. We have changed the criteria for tenure and promotion, basing both now on the theme of good teaching. Faculty members must now present a portfolio that reports their status and compliance around specifics of the M-DCC's faculty excellence and faculty values documents.

Faculty excellence is defined at M-DCC in four categories.

1. Motivation
   - Excellent faculty are enthusiastic about their work
   - They set challenging individual and collective performance goals
   - They set challenging performance goals for their students
   - They are committed to education as a profession
   - They project a positive attitude about students' ability to learn
   - They display behavior consistent with professional ethics
   - They regard students as individuals operating in a broader perspective beyond the classroom

2. Interpersonal Skills
   - Excellent faculty treat all individuals with respect
   - They respect diverse talents

- They work collaboratively with colleagues
- They are available to students
- They listen attentively to what students say
- They are responsive to student needs
- They are fair in their evaluation of student progress
- They present ideas clearly
- They create a climate that is conducive to learning

3. Knowledge Base
   - Excellent faculty are knowledgeable about their work areas and disciplines
   - They are knowledgeable about how students learn
   - They integrate current subject matter into their work
   - They provide perspectives that include a respect for diverse views
   - They do their work in a well-prepared and well-organized manner

4. Ability to Apply Knowledge
   - Excellent faculty provide students with alternative ways of learning that stimulate intellectual curiosity
   - They encourage independent thinking
   - They encourage students to be analytical thinkers
   - They provide cooperative learning opportunities among students
   - They give constructive feedback promptly to students
   - They give consideration to feedback from students and others
   - They provide clear and substantial evidence that students have learned

M-DCC is also aware of the importance of values in the community college culture and climate; the following values guide the institution in the development of its mission, goals, philosophy, and operational procedures.

Learning: to support this value, the college creates an environment conducive to teaching and learning, supports lifelong learning, encourages the free interchange of ideas, provides the resources necessary for teaching and learning, uses qualified personnel to facilitate learning, provides advisement and counseling to support the needs of students, addresses the learning needs of the community, and emphasizes communication skills.

Change: to allow for change when it is needed, the college encourages and supports innovation and creativity, responds to the changing educational needs of the community, and supports faculty and staff development.

Access: to broaden access while maintaining quality, the college provides support services to help students meet their educational needs, offers students prescriptive learning opportunities, provides occupational education that prepares graduates to work at the level expected by the community, expects students to meet defined standards, provides academic programs that prepare graduates to succeed in upper-division learning, provides eduational opportunities for personal development, structures the admissions process to encourage enrollment, and provides a variety of scholarships and financial aid programs.

Diversity: to broaden understanding and learning, the college respects individuals from a variety of cultural backgrounds, provides role models, offers interdisciplinary educational programs, provides programs and opportunities for student growth, teaches students about the cultural, economic, political, and social environments in which they live, helps students understand themselves and others, sponsors academic organizations and extracurricular activities, respects and responds to students' different learning styles, and respects and accepts different teaching styles.

Individuals: to support respect for individuals, the college encourages a positive attitude toward teaching and learning, stresses honesty and integrity, expects all individuals to interact, communicates accurately and promptly, recognizes the importance of prior learning and experience, develops realistic expectations for all individuals, publishes explicit performance expectations for faculty, staff, administrators, and students, and rewards achievements.

Systematic decision making: to make good, well-informed decisions, the college collects accurate and current data, assesses the community's learning needs, measures students' abilities on their entry to the institution, assesses program effectiveness, provides feedback to assist in meeting standards, evaluates students' progress throughout their careers at the college, encourages individuals to be aware of relevant current research, surveys students' perceptions about courses, programs, and the teaching/learning environment, and uses the expertise of faculty to improve the teaching/learning process.

Partnership with the community: to foster this partnership, the college provides accessible campus and outreach centers, cooperates with other educational systems, supports activities that enrich the community, plans educational programs with business and industry to promote the local economic development of the community, and increases the community's awareness of college programs and activities.

Virtually every element of the Teaching-Learning Project raises issues related to faculty development and support. A unified Teaching-Learning Resource Center exists on each campus to meet three areas of needs: the continuation of traditional staff and program development opportunities; a consistent, collegewide core program designed specifically to implement the outcomes of the Teaching-Learning Project; and support for instructional design, including classroom research and expanded applications of technology.

In addition, the document *Recommendations Concerning New Faculty* contains M-DCC's hiring recommendations. Standardized activities for recruitment and for the development of applicant pools that include minorities (50 percent of new employees hired will be members of racial and ethnic minorities) are also goals of the Teaching-Learning Project. New strategies that improve the competitive edge for faculty recruitment include offering competitive salaries, providing housing and mortgage information, providing assistance to spouses, helping faculty manage moving expenses, establishing child care, providing tuition reimbursement for formal study, and providing internships for graduate students and new graduates in cooperation with university programs. Screening and selection processes will also be brought into compliance with recruitment standards. Interviewing will incorporate principles of behaviorally oriented techniques, and the rights of the interviewee will be protected by accurate and complete expectations and conditions for employment made available by the college. After being hired, all new faculty will participate in a formal orientation program, obtain a faculty handbook, will have a limit on the number of course preparations, and be provided resources for individual development (such as those found at the Teaching-Learning Resource Center).

Bob McCabe and M-DCC are now looking to the third phase of their ongoing college reform. Reform I examined assessment and general education—the "who do we teach?"; Reform II is the Teaching-Learning Project—the "how do we teach?"; and Reform III will emphasize "new directions" in the curriculum—the "what do we teach?". Under review are the elements of a core curriculum, with an emphasis on global awareness, cultural awareness and cultural pluralism, critical thinking, the use of computers across the curriculum, and avenues for incorporating the study of ethics into the curriculum. Betty Inclan, an M-DCC administrator working on Reform III, notes:

> The New Directions committee is an example of the cultur-
> ally diverse student body and faculty at M-DCC; this
> institution celebrates culture uniqueness in Paella celebra-
> tions, Jewish Heritage Week, and Women's Week. These weeks
> have become part of our college culture. We don't consider
> them separate; these groups are recognized for their achieve-
> ments, not their separateness. All these positive reforms and
> the development of a unique college culture emanate from the
> leadership of Dr. McCabe; he has a unique ability to read the
> environment, to envision change, to communicate needs to
> individuals and groups, to write concept papers about his
> plans, and to transform the thinking of others by always
> allowing for their input.

"I don't think it's legitimate to recruit students without programs to aid them—it isn't morally right to do so," McCabe states. In a continuation of a program called the Minority Student Opportunity Program, Miami-Dade works with other community colleges, helps dictate curriculum, and hires counselors and other professionals who are responsible for encouraging students to graduate from community colleges, to transfer to four-year institutions, and to graduate from them. M-DCC recognizes the importance of parents' or guardians' interest. It involves the community through mentors who mentor students and work with parents, it identifies sponsors who will provide funds for scholarship bank accounts for successful students, and it has established articulation agreements with at least 40 institutions.

MIDLANDS TECHNICAL COLLEGE

At Midlands Technical College in South Carolina, Blacks constitute 30 percent of the student population and about 11 percent of the college faculty. College president Jim Hudgins notes:

> The Human Affairs Commission, a state commission appointed by the governor, has been charged to monitor and confirm compliance to affirmative action goals at the college. Three zones of compliance are delineated: If an institution is in the first zone, it is in noncompliance status; in the second zone, it is in compliance; and in the third zone, it is in compliance with availability factors. Based on the availability factor in the area, the state expects 10 percent of the faculty and 15 percent of the staff to be Black.

Moreover, the University of South Carolina (USC) recently initiated a new program to increase the number of women and minorities in its sciences and engineering departments, and in a partnership program, Midlands Tech and USC are cooperating to focus on pre-engineering and technology students, who must adhere to a USC syllabus for the arts and sciences. Almost 200 Midlands Tech students are enrolled in this program. Another Midlands Tech-USC program focuses on recruitment and transfer of minority students to baccalaureate programs.

Hudgins's leadership has guided Midlands Tech to a strong relationship with business and industry as well. In partnership with the Michelin Company, technically qualified students are groomed for work. After a recent nine-month training program, almost all program graduates were hired.

In an innovative response to campus climate, Hudgins maintains a "suggestion box" approach to student needs. Postcards are widely available for students to write directly to the president to express their views, to ask for services, and to vent their frustrations. Hudgins reads every card, and many suggestions have been incorporated into campus life.

GREENVILLE TECHNICAL COLLEGE

Tom Barton, president of Greenville Technical College in South Carolina, focuses on quality:

> We built this institution on a solid bedrock of quality, derived from leadership and through its people. We want positive, "can-do" people here—people who are self-starters and self-confident—and I know we can find such people to work here.

As have all other South Carolina colleges, Greenville Tech has a mandate to meet compliance orders of the state legislature. Barton addresses the issue of hiring:

> We need more instructors in physics, sciences, and math, the very people industry grabs and entices with high salaries. At our own institution, a potential welding instructor was being wooed by General Electric, and we wanted to hire him; we learned we had to be more competitive and more aggressive in our hiring process. We cannot sit on the sidelines and watch excellent potential instructors serve business and industry only.

Greenville Tech has established a foundation through which endowed chairs have been created for exemplary faculty. The foundation is composed of members of business and industry who support the community college mission and who understand Barton's maxim: If colleges are dependent on state funds, they will always be mediocre.

Among the initiatives to which Barton points with pride are the following services:

- Greenville Tech has entered into contract training with industry, the city and county, and local hospitals
- Around-the-clock day care is offered on the campus
- Five major universities in the surrounding area offer upper-division and graduate work on the Greenville Tech campus. A Higher Education Center has enrolled 2,000 students.

PALOMAR COLLEGE

Palomar College in California has two programs that focus on inclusionary practices in the college. Although only 2 percent of the college's population is Native American, over 4,000 Native Americans reside on nine reservations within its service area. The American Indian Component-Transfer Center was initiated to identify and eliminate barriers to the transfer of underrepresented students. Beginning in 1985, intersegmental agreements with the University of California at San Diego, San Diego State University, National University, and United States International University have provided specifically for programs aimed at the transfer of Native American students. Moreover, recruitment efforts beginning at the junior year of high school, early outreach activities, dissemination of information, and counseling are an integral part of the programs that aim at the retaining and transferring of the nearly 500 Native American students at Palomar.

George Boggs, president of the college, says, "California is the first mainland state to have a nonmajoritarian population—Whites will no longer be the majority, and everybody will be minorities. My hope is for an integrated society." Palomar's High Risk Program reaches out to the community by using students to serve as mentors for other students. The objective of this innovative program is to go into "continuing" schools, alternative high schools, and prisons (which have substantial populations of high-risk students) to motivate potential students to attend college.

SANTE FE COMMUNITY COLLEGE

Sante Fe Community College in Florida points with pride to its program for recruiting both Black and Hispanic graduate students and future faculty members from campuses across North America. The program, which names Sante Fe Community College Fellows, works in cooperation with the University of Florida to recruit and attract Black doctoral students to the university and helps the community college develop its own Black faculty members. The University of Florida recruits doctoral students on a nationwide basis toward the goal of increasing the number of minority graduate students. While working for their doctorates, these students are encouraged to apply for Sante Fe Community College Board of Trustees Fellowships; each fellowship carries a stipend of $9,000 for the academic year and $1,500 for the summer. In exchange for the stipend, tuition, and fees at the University of Florida, the students serve as adjunct faculty at the community college in the English, math, chemistry, humanities, and physical sciences departments. They are required to teach four courses over a 12-month period. In addition to their teaching duties, the Fellows assist in advisement, counseling, recruiting, and retaining minority students at the college.

PRINCE GEORGE'S COMMUNITY COLLEGE

At Prince George's Community College (PGCC) in Maryland, the applicant pool for professional positions must be representative of the availability of minorities in related occupations within the region. The college institutional research office has developed a set of indices for minority employment based on census data. If the applicant pool is not representative of minority involvement in related occupations in the work force, the position is advertised again. Moreover, to increase the college's contacts with minorities in the community, PGCC regularly meets with minority representatives of civic organizations, fraternities, sororities, churches, and businesses. This group acts as an advisory council to the college, advising it of the availability of minorities for faculty and administrative positions. Finally, PGCC and Bowie State University, a predominantly Black four-year college, have instituted a faculty exchange program designed to increase the number of minorities on campus.

EAST LOS ANGELES COLLEGE

The service area of East Los Angeles College in the Los Angeles Community College District has a 95 percent Hispanic population; moreover, the college is located in a low-income area with a declining industrial base. The Minority Biomedical Research Support Program (MBRS) was initiated by a dedicated chemistry instructor, Carcy Chan. Chan, concerned about the 150 students who annually enrolled in her classes but were not transferring to senior institutions, applied for and won a National Institutes of Health (NIH) grant to establish a biomedical research project. Initially, six students were funded, and although the NIH normally funds only senior institutions, it has continued to fund Chan's program since 1980. Program staff look for potential and interest in students as well as good performance records. Approximately 25 students are trained in a campus research lab as undergraduate researchers. Area universities support this program and offer MBRS internships in the summer. Students are paid $4,200 for their research activities and may earn up to $1,500 in summer programs. Over 85 percent of the students who participate in the MBRS program transfer to senior institutions, and several students are enrolled in Ph.D. or M.D. programs.

MADISON AREA TECHNICAL COLLEGE

Madison Area Technical College in Wisconsin hosts a Minority Pre-

Collegiate Program for junior-level minority high school students. The program extends through the students' senior year in high school and encourages borderline students to graduate from high school and attend college. The summer program offers the opportunity to attend class 15 hours per week and work 20 hours per week (jobs are those in which minorities are not typically employed). Counselors, parents, and faculty work cooperatively in this program.

CITY COLLEGE OF SAN FRANCISCO

City College of San Francisco in California has enrolled Hispanic and Black students in a Math Bridge Program that provides special instruction to strengthen their preparation for transfer to a four-year institution. Black and Hispanic professionals serve as role models, lecturing on careers in science, engineering, computer science, and other math-related fields. A grant from Pacific Telesis Foundation funds the coordination and evaluation of the program.

CLOVIS COMMUNITY COLLEGE DISTRICT

At Clovis Community College District in New Mexico, an Hispanic Advisory Council (made up of Hispanic citizens and staff) targets Hispanic students for recruitment. The council actively recruits from various community and external markets or enclaves of Hispanic students. Through Project Forward, the district tries to mainstream women with dependent children into the work force and away from welfare dependency. Over 600 women are enrolled in a 20-hour-per-week program in which intensive counseling and career development programs are offered in addition to general and adult basic education courses. President Jay Gurley believes that "community college education is an all-encompassing endeavor which must respond to the needs of the people who live in the community."

FOND DU LAC COMMUNITY COLLEGE

Fond du Lac Community College Center in Minnesota, named for the Fond du Lac tribe, is located on a Native American reservation. The center, an extension of the Mesabi Community College campus, is well known for its "Indian People" focus; it trains in the Ojibwe language and provides bilingual training for potential teachers. The effectiveness of the Arrowhead Community College Region's Services to Indian People Program is demonstrated by its recruitment and support services orientation, but it is lauded for its 70 percent retention rate of Native American students (who also can boast of high GPAs). Jack Briggs, director of the Fond du Lac Center, was one of the original participants of the Minority Fellows Project (a project sponsored by the League for Innovation in the Community College and The University of Texas at Austin).

VALENCIA COMMUNITY COLLEGE

Valencia Community College in Florida has signed agreements with five historically Black colleges to encourage academically talented minority students to complete four years of college. The scholarship program covers two years at Valencia and the remaining two years at one of the five colleges. The program specifically recognizes that the majority of Black students begin their higher education at the community college and earn degrees from traditionally Black colleges.

CONCLUSION

Exemplary programs nationwide convince us that serious and powerful efforts to address the issues and realities of demographic changes that demand diversification do exist. They further convince us that community colleges are committed to meeting challenges and to offering innovative and constructive practices by which to encourage diversity and representation. We offer these programs as examples of challenges to current environments and policies relating to the issues of underrepresentation and cultural diversity.

In the next chapter, leaders speak to these issues in their own voices; their words are visionary and practical, straightforward and candid, and absolutely essential in positing the values of their cultures and identities.

CHAPTER SEVEN

❧

WHAT THE LEADERS
ARE SAYING:
THE VOICES OF DIVERSITY

❧

Tom Gonzales: Embracing Diversity

Juliet Garcia: Looking to Potential

Nelvia Brady: Embracing Diversity's Demands

Alfredo de los Santos, Jr.: Planning for Diversity

Augusta Souza Kappner: Supporting Diversity

Charles Green: Answering the Challenges of Change

Ruth Burgos-Sasscer: Benefitting from Diversity

Al Fernandez: Confronting the Issues of Hiring

Judith Valles: Addressing the Hispanic Agenda

Donald Phelps: Shaping the Standards for Growth

Tessa Tagle: Creating Campus/Community Partnerships

Raul Cardenas: Creating Opportunities

Ruth Shaw: Examining the Strengths in Diversity

Eduardo Padron: Designing Valuable Environments

Patsy Fulton: Facing the Challenge of Diversity

Nolen Ellison: Risking for Diversity

Conclusion

There is no better way to capture the essence of the issues surrounding underrepresentation and underutilization of women and minorities in American community colleges than to hear from leaders of these institutions. We listen to their voices, we involve them in the testimony about changes in the American community college, and we celebrate the excellence by which they have become leaders of merit and leaders of competence. These are leaders involved in the transformation away from a limited, exclusionary cultural point of view and toward a more pluralistic or multicultural view.

In this chapter, the words of some community college presidents and leaders who were interviewed extensively around the issues and questions of underrepresentation will be heard. The leaders interviewed represent colleges around the nation. In some cases, their vision is an intricate part of the college's policies and programs and, therefore, it is reality. In other cases, we hear the articulation of the "vision," the laying of the groundwork of those institutional goals that the community college leader seeks to implement—essentially, to exercise inclusionary practices in the American community college. And, finally, we hear the articulation of the dreams of those who, in the words of John Lennon, envision "a brotherhood of man:"

Imagine all the people sharing all the world...
You may say I'm a dreamer,
But I'm not the only one.
I hope some day you'll join us,
And the world will live as one.
(from "Imagine" by John Lennon)

If there is an integrating characteristic of all those whom we interviewed, it is the view that the American community college is one of the best places to develop cultural pluralism. Jerry Sue Owens, president of Lakewood Community College in Minnesota, asserts:

> There is no better place to value culture diversity than in the American community college. There is no better place to celebrate the convergence of cultures than to look at the students; than to reflect those students in the staff, the faculty, and the administration, and to celebrate how that reflection is a microcosm of American society.

Her words are eloquent, her ideas are timely, and her vision reflects that of the leaders whose voices embody the current community college milieu.

TOM GONZALES: EMBRACING DIVERSITY

Tom Gonzales, chancellor of Seattle Community Colleges, discusses diversity:

> Everything we do focuses around people, not bricks and mortar or growth. It focuses on how we deal with the people in diversifying institutions. Diversity is a thing for leadership, for future change in education and the work force and in society.

Gonzales questions how we change culture and how we embrace diversity; he wonders what imperative is involved in embracing diversity. He answers:

> We must go back to basics—to look at the values and missions of the community colleges, to redefine the values of culture and to make certain that everyone understands that the value of diversity is represented in voice, in words, in conversation, in convocation in the American community college. Change is inevitable in the American community college; we must do everything possible to incorporate needed change. People— who they represent, who they are, what their needs might

be—are assets that must find their markets.

> We must move from looking at people as expenses to looking at people as assets. We must move from looking at the idea of control to the idea of an open system. We have to move from the idea of being the same to being flexible. We have to move from being individuals and a separate system to being open kinds of systems. But most of all, we have to bring people through the process—we have to look at our own colleges and discover the real self as leader.

Gonzales maintains that the inner self needs to be incorporated into leadership, that one must discover it because self is important to leadership—not just in times of crisis, but in times of normalcy. Perhaps reflecting on Bennis's (1989) notion of leaders who are on the pathway to self-discovery, he proposes that we must examine our own values as leaders. And he asks important questions: How do we feel about what we do? How do we transmit our values? How do we embrace diversity as a whole? How do we encourage a spirit of understanding?

The very premises on which American community colleges are based evolved from the idea of egalitarianism. But the quality of this idea is connected to the beliefs of providing education for all—a fundamental precept of the American nation. If we celebrate our entrepreneurial activity, if we celebrate our technological advancement, if we celebrate our democracy, we can also celebrate our contribution to the American public through education.

Gonzales provides a personal view on getting to the top. There is a price for leadership for minorities; the price is sometimes risk taking, sometimes insecurity, and sometimes going against the values of your own culture. He observes that there is a level of intensity among people who want to move fast, that one's family may suffer, and that people who put great value on family may be offended by that. But if you want to be a leader, if you have an agenda, if you have social responsibility, if you understand self, then you must move ahead. He calls his counterparts "pioneers" in the field—people who are in the spotlight, people who have been placed "on the spot." However, if someone in the spotlight stumbles or falls, it is easy for others to consider him or her a failure. So he cautions members of ethnic minorities against stumbling, falling, and failing, and he advises that they become more supportive of each other.

JULIET GARCIA: LOOKING TO POTENTIAL

Juliet Garcia, president of Texas Southmost College, lists as her two primary concerns her faculty and administrators, and her students. The 20 poorest counties in the nation are in southern Texas, and the college is located in an area where there are few postsecondary schools. The population is indigenous Hispanics (there since Texas's early development days), and there are few facilities for developing that society. In many political science textbooks, authors suggest that there has been overt discrimination aimed at Hispanics who live in southern Texas. But we leave that issue to the textbooks for the moment.

Garcia notes that hiring and selection procedures at the college are directed at seeking out diversity. Early in her term as president, she found it obvious that faculty hired people who looked like themselves, the classic concept of selection of sameness. She has now instituted an intensive recruitment policy, combined with a new recruitment initiative: Applicants who have a master's degree in education can be hired only if they agree to abide by the firm directive that within the next two years they complete a required 18 hours of coursework in their discipline; when the requirement is met, the faculty member is then, and only then, eligible for tenure. This new policy has provided recruiting and hiring alternatives that allow the college to seriously attract more Hispanic candidates, both male and female.

Garcia directs college selection committees to look for—from all the people applying for a job—the individual who can do the best job for the college right now. Sometimes, she adds, that selection requirement compels the committee to ignore some variables and look to people who have a potential for production. When one looks at potential and dares to take a difficult stand, the outcome can be diversity. Garcia notes:

My goal is to try to expand diversity. I try to never inject into

the hiring process selection factors that narrow the pool and
limit diversity. I am aware of those factors, but I attempt to
eliminate them so that the "cream rises."

Her interest in students is keen. Entering with, on average, seventh-
grade reading levels and eighth-grade math levels, 92 percent of her
students cannot enter regular college courses at her college. Garcia
undertook a "mission impossible:" to raise reading levels by two to four
years in one semester. After raising $1 million in her own area in 18
months, also a "mission impossible," she received $2 million from the
Department of Education.

Thus began Texas Southmost's scholarship endowment program.
Beginning in the seventh grade, students taking college preparatory
courses begin to receive credit for tuition and earn money for entry into
Texas Southmost College. In this last year, old people, young people, and
students on the brink of entering college have begun to earn scholarship
money. As Garcia points out, "To effect change you have to do more than
develop the student."

Moreover, in a direct 2 + 2 relationship with the high schools, Garcia
was able to effect a curriculum change in the local high school that
provides for more courses that meet transfer requirements into the
college. Garcia has looked realistically at her special situation, the social
milieu, the economic hardships, and has decided to effect change. She
can now say with pride:

> We have made massive change. It's no accident that Harvard
> and Stanford come in yearly to recruit our top 1 percent. We
> have been a long time waiting for education to come to our
> community. We won't see change unless we do some drastic
> things to cause that change to occur.

NELVIA BRADY: EMBRACING DIVERSITY'S DEMANDS

Nelvia Brady, chancellor of City Colleges of Chicago in Illinois, is
the only female chancellor in the Illinois Community College System.
She offers some sociological observations about her role, noting that it

takes time to become part of the club, to build contacts, and to develop networks.

Brady finds that role modeling is important. She must acquaint others, especially young women and minority women, with goals that have not been there in the past and with the feeling that "if she can do it, I can do it." But she emphasizes a critical point about this role modeling: She must make certain that the model she presents is realistic and that others understand that achieving a presidency or a chancellorship requires certain steps—steps that must be taken wisely, with the understanding that a certain amount of risk is involved.

Brady handles her job in a much different fashion than did her male predecessors. She is told that she is more open, more accessible, more "down-to-earth;" that her policies are more inclusive; and that she is less tied to the status than to the promise of her position. Some view these behaviors as diminishing the position; in the old style of thinking, the position should be an ivory tower, and there should be distance between the chancellor and others because leadership is a lonely system. These are not her views. She believes that those are the old yardsticks and that they don't apply to her or to her style as the leader of her district:

> My style is related to my gender. I have a struggle to maintain
> my position. I have a struggle to understand and to make
> others understand my style. I have a struggle to maintain the
> difference between me and others who have served in this
> position.

Brady sees that a tremendous additional burden is sometimes placed on women as leaders because they are called on so many times to do so many things. She is always on call to address constituencies as a speaker and to serve as a representative or role model. With so few women in the pipeline and with a woman as leader still being such a novel situation, women in positions of power, especially minority women, have a tremendous responsibility to represent themselves to constituent groups and to others who want to emulate them.

Brady has what she calls a "three-square job:" (1) she responds to her constituencies and is on call to them at all times; (2) she fulfills her role as CEO of her college district, cleaning up problems and moving forward; and (3) she plays the role of being Black. She accepts the demands that all these roles create.

ALFREDO DE LOS SANTOS, JR.: PLANNING FOR DIVERSITY

As vice chancellor for educational development of the Maricopa County Community College District in Arizona, Alfredo de los Santos, Jr. is driven by his father's advice to "let people grow." He believes his job has two components: to study human nature; and to study how organizations do and do not work.

The first Hispanic president of a U.S. community college, de los Santos believes that by extending time and information to people, by discussing hiring procedures that emphasize affirmative action, and by having a board that is conscientiously committed to affirmative action, appropriate and acceptable representation can be achieved. Maricopa County Community College District has come a long way: It is now staffed by 50 percent men and 50 percent women, with good racial and ethnic representation and with a close reflection to the ethnic distribution in the state. Efforts to create similar conditions in its various colleges are major agenda items as de los Santos spearheads a task force to plan and coordinate a comprehensive plan for the Maricopa District in the twenty-first century.

AUGUSTA SOUZA KAPPNER: SUPPORTING DIVERSITY

Augusta Souza Kappner, president of Borough of Manhattan Community College (BMCC) in New York, speaks to the issues of supporting diversity and putting new faces in the workplace—the faces of women, ethnic minorities, and the disabled. Kappner addresses problems at her own college with the simple philosophy of "we have to do a better job." She has found the following problems to be critical at BMCC and the following solutions to be effective.

Problems implementing diversity, as related to retention: Attend to the specific problems of women and ethnic groups. Fifty percent of all minorities who enroll in higher education enroll in community colleges; retention and the promotion of excellence among minorities and women are critical issues. They are especially so for Kappner in a college where 52 percent of the students are Black, 30 percent are Hispanic, 8 percent are Asian, 10 percent are White, 67 percent are women, 48 percent are part-time, and 20 percent are non-native speakers.

When a freshman skills assessment test became a critical part of the policy and program at BMCC (in fall 1989), faculty leaders, the president, and the administration realized that there had to be a program that addressed the freshman population and its special needs. They began a pre-freshman immersion program, now in its fifth year. In this program, there is an esprit de corps, an enforcement of the spirit of success, and an active attempt to retain students before freshmen ever come to class. Initially, in 1986, approximately 70 students enrolled; in 1987 there were 700 students; in 1988, 1,200 students; in 1989, 1,419 students; and in 1990, over 1,500 students will enroll in the pre-freshman immersion program. The outcomes: 92 percent of the students completed their pre-freshman program, and 93 percent of those students completed their first semester—an increase of almost 30 percent in first-semester completions over previous years. The pre-freshman immersion program works. It retains students, it has the support of the governor of New York and the state legislature, and it has been recognized for excellence in student support and retention by the City University of New York.

Problems with hiring procedures: Create an expanded applicant pool. In 1989 the goal of hiring to reflect student body population was critical at BMCC. Reach-out programs, advertisements, and networking reflected efforts at expanding the applicant pool. Moreover, new techniques for hiring and for interviews focused on diversity. Of the 43 new employees hired that year, 22 were minorities.

Problems with cultural integration: Reach out to the ethnic community. Kappner invited her parent campus, City University of New York (CUNY), to become involved in the problems on her campus. She talked to administrators about training and about key individuals who needed to be trained in administration. She sensitized her staff to confront their present behavior, to confront change, and to understand student needs. She invited an Institute for American Pluralism team to train college administrators and to communicate with them for one year about cross-cultural integration.

Problems with professional development: Provide support for professional growth. In 1988 Kappner began the All But Dissertation (ABD) Seminar Program—tenured faculty were encouraged to pursue and complete their doctoral programs. She identified those faculty who had not completed their degrees, especially women and minorities, and invited David Sternburg, author of *How to Complete and Survive a Dissertation,* to consult with them. She released faculty from courses for as many as two semesters. A peer seminar met weekly to stimulate and motivate each other and to share problems. Since the BMCC program began, five faculty—one Black man, three Black women, and one White woman—have completed Ph.D.s. This year five faculty members are participating. Observing BMCC's success, the City University of New York has implemented its own Faculty Advancement Program.

Problems with curriculum: Provide support for cultural balance. Kappner invited CUNY to talk to BMCC about a balanced curriculum seminar based on gender, race, and social diversity. She gave individuals and representatives release time to develop this more comprehensive curricula view. Classes were held on campus. From that initiative, a permanent faculty Committee on Enhancing Pluralism was established to look at links between curriculum and noncurriculum events around the issues of pluralism, to look for faculty activities to enhance diversity, and to promote gender, ethnic, and racial balance in course content.

One day of faculty development is devoted annually to enhancing diversity. The recommendations of the faculty committee on enhancing pluralism include institutional accountability, developing strong ethnic and women's studies programs, increasing faculty development, keeping an emphasis on students, and recruiting minority faculty. The intent of these suggestions is to incorporate culturalism, pluralism, and diversity not only into the consciousness of the faculty, students, staff, and administrators, but also into the curriculum. The committee believes that faculty must look at texts in which there are topics related to pluralism and diversity and that they must look at ways to encourage students to celebrate their pasts, their accomplishments, and their unique contributions. They want to "infuse" pluralism and diversity into their courses, thus changing their curriculum.

CHARLES GREEN: ANSWERING THE
CHALLENGES OF CHANGE

Charles Green, formerly president of Rio Salado Community College in Arizona and currently chancellor of Houston Community College System in Texas, says:

> We need to grow into situations. We need to have colleges, universities, who are aware of the necessity of the education reality—student and faculty cultural diversity is upon us.
>
> People must have opportunities to be in training, in leadership training; you have to encourage people who exhibit talent; you must, as a CEO, and especially as a minority CEO, look specifically for those people who exhibit talent and then try to lead, try to bolster, try to encourage their own training.

In particular, Green looks to the Minority Mentoring Program instituted by the League for Innovation and The University of Texas at Austin (he is a responsible mentor for several Kellogg Fellows in that group), to the Texas Minority Program at Texas A&M University, and to The University of Texas Community College Leadership Program. He is optimistic about the role of women and minorities in positions of leadership. He is even optimistic when he talks about the dilemma in the minds of nonminority people who are saying to themselves, "Why am I not the one who gets promoted? I work hard. Why should affirmative action, a quota system, a set-aside system, encourage and promote someone over me?" The concern about backlash is real and is an important consideration when offering leadership opportunities and quality and excellence for women and minorities in the American community college. Green says:

I love people. I am in this business because I love people. I can even count on those people in spite of the backlash. I have greater hope for the ending than history has given us. More people today are aware. More people today want change. More people understand what we are working for. And more people know who we are working for. And more people believe that we are working for them.

RUTH BURGOS-SASSCER: BENEFITTING FROM DIVERSITY

Ruth Burgos-Sasscer, vice president of Harry S. Truman College in Illinois, asks the question: What does it take for Hispanics to succeed in the American community college? She notes that the number of Hispanics in community colleges is well below their numbers in the general population, not only among students and faculty, but among administrators. The American Council on Education documents that only 18 percent of students and 12 percent of administrators are members of minorities (7.6 percent Black, 2 percent Hispanic, 1.5 percent Asian, and 0.4 percent Native American). The Illinois system includes 49 community colleges, and minorities represent 62 percent of the student population. Only five of the 49 community colleges have minority presidents, all of whom are Black. There are only two women community college presidents and no Hispanic community college presidents. In an area around Chicago, where 20 percent of the total population and 27 percent of the student population is Hispanic, there are very few representatives in administration or faculty, and thus few role models. In the entire state there is only one Hispanic vice president and one Hispanic chancellor. There are no Hispanic deans of instruction.

Burgos-Sasscer questions why Hispanic representation is so low. Is the pool limited? Are the qualifications such that no Hispanic can enter these positions? Is there not enough being done for those who are qualified? Is it important to demonstrate extra effort? She answers:

Yes, extra effort must be made. We must reach out, welcome, and employ affirmative action so that minorities can get to the interview. But when we get to the interview stage, we few get jobs—perhaps it's because we do not fit the standard image. This circumstance must change; we must examine what is occurring during the interview itself.

In Burgos-Sasscer's own college, data demonstrate that there are 20 percent Asians; 9 percent Black and Caribbean students; 14 percent Hispanic and Central and South American students; and 1.9 percent Native Americans. The remaining minority students come from the Middle East and Eastern Europe. There are 1,300 Soviet Jews. Interestingly, only 10 percent of the faculty are minorities, and there are rarely new hires.

Burgos-Sasscer relates a story that speaks to the issue of insensitivity and misunderstanding of minorities at the administrative level. In a neighboring community college where minority students are not in the majority, there was a pronounced concern about hiring a minority leader and an immediate reaction of faculty and staff to this effect: "We don't want a president who speaks with an accent. We don't want to focus on the fit into the community. We want to focus on image!"

Burgos-Sasscer believes colleges should focus on skills and talent, and institutions will benefit from diversity. Institutions must embrace cultural pluralism as a cultural value. Her image of the melting pot is a salad bowl filled with various types of vegetables, blended and united by a dressing: The various vegetables in the salad represent various groups of people and the dressing symbolizes common goals and ideals. She cautions about assigning inflexible characteristics to management styles, and she urges everyone involved with community colleges to expand their understanding of the contributions of ethnic minorities.

AL FERNANDEZ: CONFRONTING THE ISSUES OF HIRING

Al Fernandez, chancellor of Coast Community College District in California, has confronted the critical issues of hiring. California Assembly Bill 1725 and the changing nature of the state's demography are forcing California community colleges to change their hiring practices.

AB 1725 dictates that one-third of a community college's faculty must represent its area's minority population by the year 1992. Aware that there are few minorities in the pipeline and concerned that the attention to this problem is focused primarily on Hispanics and Blacks rather than on women or Asians, Fernandez has made hiring reforms in his district. He has asked his faculty to establish recruitment teams to search for and talk to perspective candidates and to make a preliminary offer to the best candidate. Fernandez has also established, with UC-Irvine, an internship for doctoral studies that is open to everyone but focuses on minority students.

Fernandez believes that "community colleges are the key to the future of the nation" and that it is important for community colleges to develop a future work force, to evaluate their curricula, and to identify global goals. To these ends, Fernandez has made the following changes:

- The college has established relationships with groups in London, Paris, Costa Rica, and Japan
- Coastline will begin to offer courses at three sites in Japan in the near future
- The district is aligned with the World Trade Center
- More international students have been attracted to Coastline by the International Culture Center
- The college has started a training program with local police departments to recruit from minority groups and to develop basic school programs

How are all of these initiatives managed? Fernandez points to a shared governance model, identifying it as the key to what is happening in California. He points to the critical need for faculty, staff, and administration to develop a working paper for shared governance, particularly in light of the new initiatives encouraged by new budget allocations for more work on retention, marketing, and recruiting. He recommends that this working paper, and all eventual initiatives, be designed by a culturally diverse population.

Fernandez views this diversity as inevitable. His analogy is simple: The obstacles that have limited representation by minorities have acted as debris clogging a dam. As the water rises behind that dam, it will wash the debris away. That forward movement cannot be stopped.

JUDITH VALLES: ADDRESSING THE HISPANIC AGENDA

Judith Valles, president of Orange Coast College in California, provides a personal view of what happens in the struggle to become a leader. While influenced by the North American ideas of pragmatism and the practical approach that deals with goals, preparation, and looking to the future, she views the South American approach as critical to her way of thinking—thinking motivated not from pragmatism or rationalism, but from pathos, from the intuitive necessity of and the sensitive appreciation for empathy and for understanding people's actions and innate qualities. Her views reflect both the rational, goal-oriented approach and the learning-through-pathos approach. While goals can be future-oriented, they can also incorporate the pathos approach in a critical combination of the best of the North and the best of the South.

In her own struggle to become a leader in the community college, Valles has been awakened to the political realities of class and society. Her first work experiences were as a fifth-grade teacher; through hard work and active competition, she quickly moved into teaching junior high students and serving as coordinator and department head for languages. She then moved to the community college and began her rise—first as an adjunct professor, then a department head, and then a division chairperson. As she progressed beyond division chairperson, she was increasingly confronted by the issue of racism. She interviewed for dean and was subsequently named to the position; many people said that she was named because she was Hispanic. This accusation taught her that moving up the ladder, working harder, being active, and competing carried with it a political struggle. Valles tells a story, a myth about that struggle that has become for her an analogy for Hispanic cooperation:

An old man and a little boy were leaving the beach, carrying a bucket of crabs between them. The little boy, worried that he would lose their catch, kept pushing any escaping crab back into the pail. The grandfather warned him not to be so concerned about the crab that was getting to the top of the pail, but to observe the process that involved all of the crabs. He wisely observed the way the crab had of escaping, that perhaps the crabs were pushing together so that one could make an escape.

Valles appreciates the lesson in this story. Rather than sabotaging each others' attempts to rise to the top, Hispanics are joining together to push upward those who seek to climb the ladder of success.

Valles raised another issue with which she has had to contend: the "Hispanic agenda." Accusations that nontraditional groups—whether Hispanic, Black, or female—are unable to see outside their own group and do not value the dominant culture must be answered. She answers with the following advice: People may want you to be their agenda, and you cannot; you must be professional and have no particularities, you must balance all situations, you must survive unpopular decisions, and you must have a clear idea of who you are, where you intend to go, and why you plan to go there.

DONALD PHELPS: SHAPING THE STANDARDS FOR GROWTH

Donald Phelps, chancellor of Los Angeles Community College District, California, acknowledged that the key to his growth and development, and his education, was his decision to "believe and be persistent and organized and just do it." When he began college, he looked at going there as something he could do "one day at a time," and he did. This philosophy of deciding to do something and then being persistent about accomplishing it pervades his thinking.

Phelps believes that more is to be gained by being inside working than outside fighting. He speaks of the critical role of networks and camaraderie, stating that it is important to find out what the Black community is capable of doing, and it is important that Black people laugh and talk to enrich each other's souls because this camaraderie provides energy and allows Blacks to talk about their unique problems. Phelps speaks of his own mentors: a former vice president at Boeing, who taught him that Blacks as industrial leaders should learn about politics, parties, and issues; another mentor who nurtured his musical talent, which later opened doors for him; a "stately, classy, White woman whose husband had been a professor at Howard University," who provoked him to open books and who made him interested in the nation and the world as a whole; and his predecessor as chancellor of the Seattle Community College District, who encouraged him to think broadly and, on hiring him, acknowledged Phelps's leadership abilities by saying, "I am sure you will succeed me."

Now, as chancellor of the largest community college district in the nation, Phelps recognizes the inherent power of his position and the responsibility for using it judiciously—to move people toward acceptable behavior and to educate them to understand the rationale for and the importance of such behavior. He maintains that one should not use power to make people mad or sad. For example, he believes he can get faculty to seek minority candidates by wielding the power of his position, but also by explaining, by educating, and by learning all there is to know about the hiring "facts" at the college.

TESSA TAGLE: CREATING CAMPUS/COMMUNITY PARTNERSHIPS

Tessa Tagle, vice president and chief academic officer of the Medical Center Campus of Miami-Dade Community College in Florida, has a unique theory about belief and truth: "Belief is truth as I would like it to be, but truth is truth as it turns out to be." One can wish for the moon, but must deal with the environment as it really is. Her campus, a health care specialty facility, trains nurses and medical technicians. Although the school provides more than two-thirds of the registered nurses in Dade County, Tagle knows the need is greater and that she will have to do a better job. The truth of her situation is that Dade County has high unemployment, and her campus is in a disadvantaged neighborhood and is located near a number of medical complexes. Tagle has used that critical data to change the direction and focus of her campus.

Tagle recognizes the importance of a strong relationship between her campus and the community. She realizes that the campus should be a nexus for the community—something not easily accomplished. To accomplish this, one must take on a new set of problems—problems not normally found in a campus environment. This action, of course, creates a conflict—in terms of what one expects from a campus climate and the restructuring of that climate in the community. As a potential support for creating such a nexus, Tagle has looked to the neighborhood to identify neighborhood leaders and to have them discuss with leaders of the medical school what can be done to improve their relationship and to establish a community nexus.

One sterling outcome of this strategy is a "new" medical school: Support and money from Southwestern Bell has created a medical school for kids. Featured on the "Today" show, Tagle explained that one cannot begin too early to interest children in continuing their education. Her program is designed for youngsters between the ages of 11 and 14 (one-third of the youth are Black, one-third are White, and one-third Hispanic). Bringing disadvantaged children in from the neighborhood, Tagle has sought to enliven, encourage, and draw out desires that students do not even know they have and introduce children to an exciting academic environment in which they might continue.

The relationship with the community is further enhanced when that community sees reflections of its own diversity in the college personnel. But Tagle experiences difficulty in finding minorities to hire, especially in the market as it exists today, and especially considering that there are no large numbers of minorities in the pipeline. Yet Miami-Dade Community College mandates that 50 percent of its new hires be minorities. Tagle characteristically focuses on the specifics of a plan: goals must be accompanied by expectations; keep your faculty and administration aware of your plans and goals; hire at mid-level positions; have a plan that includes finding the funds neccessary for locating and seeking out eligible and competent new minority hires.

An important initiative to identify and recruit minorities has been implemented at Miami-Dade: a collegewide minority fellowship program to recruit bachelor's degree holders, to fund their master's degrees in selected disciplines, and then to hire them to teach at Miami-Dade. A $10,000 stipend is provided to the minority recipient for one year; in return, the faculty member must commit to three years of teaching in the district.

With such an interest and emphasis on diversity at Miami-Dade Community College, Tagle has organized cross-cultural workshops in which faculty, administration, and students—and often outside speakers—come together to talk about their perceptions and the social characteristics of culture. Candid conversations reveal amazing sets of filters that people bring to situations. Objectives of the workshops are to encourage people to be open and receptive to others and to change those filters in terms of gender, ethnicity, economic status, or social status. The ultimate goal is to limit tensions that exist on campus.

Finally, Tagle asserts that it is important to afford minorities opportunities to get a universal view of the world. In her experience, minorities come in the back door, even in the community college, and they are "victims of special programs or community education or student services." Therefore, we must do more to provide them an opportunity to see the world at large, to see the college as a whole, and to give them a bird's eye view. We must serve their needs beyond the little worlds that they have experienced, to give them a broad-based socializing experience.

Another outcome of Tagle's relationship-building strategies is "Hands for Health," a program designed to fund more scholarships, to call attention to her medical complex, and to give some identity and image to the area of town in which she lives. Tagle invites a celebrity to attend a particular gala and uses that occasion to cast the celebrity's hand in bronze. Among those so "bronzed" are the musical conductor of the Miami Opera, Willie Walters; Gloria Estefan, a Miami-based, internationally known singer; and medical professionals, such as Joe Lesock or Michael DeBakey. The celebrity hands are displayed at the college, indicating that these celebrities will give a helping hand to the college and to the community by specifically raising money for medical scholarships.

RAUL CARDENAS: CREATING OPPORTUNITIES

Raul Cardenas, president of South Mountain Community College, Maricopa County Community College District in Arizona, was hired as its first president—he was to head a college that was to be built in an area desperately in need of urban renewal. He struggled with the mind-set of the people in this area that the college would not be of any use to them and that they would not have any permanent involvement with it. The college has had to work very hard to overcome a generalized perception that it is not quite as good as the other college campuses. Although many of the early concerns about the negative aspects of the community have never been realized, Cardenas recognizes that this concern has not entirely disappeared.

Cardenas sees the relationship between the college and the community as critical to the success of both. He believes that the goals of the college should be drawn from and reflect the needs of the community—for example, the drop-out problem and other social problems that exist in the community must be recognized by the college and dealt with in innovative ways.

Cardenas has initiated several programs to address community problems. The GED program provides high school drop-outs the opportunity to earn a diploma, and it allows them to march at a graduation ceremony at their own high school. One of the benefits of this program, Cardenas agrees, is that the parents love to see their sons and daughters graduating, frequently being the first in their families to do so.

The Achieving College Education (ACE) Program began as a Ford Foundation project in 1984 and facilitates the transfer of minorities and disadvantaged students to college. The high percentage of drop-outs among Hispanics and Native Americans drove Cardenas's initial interest in this project. Using data from a tracking procedure that identifies the lower quartile of high school students in several high schools in his service area, Cardenas and his team visit the schools to interest these students in going to college. By the end of their sophomore year, the students are invited into the college to see what is happening and to go through a summer bridge experience that will get them jobs, computer training, personal development training, and an active learning course that earns them college credit. Classes are provided on the high school campuses. After the students' junior year there is a second summer experience, somewhat broader than the first. The students are allowed to take courses at the college, and the college continues its serious approach to computer tracking—student attendance is constantly monitored, and counselors follow up on those students whose absences warrant intervention.

What is the effect of the ACE program? Cardenas believes that students are motivated by this program to complete high school, to go to college, and to be successful there. The program gets parents involved and it allows integration of high school facilities, college facilities, and university facilities in developing the program (a 2+2+2 program). It involves faculty from all three institutions working together to increase the likelihood that students will be monitored along the way to be successful in all of these areas.

But Cardenas sees an ongoing problem with the inherent mind-set of the community. People in the community must be brought to understand, by example and by experience, that the college can be a factor for success in their lives. Changing the minds of this population, creating confidence or even a willingness to consider that the college can make a difference, is slow and tedious. As an example, Cardenas noted that Paradise Valley Community College, set in a very affluent community, invited high school seniors and their parents to a Saturday meeting. Three thousand invitations were extended and 1,000 people participated. Cardenas and South Mountain Community College extended the same invitation to their community; 8,000 invitations were mailed and 10 people participated. Such occurrences indicate that the college must work harder and be even more motivated to change the mind-set against it.

RUTH SHAW: EXAMINING THE STRENGTHS IN DIVERSITY

Ruth Shaw, president of Central Piedmont Community College in North Carolina, speaks of a future in which the strengths of a diverse culture are its most prominent features. She identifies hiring as a critical effort in increasing diversity in colleges. Questions about who should be involved in the hiring process and under what conditions raise thorny issues. But they should be answered by providing open forums for discussion, establishing selection advisory committees, and knowing what you are looking for and how to recruit. Shaw believes underrepresentation in the legislature, in the community, and in leadership positions can change only when there are shifts in those who govern and who control money and programs that will expedite change, and that these shifts have not yet occurred.

In response to this need for change, Shaw feels community colleges must have a genuine commitment to build diversity, to nurture good and developing leaders, to allow change to occur incrementally, to help teachers develop a more institutional view, to model valuing diversity, and to incorporate these ideas into the fabric or culture or climate of the college community. While she acknowledges that diversity brings problems—such as differences in points of view and polarities in perspectives—she feels the problems can be healthy; sometimes tension, turmoil, and vastly different perspectives are best dealt with when they are finally brought out in the open. It is these differences that provide a realistic view of the world—a view to which people must, and will, become accustomed. We must assess the strength that lies in being different and encourage the freedom to be so.

Shaw warns against creating an unhealthy environment by thinking that bad things happen to us because we are women, because we are Black, or because we are Hispanic. If we think in this way, if we create this unhealthy environment, we inhibit our ability to examine ourselves; and it becomes difficult to get honest feedback. Thus, we establish a negative fantasy notion—we fulfill our own fantasies and behave in ways destructive to all parties.

EDUARDO PADRON: DESIGNING VALUABLE ENVIRONMENTS

Eduardo Padron, vice president and chief executive officer of the Wolfson Campus of Miami-Dade Community College in Florida, strives to develop the relationship between a campus and its community. Padron appreciates the decentralized structure of the various campuses of Miami-Dade Community College. This structure gives each campus a unique opportunity to reflect the community it serves and provides him the unique opportunity to direct that service. Padron's beliefs about community college education include:

- The campus is a microcosm of the community and the community environment. International flags are flown on Padron's campus.
- Impressions are valuable. Staff members are national models, representative of the people being served. Padron thinks they create harmony and provide a family-type atmosphere. He hopes that faculty and staff reflect the student body, that students find education to be an enriching growth exercise, that people feel they belong, that they find that others care, and that they find comfort in the college environment. "I get encouraging letters from students," Padron says, congratulating him about the programs that motivate and stimulate them and about exceptional faculty who recognize the needs of this diverse population.
- High school students need early encouragement. There is a strong relationship between the Wolfson Campus and its feeder schools.
- Special programs reflect responses to the community's needs. At the Wolfson Campus, a college bilingual program enrolls 3,000 students; its curriculum and faculty are entirely bilingual. A business program serves the needs of the businesses that surround the area. Strong in the humanities and the arts, Wolfson supports programs in architecture, computers, and legal assistance. Enrichment programs offer special experiences

for students beyond the classroom. An outstanding example is the Miami Book Fair International, which draws famous authors from all over the world into Miami and to the Wolfson Campus to exhibit and sell their books. Open to the community, the fair provides an incredible opportunity to work with major literary people and authors of the world. Included in the activities are authors' workshops, lectures, and panels. This extracurricular affair, supported by the help of 1,000 volunteers, has received worldwide recognition. (This year the American Book Awards moved their capital to Miami from New York.)

When asked about his heroes and models for living, Padron responds, "I admire a lot of people, but my heroes are very few. But there are those who make a difference, those who teach you by example; they are not celebrities, but people who make a difference in everyday life wherever they live within society and within communities."

PATSY FULTON: FACING THE CHALLENGE OF DIVERSITY

Patsy Fulton, president of Brookhaven College in Dallas County Community College District (DCCCD) in Texas, identifies perception as a major barrier to representation. But she notes that simply having a perception about someone else or some group is not the obstacle to underrepresentation: The obstacle is that our perceptions are played out by our behaviors. If many people believe that leaders who are hired on the basis of a quota system, for example, are less capable, and that hiring practices suffer from the "reverse discrimination" involved in a quota system, then bad behaviors follow. And another, larger barrier, the environmental barrier, exists outside of the perceptions of people. Once a minority person is employed, then there may be a barrier in terms of that person's feeling or attitudes toward the environment he or she has entered. This is a barrier to retention. We may not be able to hold on to our new leaders because we have not treated them professionally and they have not been accepted. It is difficult to see whether these actions are overt or covert or perhaps both.

DCCCD has a hiring goal of 40 percent of what is called the "under-represented population"—a goal aimed primarily at faculty because in the district as a whole the numbers seem fairly good in professional staff, in support staff, and in administration, but very low in terms of faculty.

Fulton has several views on cultural pluralism. She strongly values people being given a chance to do whatever they can, and she believes all people have the right to be represented and that achieving diversity should be education's number one priority. Education exists for all people, and failure to allow access to education to all people means that societal and economic problems will continue to grow in magnitude and to negatively affect our society. Fulton states:

> I value diversity. I value that our total population accepts that diversity is important. I value looking at the broader picture of the state and the nation. I value that what we need to do is to ensure that the United States is a good place to live in the future. I value that without education the work force will not be a place that will support future generations. Perhaps it will destroy the value that the United States will be a good place to live in the future.
>
> I don't think underrepresented people have had equal opportunity. I don't accept that they have equal opportunity. We must redress the grievance in terms of providing oppor-tunity. We have a target at Brookhaven that 40 percent of our new hires will be represented by women and members of racial and ethnic minorities. We have looked at our numbers and talked about the importance of achieving diversity, that achieving diversity is an element of the concept of role-modeling, and where we are headed in the future in our state. We never pushed the idea of hiring the best, and that is a goal that we will achieve in addition to achieving diversity.

Fulton attacks problems as they exist. Not only is she open to her faculty and assertive in her statements about the underrepresentation of groups, but she also contacts "people who grumble" about issues of hiring and underrepresentation. She talks to individuals about their dissatisfaction and brings issues out into the open. She talks about what is the best policy. More important, she notes that if the response of the community college fails to move it toward this diversity, if there is failure at the local level, then obviously control will come from above. Agencies, state legislatures, or national laws will step in, probably instituting policies that are out of sync with the individual needs, environments, and special differences that make campuses unique.

At Brookhaven College, there are special programs to encourage retention of underrepresented faculty and students:

- Clubs have been organized: the International Club, the Hispanic Club, and the Black Club help to form support groups for faculty and students.
- Black mentors from the faculty, from business, and from the area around Brookhaven College are encouraged to become involved in activities on and off campus.
- Two directories—one for Blacks and one for Hispanics—have been developed to provide some interconnection among these groups.
- Administrators and faculty have looked at their curriculum—at what the curriculum looked like to the average student and what it didn't look like to the average student. Where the curriculum seems one-sided, they have integrated the curriculum to include those who had been underrepresented.
- Fulton devised a survey instrument to assess the issues of racism. Used as a pre- and post-test, the survey indicated that while some people at the college initially believed that racism existed, the post-test showed that students were becoming more and more integrated, that they didn't feel segregated, and that they felt that the college gave them a good learning environment. Most important, students said, "I want to stay at Brookhaven."
- Faculty and administration identified the "American Values" class as an important part of the college curriculum and began to look at stereotypes in the class and discuss them. These are powerful experiences for the students.

Fulton maintains that everyone must see that what they do is their own responsibility. We are all responsible and obliged to establish diversity. Education serves as a catalyst for change within the community, and we must allow that change to occur. She recognizes that change is not easy. People need to work on core values, and there are not any shortcuts. One cannot just meet affirmative action requirements without comment and without commitment. Fulton's message is: You meet, you address, you understand, but you do so with your heart in it.

Fulton believes that there is an issue of race, not just at the college level, but in the community. Moreover, she believes that if her institution and the Dallas County Community College District as a whole show diversity and prove that education is an avenue for people to come together and talk to each other, then others may begin to do so as well. It is important that the circles produced by this ripple effect move out from the educational institution into the society.

NOLEN ELLISON: RISKING FOR DIVERSITY

Nolen Ellison, president of Cuyahoga Community College in Ohio, is a man who speaks specifically to the unique perspective of the community college located in a dense urban setting.

The challenges are especially keen in such a setting. They are the challenges created by multiculturalism, by the need to build consensus, and by the need for great vision. Ellison explains that "we have been whiplashed by events of the environment we don't control"—the movement from rural to urban areas, the movement from an agrarian to an industrial to a postindustrial society, and the movement from a manual to a technical to a technological society. Ellison sees community colleges at the margins—ready to excel, ready to look at the urban dilemma, ready to be reflective of that dilemma and to welcome Hispanics, Blacks, Asians, and Native Americans in terms of their open-door, open-access policies. He believes that no place else is the issue, the idea, and the ideal of diversity brought together as it is in the community college.

However, all is not a bed of roses. What happens in the urban areas—the problems of poverty, drugs, and teenage pregnancy—is augmented and fragmented in the community. Ellison calls the situation a political, governmental, educational, and economical morass in which it is difficult to find a sense of direction. He cites the meandering behavior of many school districts as an especially critical concern for the community college and the university. There is a sense of urgency around urban education, around the metropolitan centers, and around the notion that the ghetto may become a way of life in these urban areas. Studies of large urban areas clearly identify a rising underclass, and this underclass can no longer be neglected.

These problems must become the community college's problems if it is to effectively serve its community. Literacy, social welfare, training, the issue of prisons, and the problems of families all have to be addressed; perhaps more important, the number of children who fail in high school (and the frightening retention rate) has to be addressed. Although these seem to be challenges of insurmountable proportions, Ellison notes that there are community college programs that address these issues.

Leadership has a unique dimension in the community college, and it has an especially important dimension in the urban setting. Ellison speaks of the fragmentation, disorientation, and disconnection of people, that we are a nation of strangers, and that our mobility causes us great disparity. Community colleges must serve, especially in the urban area, vocational and technical education, continuing education, and community service. These dimensions are ones that reflect the social forces, reflect the society as it is, and reveal that there is such social disorientation in our society that community colleges must become managers of these problems and become a hope for the future.

CONCLUSION

Gilligan (1982) suggests that we have become cognizant of those "who speak in a different voice." And Freire (1972) has convinced us that "every human being, no matter how submerged in the culture of silence," is capable of looking critically at the world in a dialogical encounter with others and can be educated through words and voice as a means by which they discover their potential. Freire asserts that "through education, each man and woman wins back their right to say their own words, to name the world" (p. 13). These are the voices of educators, and they have won their right to name the world.

CHAPTER EIGHT

ॐ

GETTING THERE
FROM WHERE YOU ARE:
INCREASING REPRESENTATION
AND RECOGNITION

ॐ

What is especially disturbing about the social and economic
disadvantages of Blacks and Hispanics is that they are precisely
the group with whom most of our nation's schools and colleges
have been least successful.
Community colleges enroll 55 percent of all Hispanic undergraduates,
57 percent of Native American college students,
43 percent of all Black students, and 42 percent of all Asian students...
we must reaffirm to minority students the promise of
empowerment through education—
equality of opportunity for all ages and racial and ethnic groups
is an essential goal
(Commission on the Future of Community Colleges, 1988, p. 9).

さ

Disturbed by the faltering pace of minority advancement
in American life and by the discouraging
decline of participation of minority individuals,
higher education should take a leadership role
in rekindling the nation's commitment
to the full participation of minority students.
ACE recognizes the effect of the 1980s' lost momentum
in the efforts to ensure that minority groups are fully represented,
welcomed, and involved in higher education and on the campuses.
This fact cannot result in an attitude of resignation and defeat—
but success in creating a truly pluralistic campus
(Green, 1989, p. vii).

There is little doubt about the nature or size of the problem of racial-ethnic minorities in higher education today. Participation in college doesn't mean enrollment; it means graduation, and it means getting jobs. Colleges must retain minority students, and they must provide them with role models whose success becomes a pattern for student achievement and student goals. How does this happen? Obviously, it happens in spite of what occurs today, and it happens because of the dreams, commitments, and vision of leaders. Leaders (such as CEOs, boards of trustees, and legislators) must refocus their vision and build a sense of shared purpose while developing an integrated approach to change. Minority participation must be integral to the mission and the workings of higher education institutions.

Minorities seem to bear the entire burden of adaptation to the "dominant" culture on campuses today. Acquiring cultural pluralism based on diversity requires great energy and the necessity, or perhaps the threat, of institutional change. If campuses are to reflect their represented cultural pluralism, then the assumptions and priorities of higher education must be examined. As Green (1989) notes:

> Strategies must go beyond putting old wine in new bottles
> and will require fighting the temptation to look for new roads
> to travel when we have not really charted or navigated the
> existing ones—"We've tried that and it didn't work" should
> be the beginning of the voyage, not the end (p. xv).

In the 15 years between 1950 and 1965, enrollment of Black students in higher education went from 150,000 to 1,000,000. From those amazing data, one would expect a continued increase of Black students in higher education. But time and history did not bear out that promise; by the mid-'70s, enrollment for Blacks, Hispanics, and Native Americans began to decline or to stagnate rather than grow. Green (1989) and Carter and Wilson (1989) suggest this is a problem of "lost momentum" beginning with poverty and shaped by piecemeal, slow-to-respond social and educational institutions. Green notes that "Black and Hispanic students are more likely to be poor, to live in urban areas and attend inner-city public schools and receive inferior education to that of affluent Whites"

(p. 1). And researchers Carter and Wilson assert that "isolated programs to attract and retain minority students, faculty, and staff keep the effort (to increase minority participation) marginal to the central mission of the institution" (p. 17).

Moreover, between 1976 and 1988 data demonstrated that family income and gender were critical to Black and Hispanic enrollment in college; low-income Black and Hispanic men lagged behind and then dropped below female enrollment for those same groups (Carter and Wilson, 1989). And, despite losses at nearly all levels for Black men, minorities collectively made gains in earning degrees from 1985 to 1988: a 3 percent increase for both associate and master's degrees, a 6 percent increase for bachelor's degrees, and a 15 percent increase in first-professional awards (Carter and Wilson, 1989, p. iv). In 1987 the U.S. Department of Education, in a report titled *Highest Educational Degree Attained by 1980 High School Seniors by Sex, Race, Type of Community, and Type of High School*, contained the following data:

1986 Degrees Held by 1980 High School Seniors

	Associate	Bachelor's	Master's
Hispanic	7.3%	6.8%	.1%
Native American	9.3	10.8	.0
Asian	8.7	27.3	1.7
Black	5.3	10.0	.2
White	6.6	20.2	.9

Source: Center for Educational Statistics, 1987

Green (1989), in *Minorities on Campus: A Handbook for Enhancing Diversity*, seeks to increase minority participation by examining institutions and their students, faculty, and administrators; by improving campus climate; and by exploring teaching, learning, and the curriculum. Her assumptions are that all institutions are different—each has a different culture, history, and structure and has devoted varying amounts of attention to the issue of minority participation; that institutions must change to adapt to a new population of students, with building a pluralistic environment and culture as their goal; and that in this emotionally charged and value-laden area, constructive efforts are required to dispel anger and frustration and to address the "values" issues. The goal of the *Handbook* is that benefits address the entire campus community, not simply minority individuals.

The American Council on Education offers a longitudinal study of minorities in higher education in its annual *Status Report on Minorities in Higher Education.* The data in these reports trace trends and circumstances of "the underserved" in higher education. Blandina Ramirez, director of ACE's Office of Minorities in Higher Education, notes:

> High school completion and college participation for minorities in education has decreased in the last 10 years. For example, although Hispanic high school enrollment data demonstrate an overall increase from 1978 of 10 percent—this does not begin to reflect the 6.7 percent yearly increase in Hispanic population in the last decade. Moreover, in the last 12 years Hispanic enrollment in college fell by 15 percentage points.

There are approximately 28 million 18- to 24-year-olds in the nation; they make up the traditional college cohort. Fourteen percent (3.5 million) of this group are Black, and 10 percent (2.6 million) are Hispanic (Carter and Wilson, 1989). In 1988 the college participation rate for Blacks was 28 percent and the rate for Hispanics was 31 percent—their highest rate since 1983 (National Center for Educational Statistics, 1990). The participation rates of 25- to 34-year-old high school graduates—the older student cohort—showed a slightly downward trend after 1978, averaging just under 10 percent throughout the 1980s; however, college participation rates for Blacks and Hispanics in this age range exceed those of Whites.

Taking into consideration socioeconomic status reveals substantial declines in the high school attendance of racial-ethnic minority groups: 61 and 51 percent respectively, of poor Blacks and Hispanics complete high school; for middle-income Blacks and Hispanics, that figure increases considerably to 84 and 76 percent respectively. This discrepancy may be demonstrated in college enrollment as well, although men demonstrate more decline. According to ACE's 1989 study, *Campus Trends*, indications are that a majority of colleges and universities have activities underway to increase minority participation, but administrators rated their ability to attract Black and Hispanic students as "fair" or "poor." Most administrators who were polled perceive more commitment to minority participation on campus compared to 10 years ago; yet when they ranked their personal commitment to minority participation, less than one-third of the campus leaders rated this commitment as "high."

Trends underscore the need for more aggressive measures to increase college access and degree attainment by minority students on every college campus. Campuses must begin to address these problems reported by Carter and Wilson: only "some" campus activity around increasing enrollment, retention, financial aid, and faculty for minorities; "infrequent" assistance to minority faculty; little demonstrated effort to increase numbers of minority senior administrators; and few examples of monitored tracking of minority students' enrollment, participation, and completion rates (1989, p. 17).

Data compiled from the *1989-1990 Fact Book on Higher Education* reveal the depth of the problem:

> There are approximately 5 million students enrolled in community colleges—2.1 million are male students, and 2.7 million are female. Half of the community colleges are located in the Southeast and Far West regions; these two regions contain one-third of all higher education institutions. In 1986, women represented 56 percent of all students enrolled in community colleges, increasing 36 percent in 10 years.
>
> Thirty-eight percent of all higher education institutions (3,434) are community or junior colleges (1,305); this figure

represents a doubling in the last 25 years. Twenty-three percent of the traditional college-age population is Black or Hispanic; their family median incomes were $16,786 and $19,027, compared to $29,152 for White families. The percentages of those families with incomes over $30,000 was 30 percent for Blacks, 36 percent for Hispanics, and 69 percent for Whites. Median income for Black men with a high school education was $18,452; for Black women with a high school education, median income was $13,806. Unemployment rates for Blacks and Hispanics were 13.0 percent and 8.8 percent, respectively; the rate for Whites was 5.3 percent.

2.2 million minority students were enrolled in higher education institutions; this represents 18 percent of the total enrollment. The racial-ethnic backgrounds of men who were first-time, full-time freshmen in fall 1987 were 87.6 percent White, 7.2 percent Black, 2.6 percent Asian, 0.9 percent Hispanic, and 0.9 percent Native American (1.6 percent were "other"). Women were 84.5 percent White, 10 percent Black, 2.1 percent Asian, 1.5 percent Hispanic, 0.9 percent Native American, and 1.7 percent other.

There are 1,081,000 Black students, 624,000 Hispanic students, 448,000 Asian or Pacific Islander students, and 90,000 Native and Alaskan American students. In 1986, 7.8 million students attended senior institutions and approximately 4.7 million students attended community colleges. Hispanic, Native American, and Asian students are most heavily concentrated in New York, New Jersey, Florida, Texas, New Mexico, Arizona, Colorado, California, Alaska, Hawaii, and Washington. The heaviest concentrations of Black students are in the states of North and South Carolina, Georgia, Alabama, Mississippi, and Louisiana—all Southern states.

In 1987, there were 296 institutions, out of 3,434, headed by women; 195 were four-year colleges and universities, and 101 were community and junior colleges. Approximately 20 percent of all ranks of faculty of four-year colleges and universities are women; 38 percent of faculty are women in community and junior colleges.

GETTING STARTED: TIMELINE FOR TRANSFORMING INSTITUTIONS

How do campuses get started? They begin with leaders' commitments and broad institutional involvement, with assignment of administrative responsibility, and with planning that takes stock of individual campuses and examines their cultures and climates. Planning should involve the fundamental "statement of philosophy" and mission statement of the college and should provide mechanisms for monitoring conflict, accountability, and evaluation.

Assuming that community colleges are working toward realizing cultural diversity, we suggest a timeline for stages and goals:

- *Beginning Stages: Campus Culture and Climate*
  Beginning now and where you are
  Defining and understanding campus culture
  Valuing pluralism and diversity
  Challenging beliefs and motives
  Confronting issues: thinking and rethinking
  Questioning losses and gains
- *Intermediate Stages: Teaching, Learning, and the Curriculum; and Addressing Faculty and Leadership Shortages*
  Seeking cooperation and like-mindedness
  Employing catalysts in people and information
  Allowing nonperfection of strategies and ideas
  Identifying successes: large or small, immediate and visible
- *Future Goals*
  Valuing diversity and individual differences and receptivity to change
  Recognizing contributions

Making a long-term commitment to change (strategies for graduate preparation)

CAMPUS CULTURE AND CLIMATE: BEGINNING NOW AND WHERE YOU ARE

Higher educational institutions have their own culture. Campus cultures can be an environment for fostering student involvement, but they can also alienate students. Students, faculty, and staff are sensitive to the values, attitudes, and behaviors that set the tone of their campus environment. This environment is also referred to as campus climate. Green (1989) examines the concept of "climate."

> Campus climate embraces the culture, habits, decisions, practices, and policies that make up campus life. It is the sum total of the daily environment and central to the comfort factor that minority students, staff, faculty and administrators experience on campus. Students and other members of the campus community who feel unwelcome or alienated from the mainstream campus life are unlikely to remain. If they do remain, they are unlikely to be successful.
>
> The culture or climate of an organization cannot be quantified or legislated. It is shaped by tradition, values, attitudes, many of which are unexpressed. Thus, changing the campus climate can be a difficult and elusive task. But, because the climate is so central to all other efforts to improve minority participation, it is both the point of departure and the culmination of all other efforts (p. 113).

Recalling the works of Schein (1985b), Deal and Kennedy (1983), and Ouchi (1981), attention to the "organizational culture" of community colleges is paramount. When Schein wrote *Organizational Culture and Leadership*, a clear view of the relationship between the values, identity, and norms of organizations began to emerge. His intent was to posit a model in which leaders not only were aware of their role in embedding culture in the organization or institution, but also were aware of the circumstances, particularities, and nuances of their own institution's culture or cultures. The structure of culture—how it works, how it begins, what functions it serves, what problems it solves, why it survives, why and how it changes, and whether it can be managed—provides a dynamic model that tells us what a culture does as well as what a culture is. According to Schein (1985b), culture is a deeper level of basic assumptions and beliefs that are shared, that operate unconsciously, and that define in a basic taken-for-granted fashion an organization's view of itself and its environment (p.6). As a conceptual tool of analysis, culture research illuminates individual, group, and institutional behavior by:

- Demonstrating observed behavioral regularities of personal interaction, language, and rituals
- Uncovering the norms that evolve in a particular society or setting regarding working conditions
- Revealing the dominant values espoused by an organization
- Examining the philosophy that guides an organization's policy toward its constituent groups
- Divulging the rules of the game for getting along in the organization, the ropes that a newcomer must learn to become an accepted member
- Ascertaining the feeling or climate that is conveyed in an organization by the physical lay-out and the way in which members of the organization interact with outsiders (Schein, 1985b, pp. 5-6)

Although an examination of the culture of an organization is essential, emphasis must be placed on climate as a creation by leaders in their particular institutions. If their task as leader is modified by observing behavioral patterns, by uncovering the norms of the working environment, or by questioning the dominant values and philosophy that guide the organization, then the leader is equipped with the tools of analysis about his or her college campus.

The leader must posit those findings with new and challenging epistemologies, must recognize paradigmatic shifts, and must accommodate social needs and demands. Moreover, if the leader is to "transform" his or her constituent groups, rather than act as a transactional exchange agent, then his or her moral obligation is to meet the demands and needs of constituent groups. The leader is called on to become teacher and coach—to reduce the barriers and obstacles that stand in the way of successful behavior.

Not since the 1960s have campuses seen the racially and ethnically motivated conflict that is occurring now. Events are particularized to senior college institutions where the focus is on perceived racism and discrimination, and specifically on universities' failures to recruit greater numbers of minority students and faculty. Between 1978 and 1988 minority enrollment in two-year institutions increased more dramatically than enrollment in senior institutions—20.8 percent versus 13.5 percent. Community colleges have a "disproportionate share of minority enrollment; although two-year schools accounted for 37 percent of total enrollment in higher education, they accounted for 46 percent of the total minority enrollment in 1988" (National Center for Education Statistics, 1990). Race-related events dramatize overt situations; they do not speak to the attitudes and perceptions or the climate of a campus.

An inhospitable campus environment can be overt and noticeable or quite subtle. Minority students often feel conspicuous and isolated from the mainstream; many would say they feel marginal to the predominantly White student body and prevailing culture. Scarcity of minorities is seen as evidence of institutional indifference to minority issues. The absence of minority focus in the curriculum is interpreted as a devaluation of diversity. According to Nettles (1988), 76 percent of Black college students still believe discrimination is a problem on campus. Moreover, minority student cohesiveness or gatherings are still perceived as threatening, hostile, or separatist by Whites.

Changing the climate may be difficult and confrontational—leaders must recognize climate as an issue and set the tone and pace for efforts to recruit and retain minority students, faculty, and administration; they must recognize that the issue belongs to everyone on campus; and they must provide education and training in the form of workshops, symposia, and other activities to cultivate pluralism in cultural and extracurricular activities. Schein would suggest that changing group behavior is best represented by a "paradoxical model" in which opposition and conflict are known to be perpetually present, such as dealing with underlying emotional issues that continually surface and resurface and dominate the attention of groups at any stage of cultural or climate change. The stages Schein proposes involve confrontation of:

1. Dependency/authority issues. This is the group's ability to deal with the issue of leadership (who will lead, with how much authority, power, and influence, and who will be dependent on whom), the resolution of external problems, and the creation of comfortable internal environments.

2. Intimacy, role differentiation, peer relationship issues. It is possible for the group to fall into the "fusion" principle, making euphoric and unrealistic assumptions about how good the group is and how much the members love one another, rather than the realistic principle, which allows appraisal of the division of labor, the tasks at hand, and the interdynamics of group interrelationships.

3. Creativity/stability issues. As the group learns to deal with its problems, to accomplish its mission, and to build an internal system that is acceptable, it begins to face the problems of institutionalization. Where creativity and innovation characterized the group's first efforts, these same factors now become the source of disruption and anxiety. The paradox now is that the group cannot succeed without continued ability to create and innovate, but neither can it feel comfortable with abandoning old solutions. The cultural assumptions already adopted now can become a constraint and a barrier to further growth. The dilemma at this stage is how to maintain adaptiveness without feeling too threatened internally.

4. Survival/growth issues. As the group matures and continues to interact with a dynamic external environment, it will sooner or later discover whether its culture can provide solutions to the new survival problems. And at that stage, the question arises of whether the group serves important functions and should survive, or whether it should allow itself to die or be terminated so that a more adaptive set of solutions can be created by a new group (Schein, 1985, pp. 164-165).

The process by which basic assumptions become explicit, new insights are gained, new common understandings are created, and norms are formed may be understood by examining a group's history and by determining that all these things occur around catalytic marker events or critical incidents—this is the "reaction to dramatic events" concept that forces change to meet exigencies, emergencies, and pressures. These circumstances are noted by leadership (and at this point, a sense of shared purpose can be developed between leaders and constituent groups). Anxieties, emotional response and release, and emotional regression are integrating factors for understanding common experiences and feelings. Joint problem-solving activities and shared consensus circumscribe differences in interpersonal styles; emotional make-up and cognitive styles build communication systems in which all parties have the same sense of the "meaning" of events.

Thus, the embedding process is difficult and demands a visionary leader. Leaders focus on crises in the external environment to make the internal zone consistent with the needs of the various constituencies. A plurality of interests, a multicultural student body and community, and the mounting needs of urban environments all affect the leader of the community college campus. Diversity is not just an issue of the "nontraditional student" on community college campuses; it is a way of life, a *sine qua non* explanation of community colleges in America.

Strategies have been suggested for successfully meeting the needs of the modern community college and its collective culture and norms—strategies that presuppose and assume the condition of egalitarianism and open access. Many of these strategies are offered in great detail in Green's *Minorities on Campus: A Handbook for Enhancing Diversity* (1989). This American Council on Education publication provides an excellent and detailed discussion of specific strategies for use in higher education institutions. Most of the remarks that follow focus specifically on racial-ethnic minorities, primarily because women now constitute one-half of all undergraduate and master's degree recipients and receive 34 percent of all Ph.D.'s. They also represent 38 percent of all new law school graduates, 30 percent of new medical school graduates, and 21 percent of new dental school graduates (National Center for Educational Statistics, 1987). Where they are underrepresented and underutilized is in faculty positions in senior institutions (presently they hold approximately one-fourth of those positions) and in leadership positions at both community colleges and senior higher education institutions (they hold approximately 10 percent of those positions).

We are suggesting strategies for improving the culture and climate of community colleges to make them more inclusive of racial-ethnic minorities and women. Some of the ideas represented here are gathered from programs and practices now in place in community colleges around the nation; other ideas emanate from research findings and from the demands of changing demography—from the individual and group needs of the underutilized and the underrepresented.

1. *Recognizing individual differences among institutions.* Consideration should be given to external and internal environments including geographic location; urban, interurban, or rural setting; population statistics and future trends; community needs; requirements and interrelationships; governmental relations; and economic needs.

2. *Leading from the top.* The goals, purpose, and ultimate planning for redirection emanate from the office of the CEO; moreover, commitment from the leadership, clarity around goals, and enthusiasm for constructive change guide the institution and its constituent groups. The leader's initiatives in promoting racial-ethnic and gender diversity become signposts for others' directions and attitudes toward underrepresented groups. Communicating minority concerns freely and openly to constituent groups is a fundamental goal.

3. *Organizing representative groups and constituencies.* Discuss, confront, and raise issues around your campus culture, the climate weathervane, how you specifically (as individuals or groups) work to achieve cultural diversity and pluralism on campus. This can be done by:

- Defining diversity, cultural pluralism, and multicultural groups
- Questioning the issues of racial-ethnic and gender discrimination and prejudice that may exist on campus
- Developing policies for dispute resolution, harassment, bias,

discrimination, and grievances
- Discussing issues related to justice-injustice, equality-inequality, the ethics of choice, dominant-subgroup culture, and political choices about controversial topics like affirmative action or quotas
- Examining the existing strata for numbers of leaders, faculty, and students representing various constituencies in the college and determining underrepresentation and underutilization

4. *Knowing the "costs" of changing.* Consider the opponents, the research required, the financial and human resources needed, the political spectrum, the role of leadership, faculty reactions, and relations to other constituencies and other colleges. Consider forming information-sharing networks with other institutions and other colleges.

5. *Offering guideline strategies.* Constituent college groups should work toward goals to be modified for individual campus needs. Such goals may include:
- Planning special orientations, such as summer orientations, or 2+2 programs for new minority students
- Ensuring faculty, staff, and student awareness of services
- Holding workshops on college climate for faculty and students and integrating academic concerns with student life
- Implementing special counseling and peer counseling programs
- Providing minority students with opportunities and mentors to acquire the skills necessary to seek leadership positions at various levels, including leadership positions in extracurricular activities
- Sponsoring cultural events featuring minority individuals and issues
- Maintaining a student success model for instant tracking of students
- Interviewing students who transfer, drop out, or change majors

6. *Developing criteria for climate.* Develop the issues to be used in evaluations, both in evaluating applications for faculty and staff positions and in evaluating faculty performance.

7. *Rewarding and recognizing individuals and organizational units.* Celebrate exceptional progress in creating a positive climate for minority concerns.

TEACHING, LEARNING, AND THE CURRICULUM

What is at the heart of the matter is what happens in the classroom: Quality teaching benefits all students. A curriculum that broadens students' horizons and enables them to appreciate different cultures, different modes of thinking and inquiry, and different values and aesthetics will benefit all students. Women's studies and ethnic studies serve to inform the curriculum and enrich the academic experience. The role of the faculty, faculty leadership, and the receptiveness of individual faculty members to new ideas and commitment to continued professional growth are essential to positive change. As Green (1989) maintains, "teaching and learning encompasses inquiry, pedagogy, educational theory, learning styles and preferences, and personal growth and development" (p. 133).

What do we know about effective teaching? According to Baker, Roueche, and Gillett-Karam's work, *Teaching as Leading* (1990), it is the teacher who accepts responsibility for the learning process and for motivating and influencing students to learn how to learn. Teachers are urged to examine themselves to discover whether their predominant teaching style is as a Supporter, Theorist, Achiever, or Influencer—only by discovering this proclivity can the teacher modify his or her behaviors in the classroom to accommodate the readiness of the students. Teachers are leaders who, of course, recognize the importance of subject matter, but they are also leaders who recognize the strategic functions of leadership in the classroom, including: engaging the desire to learn; eliminating obstacles to learning; increasing opportunities for success; offering positive guidance and direction; empowering through high expectations; and motivating toward independence.

Observation and research on faculty attitudes and behaviors toward minority students suggest that although teachers may demonstrate "good practices" by encouraging student-faculty contact, cooperation among students, and active learning; giving prompt feedback and emphasizing time on task; and communicating high expectations and respecting diverse talents and ways of learning (Chickering and Gamson, 1987), few instructors actually change their teaching methods—primarily because they emulate the traditional ways they were taught in their own under-graduate and graduate experiences. Many of these practices produce unconscious attitudes and behaviors, many of which are covertly discriminatory. More important, although a wealth of materials exists for good teaching practices, there are few training courses for college instructors in any discipline. Findings indicate a need for such training experience.

We suggest that training programs teach teachers to teach and that exemplary teachers serve as models for teachers in these training experiences.

Teachers as leaders understand that only by recognizing the reality of the teaching situation can teachers modify their teaching behaviors. Situational teaching requires the instructor to become aware of the circumstances of the college environment and to act as a leader in the classroom, invoking the same direction, plans, and strategies that the CEO does for the entire campus. Thus, the exemplary college instructor plans for change, understands the environment or climate of campus and classroom, and implements a framework that allows modification of teaching style based both on student readiness and on the actual evaluated success or failure of the teacher's ability to motivate and influence students. The six functions of effective teaching will be discussed in the following pages and offered as strategies for classroom practice aimed at improving teaching and learning.

Engaging the desire to learn includes:
- Diagnosing student needs
- Communicating goal and purpose of instruction
- Providing for student input
- Being aware of the total student (Roueche, Baker, and Gillett-Karam, 1990)

As part of recognizing and being aware of the students' desire to learn, teachers should diagnose, communicate, and foster interpersonal relationships in their classrooms. Teachers should be aware of the research on cultural diversity and should integrate that research with their ability to draw out the hidden potential and self-knowledge in their students. This is the role of the leader who encourages the courage of the follower—the courage for students to find what they need to know within themselves.

Several inflammatory discussions are resurfacing around the "nature" of racial-ethnic students and their "turning their backs on education" (Keller, 1988-1989). Keller reports the views of various researchers and journalists who have attempted to address the question of Black students' attitudes toward education:

> College attendance rates and graduation rates for Blacks actually declined in the 1980s, and most preferential treatment has not prevented the decline. William Blakey says, "Education is not as high a priority within the Black community as it used to be." Reginald Wilson says, "A unique animosity toward Blacks and a lingering racism is still active." Or is there some crippling historical burden, some peculiar set of attitudes toward formal learning, or a singular confidence about the possibilities of intellectual and scientific achievement, lodged in the emotional core of an enlarging number of young Blacks? William Raspberry says, "The real problem, I suspect, is the curse of low expectations." Clifton Wharton believes that Blacks are "crying out for a massive infusion of self-esteem." And Jeff Howard and Ray Hammond suggest, "The performance gap is largely a behavioral problem. It is the result of a remediable tendency to avoid intellectual engagement and competition" (p. 44).

These accusations may have some foundation, but if this is an issue of "sudden educational erosion among Blacks," as Keller points out, then educators must recognize their own responsibilities toward this immediate crisis. Nettles (1988) reminds us that American colleges enrolled 76,554 fewer Black undergraduates in 1985 than in 1976—a decline of 8.9

percent. Studies on culture suggest it is these crises-making events that cause us to re-evaluate our practices and to direct change appropriate to environmental and societal need. Teachers should respond to Keller's accusation that the "lumping together of all minorities is intellectually questionable" and should address the issues of educational need based on individual experiences.

Blacks and Native Americans are significantly less represented in higher education, whether as students or in faculty positions, but all racial-ethnic groups and women are underrepresented in positions of leadership in higher education.

Increasing students' opportunities for success places the following requirements on the teacher:
- Has an education philosophy
- Sees learning as a valuable activity
- Relates the course to his or her experiences
- Is a facilitator of learning
- Maintains high expectations of student
- Helps student learning process
- Encourages belief in student self-worth
- Cares about the student
- Finds satisfaction in student achievement
- Allows the student to take responsibility for learning

Helping to clarify learning goals and empowering students to achieve active learning contingent on effective performance are critical instructional strategies. The need to respect diverse talents and ways of learning involves a learning theory that maintains that individuals learn differently. "Learning style" refers to how students process and retain information, how they prefer to interact with their instructors and other learners, and their preferences for learning environments.

The relationship of gender, racial, and ethnic differences to learning styles creates controversy: Is it legitimate to associate learning style with gender, race, and ethnicity, and if so, then why are there such differences? Various studies recommend that teachers become more aware of how different cultural backgrounds affect communication and learning, but there is active disagreement as to whether cultural background should be singled out for attention. The danger lies in possible stereotyping; the dilemma lies in recognizing diversity without casting a stereotypical mold. Claxton and Murrell (1987) and Anderson (1988) indicate a relationship between culture, conceptual systems, and learning styles. Perceptual and cognitive differences have been demonstrated between different minority groups and the "dominant" culture. American educational values hinge on male-oriented, Euro-American traditions.

Many researchers relate this isssue to the nature versus nurture debate, maintaining that gender or race may influence preferred learning style because the style is either valued or reinforced by that group or by the majority culture. The perception that women are collaborative rather than competitive learners may be attributable to the fact that the dominant culture reinforces these tendencies in women and discourages them in men. Hale-Benson (1982) portrays Black children as more relational than analytical in their learning styles; others would say that these differences disappear when students are acculturated to the predominant analytic style of most schools.

Resistance to culturally based learning styles stems from the assumption that what is different from the norm is deviant or less valuable. Learning styles, however, seem to be a question of preference rather than absolutes—good teachers allow students opportunities to exercise their own style while helping them develop in other areas as well. A conceptual framework for a continuum of learning styles, such as that presented in *Teaching as Leading* (Baker, Roueche, and Gillett-Karam, 1990), provides instructors a process for examining how students learn and assessing their own impact on student learning style. Preferences for personality, information processing, social interaction, and instruction can be met; teaching should be situationally perceptive so that teaching style can be modified on the basis of student need. Classroom research about teaching and learning styles, in which instructors have students take the Kolb (1976) learning style inventory, and the Baker, Roueche, and Gillett-Karam (1990) TALI (Teaching as Leading Inventory), profits everyone.

By eliminating obstacles to learning, the exemplary faculty member:

- Assesses and resolves problems individually
- Listens with an open, receptive attitude
- Explores alternatives for change
- Develops and modifies curriculum to meet needs
- Maintains supportive communication
- Is sensitive to student perceptions
- Maintains a supportive classroom environment
- Meets with students outside of the classroom
- Provides extra help
- Encourages the use of support and resource services
- Uses peer and other tutoring

Working to eliminate or at least reduce obstacles to learning is another strategic function of the teacher as leader. In this role, faculty are aware of the major barriers that confront the teaching-learning environment, and they work to eliminate or at least reduce them. Concentration here is on solutions; defining the problems is not a sufficient goal of the exemplary teacher.

Richardson and Bender (1987) address the issues of minority participation in *Fostering Minority Access and Achievement in Higher Education*. Their principal interest lies in the relationships between declining enrollments and the transfer function. Obviously, this is one area of access, but only one among many.

Richardson and Bender's criticism of the transfer function at community colleges subsumed by "middle-class values" that dominate the policies, practices, and expectations of their educational programs is particularly weak, especially since the transfer function is viewed as the only critical function of community college education. Their stated intolerance toward "different standards for courses and tailoring of courses to student capabilities" is a slap in the face of community colleges. Accusations "that minorities become vocational and technical majors because no viable alternatives are provided them" is simply inaccurate. This reference to the "cool out" function of the community college is not a new one; it is, however, an overly abused accusation. These authors do not acquit themselves by obliquely commending community colleges for their belief in the basic dignity of all human beings, their increasing sophistication in dealing with learning problems, and their success in recruiting large percentages of minority faculty members.

Community college education provides opportunities beyond the transfer function, and this is not an apologetic function. Community colleges are colleges that mirror societal and individual needs and demands, and as such they provide functions that relate to retraining the work force, working in conjunction with federal programs (e.g., the Job Training Partnership Act and the Family Assistance Act), providing prison training, and developing a large curriculum for continuing education, amnesty programs, and short-term community services.

Quality colleges and teachers work to reduce obstacles to learning by examining the status quo; by offering options to existing problems, such as students' language or reading skills deficiencies or cultures whose norms do not "value" education in the same manner as does the "dominant" culture; and by addressing the issues of underrepresentation and underutilization of racial-ethnic minorities in the classroom, among the faculty and administration, and in positions of leadership in the community college. Examples at Miami-Dade Community College and Borough of Manhattan Community College provide options, not accusations, and they provide and document successes, not failures, in overcoming and addressing obstacles for minority and gender issues in their communities and for their local populations.

Empowering through high expectations means a faculty member:
- Sets and upholds standards of behavior
- Models expected behavior
- Clarifies expectations and performance for outcomes
- Teaches student consequences of actions
- Provides appropriate feedback
- Accepts and empowers students

Questions such as the following (modified from Green, 1989) direct teachers' attention to a variety of important issues:
- What are your expectations of minority students? Do you communicate these expectations?

- Do seemingly innocuous remarks by you appear sexist or racist to students?
- Do you call on minority students as frequently as majority students?
- How do you deal with silent students?
- Do you sustain eye contact with students?
- Do you interrupt students?
- Do you solicit the input of minority students as "spokespersons" or as individuals?
- How are students seated in your classes?
- How do you give feedback to students?

Research indicates that teachers form expectations on the basis of prior achievement, physical attractiveness, sex, language, socioeconomic status, and race-ethnicity (Good, 1981; Brophy and Good, 1984). Moreover, instructors may assume that minority students are grouped at the lower end of the ability continuum and may have lower expectations of them, which leads to the self-fulfilling prophecy. Research shows differences in the way teachers interact with low achievers and high achievers. To the extent that minority students are actually underprepared, or simply stereotyped as low achievers, they may be treated differently from other students—called on less frequently, given less time to respond to questions, interrupted or criticized more often, and given insincere or generalized praise (Green, 1989). The assumptions instructors make about abilities and attitudes can and do differ for majority and minority students.

All students are sensitive to nonverbal cues; minority students are intimidated by a predominantly White environment and dominant culture and may view the instructor as an authority figure not to be questioned. These are characteristics of cultural diversity and socialization by subgroup cultures. Cultural differences and norms may be demonstrated with eye contact—for some cultures, direct and sustained eye contact represents interest and engagement; for other cultures, it may represent disrespect, and for others, it may imply personal or sexual interest (Byers and Byers, 1972). For the minority student, these factors may inhibit their participation, and faculty misinterpretation may exacerbate these problems. Pemberton (1988) discusses an interaction between a professor and student in which what the instructor perceives as interest in the student, the student perceives as her life "being ransacked for sociological evidence" of race.

Instructors model expected behavior—they "inspect what they expect." High expectations are themselves self-fulfilling prophecies; this is the so-called Pygmalion effect, and it can be demonstrated over and over again in social settings that seem desperate and unyielding. Surely the achievements of Marva Collins demonstrate this fact, but so do the achievements of other "hopeless" cases. These cases remind us of the excitement of discovering the love of learning. None of these cases is more powerful than Wright's (1945) discussion of the use of his mentor's loaned library card and how it opened his mind to books and to the world outside of being a "black boy" from the South:

> It had been my accidental reading of fiction and literary criticism that had evoked in me vague glimpses of life's possibilities. Of course, I had never seen or met the men who wrote the books I read, and the kind of world in which they lived was as alien to me as the moon. But what enabled me to overcome my chronic distrust was that these books—written by men like Dreiser, Masters, Mencken, Anderson, and Lewis—seemed defensively critical of the straitened American environment. These writers seemed to feel that America could be shaped nearer to the hearts of those who lived in it. And it was out of these novels and stories and articles, out of the emotional impact of imaginative constructions of heroic or tragic deeds, that I felt touching my face a tinge of warmth from an unseen light; and in my leaving (the South) I was groping toward that invisible light, always trying to keep my face so set and turned that I would not lose the hope of its faint promise, using it as my justification for action (p. 227).

By offering positive guidance and direction through coaching, a faculty member:
- Demonstrates well-defined course organization

- Identifies and communicates expectations
- Matches student needs with plans
- Encourages student efforts with feedback
- Repeats goals and objectives of the course and learning
- Identifies and affirms student responsibilities

Increasing the opportunities for quality educational performance and success in college, and recruiting and retaining minority undergraduates, are essential steps to ensuring equity for minority citizens and for improving the learning environment for all students. A college degree provides increased employment opportunity as well as enhanced social standing. Anything less than full access for all citizens to this important credential is clearly unjust. Educational experiences should reflect the pluralism of our country and the importance of racial-ethnic minorities as individuals and cultures. The following chart reflects trends in minority education in the 1970s and '80s:

High School Graduation, College Attendance, and Degrees (by %)

High School Graduation	Blacks	Hispanics	White
1971	62 %	52	
1981	71	56	81
1986	76	63	84
College Attendance			
1970	39	51	53
1975	48		
1985	44	47	55
1986	57	45	
Degrees	**Associate**	**Bachelor's**	**Master's**
Hispanic	7.3	6.8	.1
Native American	9.3	10.8	.0
Asian	8.7	27.3	1.7
Black	5.3	10.0	.2
White	6.6	20.2	.9

Source: Center for Educational Statistics, 1987

Between 1976 and 1986, the number of minority students in graduate schools grew by 40 percent: the number of Hispanic and Native American students doubled; the number of Black students did not grow at all; White students had a 10 percent growth. During that same period, the numbers of minority students enrolled as professional students doubled for Hispanics and Asians and increased 25 percent for Blacks; however, the numbers of Black and Hispanic graduate students are still insufficient to achieve adequate representation in the professions and in faculty positions. In 1986, of the almost 24,000 doctorates earned, 904 went to Blacks, 709 to Hispanics, 115 to Native Americans, and 1,162 to Asian Americans (National Research Council, 1987).

Both faculty and administration should be motivated to provide strategies to eliminate the gap between access and completion rates of minorities in higher education. Although this effort is being made at the community college level, there are obvious implications beyond the two-year experience. Planning should be geared toward the acquisition of 2+2+2 programs aimed at both recruitment and retention; these programs are best complemented by admissions, academic support programs, and financial aid.

PLANNING

Colleges should work cooperatively with public schools to diagnose and correct conditions and current problems; sometimes this requires adaptation of junior high and high school curricula to accommodate college entry requirements. Local schools need information about college as early as junior high; some educators are talking about including this concept in elementary schools as well. At the Medical Center Campus of Miami-Dade Community College, weekend and summer programs for minority youth are being developed with a disciplinary focus on health professions; students are invited and oriented to college-level work while still in high school. Moreover, the guidance counseling function is critical; work with high school guidance counselors, college students, and business mentors can serve primary and secondary school students well.

Outreach programs should include parents of middle, junior high, and even grade school students and should orient them to opportunities for their children. Regular meetings between high school and college instructors within the same discipline can improve communication, knowledge of requirements, and expectations at the college level. Workshops for high school teachers and business leaders to share the latest research in teaching and business can become a cooperative effort.

The most important initiative that graduate and professional schools can take to increase minority enrollment is to cultivate and enlarge the pool of potential students; they can develop programs to recruit "at home" and "grow their own."

Such programs inform minority undergraduates of the rewards of graduate study and should be aimed at reaching minority students early in their undergraduate careers. In many instances, role models from minority racial and ethnic groups and from critical university faculty provide opportunities for minority undergraduates to pursue academic research and work with employers in industry, government, and the nonprofit sector to identify needs and interests in graduate study.

RECRUITING

It is important to give careful attention to local schools, four-year institutions, and community colleges working collaboratively; to recognize differences among and within minority groups; and to develop informational materials in languages other than English. Recruitment aimed at senior institutions is also critical. The graduate faculty network often excludes minority faculty members and faculty members at colleges with large numbers of minority students. These faculty are the most influential persons in students' decisions to attend graduate and professional schools. Institute student visitation programs (at university expense). Identify colleges at which recruitment of minorities would be most productive and efficient; encourage joint ventures with minority institutions. Develop effective recruitment materials aimed at minority undergraduates, and advertise graduate and professional programs in national publications that minority undergraduates read. Colleges can also provide summer school research activities or assistantships at the graduate school for the sophomore, junior, and senior year.

ADMISSIONS AND ACADEMIC SUPPORT PROGRAMS

In admissions, it is important to use qualifying examinations judiciously and use additional evaluative criteria such as interviews, professor's recommendations, autobiographical statements, and GPAs. Give undergraduate transcripts significant weight as admission criteria, and analyze students' strengths and weaknesses. Be aware of possible bias in evaluating credentials of minority students; consider using conditional admissions procedures or multiple criteria for admissions purposes. Assist minority applicants in admissions procedures.

It is essential to emphasize teaching and learning for all students. Support programs should be related to academic majors. Provide trained, experienced teachers for underprepared students, integrate academic support programs with student service counterparts, and provide peer counseling and an early warning system.

RETENTION

Create a hospitable environment for minority students and demonstrate the importance of support services for undergraduates. Graduate programs should support discipline-based minority student interest groups, such as "Blacks in psychology," or "Hispanics in engineering." There are many ways to create academic support mechanisms: help students by reducing course loads when they need time to catch up with peers; promote programs that recognize distinctive cultural heritages; and create a system of faculty mentors. Provide training to White faculty to help them become more understanding of minority student needs, and encourage faculty members to become aware of the new issues in their disciplines that focus specifically on minority issues and concerns. Help minority students understand how the graduate and professional school system works. It is also advisable to develop financial incentives for departments, such as increased minority fellowship funds or graduate assistantships, and annual affirmative action grants.

FINANCIAL AID

Inform the student as early as possible about financial awards—preferably at the time of admission. Provide more work-study programs and fewer loans to minority students, connect work-study programs to course and workload decisions, and provide budget counseling and emergency loan services. Graduate schools should provide minority students with financial support packages that are adequate and guaranteed through the students' graduate careers, provided students make satisfactory academic progress. Colleges should also award assistantships that complement studies; ensure that sufficient scholarships are available for qualified minority students; and ensure that minority teaching fellows and research assistants are in the mainstream of academic and social activities of the department, including sharing graduate offices, working on research projects, and attending informal socials. It is important to seek financial arrangements with external sources, to support students needing part-time work, and to assist minority students with loans when necessary.

Finally, exemplary faculty incorporate the strategem of "motivating toward independence;" they:

- Motivate the student toward greater involvement
- Consider the student to be an adult
- Capitalize on student experience
- Promote trust and respect
- Encourage independent thinking
- Encourage maturation as a goal of education
- Encourage risk taking

CURRICULUM

Without heating up the controversy over curriculum, one could safely say that there is consensus around the overall purposes of a liberal education. An appreciation of humanities, sciences, and the arts, an emphasis on ethical conduct, and an understanding of knowledge implementable in theory and practice are essential for the undergraduate curriculum. But the controversy does begin to heat up around the interpretation, implementation, and relative importance of curriculum.

Moreover, there is agreement that curriculum cannot be static; new knowledge, changing conditions, and requirements of society all affect curriculum at the college campus. Sometimes new information may render existing theories totally invalid or may point out the incompleteness of existing facts. In the last three decades, the college campus itself has drastically changed and has been dramatically challenged by the entrance of women, minority students, and older students. New areas of knowledge, new disciplines, and new educational issues have resulted. Not only did women's studies, African American studies, ethnic studies, and other area studies point out the omission from the curriculum of the experiences and contributions of large segments of society, but they also challenged incomplete and unidimensional thinking. These shifts in curricula are not without their detractors, but some educators suggest that ignoring the critical need for such curriculum in American higher education is "killing the spirit" of the learner (Smith, 1990).

The current debate over curriculum centers on the question of inclusion of culturally pluralistic and global resources; it aims to ensure that all students understand the richness of the history, art, and literature of women and racial-ethnic groups. This debate talks about "transformation" of the curriculum as it is now known. Value and philosophical differences electrify the controversy. These efforts decry the "add-on" theory in which brief mention is made of cultural, racial-ethnic, or gender-related issues or contributions. Rather, the advocates of inclusion of the works and perspectives of women and minorities seek to transform the curriculum and the entire teaching and learning process;

237

it is meant to be a long-term process. Schuster and Van Dyne (1984) suggest that the current curriculum does not expose the "invisible paradigms which are the internalized assumptions, the network of unspoken agreements, the implicit contracts, that all the participants in the process of higher education have agreed to, usually unconsciously, in order to bring about learning" (p. 417). Others would suggest that transforming the curriculum makes it too political (and less neutral); they claim that proponents of a transformed curriculum seek to distort it with politically motivated reform agendas. Gates responds that transforming the curriculum is:

> ...no more political than the process that designates the existing canon...that people can maintain a straight face while they protest the eruption of politics into something that has always been political from the very beginning says something about how remarkably successful official literary histories have been at disguising all linkages between the canon, the literary past we remember, and those interests that maintain it (as quoted in Green, 1989, p. 148).

The obvious framework for such curriculum is one of an inclusionary change process. This reframing de-emphasizes political debate and instead capitalizes on dialogue that incorporates new visions while protecting the existing curriculum. McIntosh in Pearson, Shavlik, and Touchton (1989), Green (1989), and Schuster and Van Dyne (1984) suggest directly confronting the exclusive curriculum through a series of phases that transform the curriculum, integrating multicultural values and contributions. Some practical suggestions move the notion of the "add-on phase" to a more inclusionary policy that incorporates the "specialized" course, such as ethnic studies or women's studies, of which Smith (1990) says:

> There are certainly positive aspects of "counter"-education run by women for women. There are strong moral imperatives... there is passionate conviction... that women teachers take a far more personal interest in their students (p. 289).
>
> They [women] are the last utopians; they have revived the

dream of a better, more humane society, not to be achieved
this time by science or reason or objectivity, but by the keener
sensibilities and nobler character of women (p. 292).

Eventually, the environment will produce a "breakthrough" as a
transformed curriculum that incorporates new knowledge, new scholarship, new methodologies, and new ways of teaching and learning, and
that encourages new ways of thinking, is put into place. Moving from
strategies that transform the curriculum to strategies that increase representation of faculty and administrators on community college campuses
seems to be a natural step.

A diverse faculty is essential to a pluralistic campus. Faculty create
the curriculum and determine the quality of the experience in every
classroom. Currently, between 10 and 12 percent of faculty at community colleges across the nation are members of racial-ethnic minority
groups. Between 1977 and 1985, Black faculty on college campuses
declined from 4.4 to 4.2 percent of the total faculty. This figure includes
Blacks who are at historically Black colleges and universities—in
predominantly White institutions, this figure is 1.8 percent. Hispanic and
Native American faculty rose from 1.5 to 1.7 percent (1,000 more); and
Asian faculty rose from 2.7 to 4.1 percent (7,000 more). Between 1981 and
1987, the number of doctorates awarded to minorities rose from 2,728 to
2,890, and high concentrations of these degrees were in education.
Minority faculty are less likely to hold tenure: 71 percent of Whites hold
tenure; 62 percent of Blacks; 66 percent of Hispanics; and 65 percent of
Asians. Women are also less likely than men to hold tenure, and for both
racial-ethnic minorities and women, there are substantial differences in
salaries. The numbers of minorities choosing academic careers declined
from 1975 to 1985. In 1985 only about 12 percent of all administrators were
members of racial-ethnic minorities, and this figure includes all individuals who administer special minority programs in predominantly
White institutions. Data demonstrate that these numbers are relatively
stable over the last 10 years. Moreover, few of this small percentage of
minorities are presidents, vice presidents, or deans; rather they are "assistants to" or are connected to minority or affirmative action positions,

opportunity programs, bilingual education, and student services. Often, the special minority programs are funded with temporary grants and short-term funding. (These data were compiled from Mingle, 1987; Carter and Wilson, 1989; Linthicum, 1989; and Green, 1989.)

The strategies to recruit and retain racial-ethnic minority and women faculty must be tied to strategies to recruit and retain students, but increasing the number of women and minorities in the pipeline is a long-term effort. Approaches that look outside the traditional ranks to business, industry, and government, and explore innovative approaches—such as faculty exchanges with historically Black universities and colleges—demand that colleges understand, as does Greenville Technical College, that more money is needed to compete with industry and business. Approaches that tie the search process to standards and insist on results and accountability, such as those at the Foothill-DeAnza Community College District and Miami-Dade Community College, suggest that planning is a critical factor for recruitment and retention. Programs that seek out minority faculty from graduate schools, from historically Black or Hispanic colleges, and that mentor faculty, such as those at Sante Fe Community College or the Los Rios Community College District, are positive examples of what can be done to encourage diversity. What remains for the long term is that it must be the vision of our nation's community college leaders that guides us all to a college culture that values diversity.

CONCLUSION

Manuel Justiz, dean of the College of Education of The University of Texas at Austin, is an aggressive campaigner for diversity. He believes in an active search process: using personal and professional networks to identify potential candidates; telephoning potential minority candidates to invite them to apply for positions; and reaching out to the community for ideas and suggestions. In all this, he is committed to quality and to finding the best candidate for the job.

It is this conviction and this desire to do better that will strengthen and embed new cultural norms for institutions and that will establish new heroes and new artifacts that honor the contributions and talents of a broader, more comprehensive representation of our heterogeneous society in the community college.

If community colleges are to lead the way, to imagine a better world, to illuminate the darkness, to find the courage to be an egalitarian educational institution, and to demonstrate a passion for justice, then they are in the right place to:

- Begin now and where they are
- Define and understand campus culture
- Value pluralism and diversity
- Challenge beliefs and motives
- Confront issues: thinking and rethinking
- Question losses and gains
- Seek cooperation and like-mindedness
- Employ catalysts in people and information
- Accept that nonperfection of strategies and ideas is still okay
- Seek successes: large or small, immediate and visible
- Value diversity and individual differences and be receptive to change
- Recognize contributions
- Develop long-term commitment to change

Fools act on imagination without knowledge; pedants act on knowledge without imagination. The task of education is to weld together imagination and experience. (Alfred North Whitehead)

Nothing good is done without passion, nothing great with passion alone. (Paul Valery)

The pursuit of truth and beauty is a sphere of activity in which we are permitted to remain children all of our lives. (Albert Einstein)

APPENDIX

Contributors

Name	Title	College	State
Sandy Acebo	Vice President	DeAnza College	California
Baltazar Acevedo	Director	Dallas County CC District	Texas
Adrianna Barrera	Asst. to President	Austin CC	Texas
Tom Barton	President	Greenville Technical College	South Carolina
Jacquelyn Belcher	President	Minneapolis CC	Minnesota
Charlotte Biggerstaff	Director	Northeast Texas CC	Texas
Marjorie Blaha	Chancellor	Los Rios CC District	California
George Boggs	Superintendent/ President	Palomar College	California
Nelvia Brady	Chancellor	City Colleges of Chicago	Illinois
Jerry Briggs	Director	Fond du Lac College	Minnesota
Mildred Bulpitt	Director	Rio Salado College	Arizona
Ruth Burgos-Sasscer	Vice President	Harry S Truman College	Illinois
Raul Cardenas	President	South Mountain Community College	Arizona
Max Castillo	President	San Antonio College	Texas

Name	Title	College	State
Carcy Chan	Program Director	East Los Angeles College	California
Alfredo de los Santos	Vice Chancellor	Maricopa County CC District	Arizona
Wilhelmina Delco	State Legislator		Texas
Carolyn Desjardins	Director	Rio Salado College	Arizona
Ramon Dovalina	Vice President	Austin CC	Texas
Flora M. Edwards	President	Middlesex County College	New Jersey
Nolen Ellison	President	Cuyahoga CC	Ohio
Al Fernandez	Chancellor	Coast CC District	California
Pam Fisher	Vice Chancellor	Yosemite CC District	California
Carolyn Fountenberry	Affirmative Action Chair	DeAnza College	California
Tom Fryer	Chancellor	Foothill-DeAnza CC District	California
Patsy Fulton	President	Brookhaven College	Texas
Juliet Garcia	President	Texas Southmost College	Texas
Tom Gonzales	Chancellor	Seattle Community Colleges	Washington
Charles Green	Chancellor	Houston CC System	Texas
Jay Gurley	Provost	Eastern NM University-Clovis	New Mexico
Jim Hudgins	President	Midlands Technical College	South Carolina
Betty Inclan	Project Director	Miami-Dade CC	Florida
Manuel Justiz	Dean	The University of Texas	Texas
Augusta Kappner	President	Borough of Manhattan CC	New York

Name	Title	College	State
Geraldine Kaspar	Director	Foothill-DeAnza CC District	California
Yvonne Kennedy	President	S. D. Bishop State CC	Alabama
Ann Lopez	Coordinator	Texas Higher Ed. Coordinating Board	Texas
Hal McAninch	President	College of DuPage	Illinois
Robert McCabe	President	Miami-Dade CC	Florida
David Mertes	Chancellor	California CC System	California
Jerry Sue Owens	President	Lakewood CC	Minnesota
Eduardo Padron	Vice President	Miami-Dade CC	Florida
Dale Parnell	President	AACJC	Washington, DC
Donald Phelps	Chancellor	Los Angeles CC District	California
Blandina Ramirez	Director	ACE Office of Minorities in Higher Education	Washington, DC
Michael Saenz	President	Tarrant County JC-Northwest	Texas
Ruth Shaw	President	Central Piedmont CC	North Carolina
Leila Gonzales Sullivan	President	Middlesex CC	Connecticut
Tessa Tagle	Vice President	Miami-Dade CC	Florida
Judith Valles	President	Golden West College	California
Leonard Valverde	Vice President	University of Texas–San Antonio	Texas
Sharon Yaap	Dean	Grossmont College	California

BIBLIOGRAPHY

Abraham, H.J. *Freedom and the Court: Civil Rights and Liberties in the United States.* New York: Oxford University Press, 1988.

Acuna, R. *Occupied America.* San Francisco: Canfield Press, 1972.

Albrecht, K. *The Creative Corporation.* Homewood, Ill.: Dow Jones-Irwin, 1987.

Allport, G. *The Nature of Prejudice.* New York: Doubleday, 1958.

American Council on Education. *Campus Trends.* Washington, D.C.: American Council on Education, 1989.

Andersen, C. et al. *1989-1990 Fact Book on Higher Education.* New York: American Council on Education/Macmillan, 1989.

Anderson, J.A. "Cognitive Styles and Multicultural Populations." *Journal of Teacher Education,* January/February 1988, pp. 2-9.

Argyris, C. and Schon, D.A. *Theory in Practice: Increasing Professional Effectiveness.* San Francisco: Jossey-Bass, 1974.

Baier, A. "Hume, the Women's Moral Theorist?" In E. Kittay and D. Meyers (Eds.), *Women and Moral Theory.* Totowa, N.J.: Rowman and Littlefield, 1987.

Baker, G.A., Roueche, J.E., and Gillett-Karam, R. *Teaching as Leading: Profiles of Excellence in the Open-Door College.* Washington, D.C.: Community College Press, 1990.

Balandier, G. "The Colonial Situation: A Theoretical Approach." In I. Wallerstein (Ed.), *Social Change.* New York: John Wiley, 1966.

Barrera, M. *Race and Class in the Southwest.* Notre Dame, Ind.: University of Notre Dame Press, 1979.

Bass, B.M. "Some Observations About a General Theory of Leadership and Interpersonal Behavior." In W.R. Lassey and M. Sashkin (Eds.), *Leadership and Social Change.* (3rd ed.) San Diego: University Associates, 1983.

Bass, B.M. *Leadership and Performance Beyond Expectations.* New York: Free Press, 1985.

Baum, L. "The Court and Civil Liberties." In A. Cigler and B. Loomis (Eds.), *American Politics: Classic and Contemporary Readings.* Boston: Houghton Mifflin, 1989.

Belenky, M. et al. *Women's Ways of Knowing: The Development of Self, Voice, and Mind.* New York: Basic Books, 1986.

Bell, D. *The Cultural Contradictions of Capitalism.* New York: Basic Books, 1976.

Bennis, W. *On Becoming a Leader.* New York: Addison-Wesley, 1989.

Berry, M. *Women in Higher Education Administration: A Book of Readings.* Washington, D.C.: National Association for Women Deans, Administrators, and Counselors, 1979.

Biggerstaff, C. "Creating, Managing, and Transforming Organizational Culture in the Community College: Perspectives of Reputationally Effective Leaders." Unpublished dissertation, Community College Leadership Program/Educational Administration, The University of Texas at Austin, 1990.

"Black and White in America." *Newsweek,* March 7, 1988. pp. 18-24.

Blauner, R. *Racial Oppression in America.* New York: Harper and Row, 1972.

Bluestone, N. *Women and the Ideal Society: Plato's Republic and the Modern Myths of Gender.* Amherst: University of Massachusetts Press, 1987.

Bonacich, E. "Class Approaches to Ethnicity and Race." *Insurgent Sociologist,* 1980, *10,* 11-14.

Brey, R. and Gillett-Karam, R. *Understanding and Participating in Texas Government: A Citizen's Guide.* Austin, Texas: R and R, 1988.

Brint, S. and Karabel, J. *The Diverted Dream: Community Colleges and the Promise of Educational Opportunity in America, 1900-1985.* New York: Oxford University Press, 1989.

Brophy, J.E. and Good, T.L. *Teacher Behavior and Student Achievement.* Occasional Paper 73. (ED 251 422).

Brown, M. "Career Plans of College Women: Patterns and Influences." In P. Perun (Ed.), *The Undergraduate Woman.* Lexington, Mass.: Lexington Books, 1982.

Buchanan, A. "Justice: A Philosophical Review." In E. Shelp (Ed.), *Justice and Health Care*. Boston: D. Reidel Publishing Co., 1981.

Bullock, H.A. *A History of Negro Education in the South*. New York: Praeger, 1967.

Burns, J.M. *Leadership*. New York: Harper and Row, 1978.

Byers, P. and Byers, H. "Nonverbal Communication and the Education of Children." In C.B. Cazden, V.P. John, and D. Hynes (Eds.), *Functions of Language in the Classroom*. New York: Academic Press, 1972.

Cahn, E.S. *Our Brother's Keeper*. New York: World Publishing, 1969.

Cardenas, G. "United States Immigration Policy Toward Mexico: An Historical Perspective." *Chicano Law Review*, 1975, *3*, pp. 69-71.

Carmichael, S. and Hamilton, C. *Black Power*. New York: Random House, 1967.

Carter, T.P. *Mexican Americans in School*. New York: College Entrance Examination Board, 1970.

Carter, D.J. and Wilson, R. *Minorities in Higher Education*. Washington, D.C.: American Council on Education, 1989.

Center for Educational Statistics. *Highest Degree Attained by 1980 High School Seniors by Sex, Race, Type of Community, and Type of High School*. Washington, D.C.: U.S. Department of Education, September 1987.

Chickering, A.W. and Gamson, Z.F. "Seven Principles for Good Practice in Undergraduate Education." *Wingspread Journal*, 1981, 9 (2).

Chodorow, N. *The Reproduction of Mothering*. Berkeley: The University of California Press, 1978.

Clark, B. *The Open Door College: A Case Study*. New York: McGraw-Hill, 1960.

Clark, B.R. "The Organizational Saga in Higher Education." *Administrative Science Quarterly*, 1972, *17*, 178-184.

Clark, B.R. *The Higher Education System: Academic Organization in Cross-National Perspective*. Berkeley: University of California Press, 1983.

Claxton, C.S. and Murrell, P.H. (Eds.) *Learning Styles: Implications for Improving Educational Practices*. ASHE-ERIC Higher Education

Report No. 4. Washington, D.C.: Association for the Study of Higher Education, 1987.

Cohen, A. and Brawer, F. *The American Community College.* San Francisco: Jossey-Bass, 1982.

Coleman, J.S. *Equality of Educational Opportunity.* Washington, D.C.: U.S. Government Printing Office, 1966.

Commission on the Future of Community Colleges. *Building Communities: A Vision for a New Century.* Washington, D.C.: American Association of Community and Junior Colleges, 1988.

Corcoran, T. "The Coming Slums of Higher Education." *Change,* 1972, 4 (7), 30-35.

Cox, O.C. *Caste, Class, and Race.* Garden City, N.Y.: Doubleday, 1948.

Cronin, T.E. "Thinking and Learning About Leadership." *Presidential Studies Quarterly,* 1984, 14, 1.

Cross, K.P. *Accent on Learning.* San Francisco: Jossey-Bass, 1976.

Dahl, R.A. *Democracy and Its Critics.* New Haven, Conn.: Yale University Press, 1989.

Dahl, R.A. *Political Oppositions in Western Democracies.* New Haven, Conn.: Yale University Press, 1966.

Daly, M. *Beyond God the Father: Toward a Philosophy of Women's Liberation.* Boston: Beacon Press, 1973.

Deal, T.E. and Kennedy, A.A. "Culture: A New Look Through Old Lenses." *Journal of Applied Behavioral Science,* 1983, 19, 497-505.

Deglar, C. "What the Women's Movement Has Done to American History." In E. Langland and W. Grove (Eds.), *A Feminist Perspective in the Academy: The Difference It Makes.* Chicago: University of Chicago Press, 1982.

Desjardins, C. "The Meaning of Gilligan's Concept of 'Different Voice' for the Learning Environment." In C.S. Pearson, D.L. Shavlik, and J.G. Touchton (Eds.), *Educating the Majority: Women Challenge Tradition in Higher Education.* New York: American Council on Education/Macmillan, 1989a.

Desjardins, C. "Gender Issues and Community College Leadership." In *Leadership at All Levels.* Maplewood, N.J.: American Association of Women in Community and Junior Colleges, 15th Anniversary Issue, 1989b.

Dinnerstein, D. *The Mermaid and the Minotaur: Sexual Arrangements and the Human Malaise.* New York: Harper and Row, 1976.

Dugger, R. "The Community College Comes of Age." *Change,* 1976, *8* (1), 32-37.

Dworkin, R. *Taking Rights Seriously.* Cambridge, Mass.: Harvard University Press, 1977.

Dye, T.R. and Ziegler, H. *American Politics in the Media Age.* Pacific Grove, Calif.: Brooks Cole, 1989.

Eaton, J. *Women in Community Colleges.* San Francisco: Jossey-Bass, 1981.

Education Commission of the States. *Focus on Minorities: Synopsis of State Higher Education Initiatives.* Denver: Education Commission of the States, 1987.

Eisler, R. *The Chalice and the Blade: Our History, Our Future.* San Francisco: Harper and Row, 1988.

El-Khawas, E., Carter, D., and Ottinger, C. *Community College Fact Book.* New York: American Association of Community and Junior Colleges, American Council on Education, and Macmillan, 1988.

Erikson, Erik. *Childhood and Society.* New York: Morton, 1950.

Evans, N. *Facilitating the Development of Women.* San Francisco: Jossey-Bass, 1985.

Farnham, C. *The Impact of Feminist Research in the Academy.* Bloomington: Indiana University Press, 1987.

Feagin, J.R. *Racial and Ethnic Relations.* Englewood Cliffs, N.J.: Prentice-Hall, 1989.

Feagin, J.R. and Feagin, C.B. *Discrimination American Style: Institutional Racism and Sexism.* Englewood Cliffs, N.J.: Prentice-Hall, 1978.

Flanagan, J.C. "The Critical Incident Technique." *Psychological Bulletin,* 1954, *51* (4), 327-358.

Franklin, J.H. *From Slavery to Freedom.* (4th ed.) New York: Knopf, 1974.

French, M. *Beyond Power: On Women, Men, and Morals.* New York: Ballantine Books, 1985.

Freire, P. *The Pedagogy of the Oppressed.* New York: Herder and Herder, 1972.

Fryer, T. "Servants of the Dream." Speech reprinted in *Connections,* September 30, 1988, 8, 1-7.

Garcia, C.F. *La Causa Politica.* South Bend, Ind.: University of Notre Dame Press, 1974.

Geshwender, J. *Racial Stratification in America.* Dubuque, Iowa: Brown, 1978.

Gillett-Karam, R. *Transformational Leadership and the Community College President: Are There Gender Differences?* Unpublished dissertation: The University of Texas at Austin, 1988.

Gillett-Karam, R. "Women in Leadership Roles," and "Leadership Concerns: Minorities and Women." In G. Baker, J. Roueche, and R. Rose, *Shared Vision: Transformational Leadership in American Community Colleges.* Washington, D.C.: Community College Press, 1989.

Gilligan, C. *In a Different Voice: Psychological Theory and Women's Development.* Cambridge, Mass.: Harvard University Press, 1982.

Gilligan, C. "Moral Orientation and Moral Development." In E. Kittay and D. Meyers (Eds.), *Women and Moral Theory.* Totowa, N.J.: Rowman and Littlefield, 1987.

Glazer, N. *Affirmative Discrimination.* New York: Basic Books, 1975.

Glazer, N. *Affirmative Discrimination: Ethnic Inequality and Public Policy.* Cambridge, Mass.: Harvard University Press, 1987.

Glazer, N. and Moynihan, D.P. *Beyond the Melting Pot.* Cambridge, Mass.: Harvard University Press and MIT Press, 1963.

Gleazer, E.J. *The Community College: Values, Vision, and Vitality.* Washington, D.C.: Community College Press, 1980.

Good, T.L. "Teacher Expectations and Student Perceptions: A Decade of Research." *Educational Leadership,* February 1981, pp. 417-422.

Goodstein, L.D. "Managers, Values, and Organizational Development." *Group and Organizational Studies,* 1983, 8, 203-220.

Gordon, M.M. *Assimilation in American Life: The Role of Race, Religion, and National Origins.* New York: Oxford University Press, 1964.

Gordon, M.M. *Human Nature, Class, and Ethnicity.* New York: Oxford University Press, 1978.

Gordon, M.M. "Models of Pluralism: The New American Dilemma." In R.D. Lambert (Ed.), *Annals of the American Academy of Political and Social Science*, 1981, p. 454.

Grebler, L., Moore, J.W., and Guzman, R. *The Mexican American People.* New York: Free Press, 1970.

Greeley, A. *Ethnicity in the United States.* New York: John Wiley, 1974.

Green, M.F. *Leaders for a New Era: Strategies for Higher Education.* New York: Macmillan, 1988.

Green, M.F. *Minorities on Campus: A Handbook for Enhancing Diversity.* Washington, D.C.: American Council on Education, 1989.

Greenberg, S.B. *Race and State in Capitalist Development.* New Haven, Conn.: Yale University Press, 1980.

Gregory, K. "Native-View Paradigms: Multiple Cultures and Culture Conflicts in Organizations." *Administrative Science Quarterly,* 1983, *28,* 359-376.

Gutierrez, J.A. "La Raza and Revolution." In M.S. Meier and F. Rivera (Eds.), *La Raza.* New York: Hill and Wang, 1974.

Hale-Benson, J.E. *Black Children: Their Roots, Culture, and Learning Styles.* Baltimore: Johns Hopkins University Press, 1982.

Harding, S. "The Curious Coincidence of Feminine and African Moralities: Challenges for Feminist Theory." In E. Kittay and D. Meyers (Eds.) *Women and Moral Theory.* Totowa, N.J.: Rowman and Littlefield, 1987.

Harding, S. and Hintikka, M. *Discovering Reality: Feminist Perspectives on Epistemology, Metaphysics, Methodology, and Philosophy of Science.* Dordrecht, Holland: Reidel Publishers, 1983.

Helgesen, S. *The Female Advantage: Women's Ways of Leadership.* New York: Doubleday Currency, 1990.

Heller, T. *Women and Men as Leaders: In Business, Educational, and Social Service Organizations.* New York: Praeger, 1982.

Hennig, M. and Jardim, A. *The Managerial Woman.* New York: Pocket Books, 1977.

Hersey, P. and Blanchard, K.H. *Management of Organizational Behavior.* (3rd ed.) Englewood Cliffs, N.J.: Prentice-Hall, 1972.

Hispanic Policy Development Project. "U.S. Hispanics: Who They Are, Whence They Came, and Why?" In *The Hispanic Almanac.* Washington, D.C.: Hispanic Policy Development Project, 1984.

Hodgkinson, H.L. *All One System: Demographics of Education, Kindergarten Through Graduate School.* Washington, D.C.: Institute for Educational Leadership, 1985.

Holmstrom, N. "Do Women Have a Distinct Nature?" In M. Pearsall (Ed.) *Women and Values: Readings in Recent Feminist Psychology.* Belmont, Calif.: Wadsworth Publishing Co., 1986.

Horner, M. "Toward an Understanding of Achievement-Related Conflicts in Women." *Journal of Social Issues,* 1971, *28,* 157-176.

House, R.J. and Mitchell, T.R. "The Path-Goal Theory of Leadership." In P. Hersey and J. Stinson (Eds.) *Perspectives in Leadership Effectiveness.* Columbus, Ohio: Ohio University Center for Leadership Studies, 1971.

Hunter College Women's Studies Collective. *Women's Realities, Women's Choices: An Introduction to Women's Studies.* New York: Oxford University Press, 1983.

Jacobson, A. *Women in Charge: Dilemmas of Women in Authority.* New York: Van Nostrand Reinhold, 1895.

Janeway, E. "Women and the Uses of Power." In H. Eisenstein and A. Jardine (Eds.), *The Future of Difference.* New Brunswick, N.J.: Rutgers University Press, 1980.

Jelinek, M., Smircich, L., and Hirsch, P. "Introduction: A Code of Many Colors." *Administrative Science Quarterly,* 1983, *28,* 331-338.

Jencks, C. et al. *Inequality.* New York: Basic Books, 1972.

Josefowitz, N. *Paths to Power.* Reading, Mass.: Addison-Wesley, 1980.

Josefowitz, N. *You're the Boss.* New York: Warner, 1985.

Kanter, R.M. *Men and Women of the Corporation.* New York: Basic Books, 1977.

Karabel, J. "Community Colleges and Social Stratification." *Harvard Educational Review,* 1972, *42* (4), 521-562.

Keeley, C.B. "Population and Immigration Policy: State and Federal Roles." In F. Bean, J. Schmandt, and S. Weintraub (Eds.), *Mexican American and Central American Population Issues and U.S. Policy.* Austin, Texas: Center for Mexican American Studies, 1988.

Keller, E. *Reflections on Gender and Science.* New Haven, Conn.: Yale University Press, 1985.

Keller, G. "Review Essay: Black Students in Higher Education: Why So Few?" *Planning for Higher Education,* 1988-89, *17* (3), 43-56.

Kitano, H.H. *Japanese Americans: The Evolution of a Subculture.* (2nd ed.) Englewood Cliffs, N.J.: Prentice-Hall, 1976.

Kittay, E. and Meyers, D. *Women and Moral Theory.* Totowa, N.J.: Rowman and Littlefield, 1987.

Kluegel, J.R. and Smith, E.R. *Beliefs About Inequality: Americans' View of What Is and What Ought to Be.* New York: Aldine de Gruyter Press, 1986.

Kluger, R. *Simple Justice: The History of Brown v. Board of Education and Black America's Struggle for Equality.* New York: Knopf, 1976.

Kohlberg, L. *Collected Papers on Moral Development and Moral Education.* Cambridge, Mass.: Harvard University, Moral Education Research Foundation, 1971.

Kohlberg, L. *The Philosophy of Moral Development: Moral Stages and the Idea of Justice.* San Francisco: Harper and Row, 1981.

Kolb, D.A. *Learning Style Inventory.* Boston: McBer, 1976.

Komarovsky, M. *Women in College: Shaping New Feminine Identities.* New York: Basic Books, 1985.

Kuh, G.D. and Whitt, E.J. *The Invisible Tapestry: Culture in American Colleges and Universities.* AAHE-ERIC Higher Education Report No. 1. Washington, D.C.: Association for the Study of Higher Education, 1988.

Leahy, R.L. (Ed.) *The Child's Construction of Social Inequality.* New York: Academic Press, 1983.

Lewin, K. *Field Theory in Social Science.* New York: Harper, 1951.

Lieberson, S. "A Societal Theory of Racial and Ethnic Relations." *American Sociological Review,* 1961, *29,* 902-910.

Linthicum, D.S. *The Dry Pipeline: Increasing the Flow of Minority Faculty.* Washington, D.C.: National Council of State Directors of Community and Junior Colleges, 1989.

Loden, M. *Female Leadership: How to Succeed in Business Without Being One of the Boys.* New York: Cornell University Press, 1985.

Maccoby, M. *The Leader.* New York: Simon and Schuster, 1980.

Maguire, D.C. "Quotas: Unequal but Fair." *Commonweal,* October 1977, p. 648.

Maldonado-Denis, M. *Puerto Rico, A Socio-Historic Interpretation.* New York: Random House, 1972.

Manchester-Boddy, E. *Japanese in America.* San Francisco: R and E Research Associates, 1970.

Martin, J. "Excluding Women from the Educational Realm." *Harvard Educational Review,* May 1982, 52 (2), 133-147.

Masland, A.T. "Organizational Culture in the Study of Higher Education." *The Review of Higher Education,* 1985, 8, 157-168.

McClelland, D. *Guide to Behavioral Event Interviewing.* Boston: McBer, 1978.

McIntosh, P. "Curricular Re-Vision: The New Knowledge for a New Age." In C. Pearson, J. Touchton, and D. Shavlik (Eds.), *Educating the Majority: Women Challenge Tradition in Higher Education.* New York: American Council on Education/Macmillan, 1989.

McWilliams, C. *North from Mexico.* New York: Greenwood Press, 1968.

Meier, M.S. and Rivera, F. *The Chicanos: A History of Mexican Americans.* New York: Hill and Wang, 1972.

Mercer, J. *Labelling the Mentally Retarded.* Berkeley: University of California Press, 1973.

Messinger, R. "Women in Power and Politics." In H. Eisenstein and A. Jardine (Eds.), *The Future of Difference.* New Brunswick, N.J.: Rutgers University Press, 1980.

Millar, E. *Hume: Essays Moral, Political and Literary.* Indianapolis: Liberty Classics, 1985.

Miller, J. *Toward a New Psychology of Women.* Boston: Beacon Press, 1976.

Miller, J. *Women and Power.* Wellesley, Mass.: Stone Center for Development Services and Studies, 1982.

Miller, J.G. "An Examination of Women College Presidents: Career Paths, Professional Preparation, and Leadership Style." Unpublished dissertation, George Peabody College for Teachers, Vanderbilt University, 1987.

Miller, W.E., Miller, A.H., and Schneider, E.J. *American National Election Study Data Sourcebook, 1952-1978.* Cambridge, Mass.: Harvard University Press, 1980.

Mingle, J.R. *Focus on Minorities: Trends in Higher Education Participation and Success.* Denver: Education Commission of the States and the State Higher Education Executive Officers, 1987.

"Minorities in the Education Pipeline." *Educational Record,* Fall 1987-Winter 1988, p. 68.

Mintzberg, H. *The Return of Managerial Work.* New York: Harper and Row, 1973.

Mitroff, I. and Kilmann, R. *Corporate Tragedies.* New York: Praeger, 1984.

Moore, J.W. "American Minorities and 'New Nation' Perspective." *Pacific Sociological Review,* 1976, *19,* pp. 468-469.

Mulder, A. *Women in Educational Administraton: Paths and Profiles.* Unpublished dissertation, Educational Administration, University of Michigan, 1983.

Myrdal, G. *An American Dilemma.* New York: McGraw-Hill, 1944.

Nadler, D. and Tushman, M. *Strategic Organization Design: Concepts, Tools, and Processes.* Glenview, Ill.: Scott Foresman, 1988.

National Center for Educational Statistics. *Trends in Racial/Ethnic Enrollment in Higher Education: Fall 1978 Through Fall 1988.* Washington, D.C.: Office of Educational Research and Improvement, U.S. Department of Education, 1990.

National Urban League. *Initial Black Pulse Findings.* Bulletin No. 1. New York: National Urban League, 1980.

Nettles, M.T. (Ed.) *Toward Black Undergraduate Student Equality in American Higher Education.* New York: Greenwood Press, 1988.

Nicholson, L.J. *Feminism/Postmodernism.* New York: Routledge, Chapman and Hall, 1990.

Nisbet, R. "Where Do We Go From Here?" In C.D. Campbell (Ed.), *Income Redistribution.* Washington, D.C.: American Enterprise Institute, 1977.

Nisbett, R.E. and Ross, L. *Human Inference: Strategies and Shortcomings of Social Judgment.* Englewood Cliffs, N.J.: Prentice-Hall, 1980.

Noddings, N. *Caring: A Feminine Approach to Ethics and Moral Education.* Berkeley: University of California Press, 1984.

Novak, M. *The Rise of the Unmeltable Ethnics: Politics and Culture in the Seventies.* New York: Macmillan, 1973.

Oates, M. and Williamson, S. "Women's Colleges and Women Achievers." *Signs,* 1978, *3,* 795-806.

Okin, S. *Women in Western Political Thought.* Princeton, N.J.: Princeton University Press, 1979.

Olson, J.S. and Wilson, R. *Native Americans in the Twentieth Century.* Provo, Utah: Brigham Young University Press, 1984.

Omi, M. and Winant, H. *Racial Formation in the United States: From the 1960s to the 1980s.* New York: Routledge and Kegan Paul, 1986.

Orfield, G. et al. *The Chicago Study of Access and Choice in Higher Education.* Chicago: University of Chicago Press, 1984.

Ouchi, W.G. *Theory Z: How American Business Can Meet the Japanese Challenge.* Reading, Mass.: Addison-Wesley, 1981.

Paredes, A. *With His Pistol in His Hand.* Austin: The University of Texas Press, 1958.

Parenti, M. *Democracy for the Few.* New York: St. Martin's Press, 1980.

Park, R.E. and Burgess, E.W. *Introduction to the Science of Society.* Chicago: University of Chicago Press, 1924.

Park, R.E. *Race and Culture.* Glencoe, Ill.: Free Press, 1950.

Parsons, T. "Full Citizenship for the Negro American: A Sociological Problem." In T. Parsons and K. Clark (Eds.), *The Negro American.* Boston: Houghton Mifflin, 1966, p. 740.

Pascale, R. "The Paradox of 'Corporate Culture': Reconciling Ourselves to Socialization." *California Management Review,* 1985, *27* (2), 26-41.

Pearson, C.S., Shavlik, D.L., and Touchton, J.G. *Educating the Majority: Women Challenge Tradition in Higher Education.* New York: American Council on Education/Macmillan Publishing, 1989.

Peck, A.L. *The Generation of Animals.* Cambridge, Mass.: Harvard University Press, 1953.

Pemberton, G. *On Teaching the Minority Students: Problems and Strategies.* Brunswick, Maine: Bowdoin College, 1988.

Perry, W. *Forms of Intellectual and Ethical Development in the College Years.* New York: Holt, Rinehart and Winston, 1970.

Pestalozzi, J.H. *Leonard and Gertrude.* Boston: D.C. Heath and Co., 1903.

Peters, T.J. and Waterman, R.H., Jr. *In Search of Excellence: Lessons from America's Best-Run Companies.* New York: Harper and Row, 1982.

Pettigrew, T.F. *Racially Separate or Together?* New York: McGraw-Hill, 1979.

Pfeffer, J. "Management as Symbolic Action: The Creation and Maintenance of Organizational Paradigms." In L.L. Cummings and B.M. Staw (Eds.), *Research in Organizational Behavior 3.* Greenwich, Conn.: JAI Press, 1981.

Piaget, J. *The Moral Judgment of the Child.* New York: Free Press, 1965.

Portes, A. and Bach, R.L. *Latin American Journey.* Berkeley: University of California Press, 1985.

Portes, A. and Manning, R.D. "The Immigrant Enclave: Theory and Empirical Examples." In S. Olzak and J. Nagel (Eds.), *Competitive Ethnic Relations.* Orlando, Fla.: Academic Press, 1986.

Rainwater, L. and Yancey, W. *The Moynihan Report and the Politics of Controversy.* Cambridge, Mass.: MIT Press, 1967.

Ravitch, D. "Multiculturalism, Yes; Particularism, No." *Chronicle of Higher Education,* October 24, 1990, A-52.

Rawls, J. *A Theory of Justice.* Cambridge, Mass.: Harvard University Press, 1971.

Rich, A. *On Lies, Secrets, and Silence: Selected Prose—1966-78.* New York: Norton, 1979.

Richardson, R.C. and Bender, L.W. *Fostering Minority Access and Achievement in Higher Education: The Role of Urban Community Colleges and Universities.* San Francisco: Jossey-Bass, 1987.

Rokeach, M. *Beliefs, Attitudes, and Values: A Theory of Organization and Change.* San Francisco: Jossey-Bass, 1968.

Rosenberg, R. *Beyond Separate Spheres: Intellectual Roots of Modern Feminism.* New Haven, Conn.: Yale University Press, 1982.

Rosener, L. and Schwartz, P. "Women, Leadership and the '80s: What Kind of Leadership Do We Need?" In *The Report: Roundtable on New Leadership in the Public Interest.* New York: NOW Legal Defense and Education Fund, 1980.

Roueche, J. *Salvage, Redirection, or Custody? Remedial Education in the Community Junior College.* Washington, D.C.: American Association of Community and Junior Colleges, 1968.

Roueche, J. "Don't Close the Door." *Community, Technical, and Junior College Journal*, December/January 1981-82, *52* (4), 17, 21-23.

Roueche, J. and Baker, G. *Access and Excellence*. Washington, D.C.: Community College Press, 1987.

Roueche, J.E., Baker, G.A., and Rose, R.R. *Shared Vision: Transformational Leaders in American Community Colleges*. Washington, D.C.: Community College Press, 1989.

Rubio, A.G. *Stolen Heritage*. Austin, Texas: Eakin Press, 1986.

Ruddick, S. *Maternal Thinking: Toward a Politics of Peace*. New York: Ballantine Books, 1989.

Ruddick, S. "Remarks on the Sexual Politics of Reason." In E. Kittay and D. Meyers (Eds.), *Women and Moral Theory*. Totowa, N.J.: Rowman and Littlefield, 1987.

Samora, J. *Los Mojados: The Wetback Story*. South Bend, Ind.: University of Notre Dame Press, 1971.

Sanchez, G.I. "History, Culture, and Education." In J. Samora (Ed.), *La Raza*. South Bend, Ind.: University of Notre Dame Press, 1966.

Sandel, M.J. *Liberalism and the Limits of Justice*. New York: Cambridge University Press, 1982.

Sathe, V. "Implications of Corporate Culture: A Manager's Guide to Action." *Organizational Dynamics*, 1983, *12* (2), 5-23.

Schein, E.H. "The Role of the Founder in Creating Organizational Culture." *Organizational Dynamics*, 1983, *12* (1), 13-28.

Schein, E.H. "How Culture Forms, Develops, and Changes." In R.H. Kilmann, M.J. Saxton, R. Serpa, and Associates (Eds.), *Gaining Control of the Corporate Culture*. San Francisco: Jossey-Bass, 1985a.

Schein, E.H. *Organizational Culture and Leadership*. San Francisco: Jossey-Bass, 1985b.

Schermerhorn, R.A. *Comparative Ethnic Relations*. New York: Random House, 1970.

Schuster, M. and Van Dyne, S. "Placing Women in the Liberal Arts: Stages of Curriculum Transformation." *Harvard Educational Review*, 1984, *54* (4), 413-428.

Selby-Bigge, L. and Nidditch, P. *David Hume: Enquiries*. Oxford, England: Clarendon Press, 1978.

Shakeshaft, C. *Women in Educational Administration*. Newbury Park, Calif.: Sage Publications, 1987.

Sheldon, W. "Educational Research and Statistics: The Intelligence of Mexican-American Children." In L.H. Carlson and G.A. Colburn (Eds.), *In Their Place*. New York: John Wiley, 1972.

Sikora, R.I. and Barry, B. *Obligations to Future Generations*. Philadelphia: Temple University Press, 1978.

Simeone, A. *Academic Women: Working Toward Equality*. South Hadley, Mass.: Bergin and Garvey, 1987.

Sims, W.E. and de Martinez, B.B. *Perspectives in Multicultural Education*. New York: University Press of America, 1981.

Smircich, L. "Concepts of Culture and Organizational Analysis." *Administrative Science Quarterly*, 1983, 28, 339-358.

Smith, P. *Killing the Spirit: Higher Education in America*. New York: Viking Press/Penguin Books, 1990.

Solomon, B. *In the Company of Educated Women: A History of Women and Higher Education*. New Haven, Conn.: Yale University Press, 1985.

Solomon, R.C. *A Passion for Justice: Emotions and the Origins of the Social Contract*. Reading, Mass.: Addison-Wesley Publishing Company, 1990.

Spicer, E.H. et al. *Impounded People*. Tucson: University of Arizona Press, 1969.

Steinfels, P. *The Neoconservatives: The Men Who Are Changing America's Politics*. New York: Simon and Schuster, 1979.

Sterba, James P. *Justice: Alternative Political Perspectives*. Belmont, Calif.: Wadsworth Publishing Co., 1980.

Stoddard, E.R. *Mexican Americans*. New York: Random House, 1973.

Sumner, W.G. *Folkways*. New York: Mentor Books, 1960.

Taylor, S.E. "The Interface of Cognitive and Social Psychology." In J.H. Harvey (Ed.), *Cognition, Social Behavior, and the Environment*. Hillsdale, N.J.: Erlbaum, 1981.

tenBroek, J., Barnhart, E.N., and Matson, F.W. *Prejudice, War, and the Constitution*. Berkeley: University of California Press, 1968.

Tichy, N.M. and Devanna, M.A. *The Transformational Leader*. New York: John Wiley, 1986.

Tidball, M. and Kistiakowsky, V. "Baccalaureate Origins of American Scientists and Scholars." *Science,* 1976, *193,* 646-652.

Tierney, W.G. "Organizational Culture in Higher Education: Defining the Essentials." *Journal of Higher Education,* 1988, *59* (1), 2-21.

Tocqueville, A. de. *Democracy in America, Vol. II.* New York: Vintage Books/Random House, 1945.

UNESCO Statement on Race, 1950, p.154.

U.S. Bureau of Indian Affairs. *Federal Indian Policies.* Washington, D.C.: U.S. Bureau of Indian Affairs, 1975.

U.S. Commission on Civil Rights. *Mexican Americans and the Administration of Justice in the Southwest.* Washington, D.C.: Government Printing Office, 1970.

U.S. Department of Health, Education, and Welfare. *A Study of Ethnic Minorities.* Washington, D.C.: Government Printing Office, 1984.

Wellman, D.M. *Portraits of White Racism.* Cambridge, England: Cambridge University Press, 1977.

Williams, R.M. Jr. *Strangers Next Door.* Englewood Cliffs, N.J.: Prentice-Hall, 1964.

Wilson, R. and Melendez, S. "Strategies for Developing Minority Leadership." In M. Green (Ed.), *Leaders for a New Era: Strategies for Higher Education.* New York: Collier Macmillan, 1988.

Wong, E. "Asian American Middleman Minority Theory: The Framework of an American Myth." *Journal of Ethnic Studies,* 1985, *13,* 51-87.

Wright, R. *Black Boy: A Record of Childhood and Youth.* New York: Harper and Row, 1945.

Young-Eisendrath, P. and Wiedemann, F.L. *Female Authority: Empowering Women Through Psychotherapy.* New York: The Guilford Press, 1987.

Zwerling, L.S. *Second Best: The Crisis of the Community College.* New York: McGraw-Hill, 1976.

ABOUT THE
AUTHORS

Rosemary Gillett-Karam is a Kellogg postdoctoral fellow in the Community College Leadership Program at the University of Texas at Austin. She is the co-author of *Teaching as Leading: Profiles of Excellence in the Open-Door College*, and contributed two chapters to *Shared Vision: Transformational Leadership in American Community Colleges*. As a Kellogg fellow, Gillett-Karam has addressed national conferences, including the AACJC Annual Convention in Seattle in April 1990 and Leadership 2000 in June 1989. She is also an instructor of government and past division chair of social and behavioral sciences at Austin Community College, Austin, Texas.

Suanne D. Roueche is director of the National Institute for Staff and Organizational Development (NISOD), housed at the University of Texas at Austin, and is editor of *Innovation Abstracts*, the weekly teaching tips newsletter published by NISOD. She co-authored, with John E. Roueche and George A. Baker, *College Responses to Low-Achieving Students: A National Study*, which received the 1984 Outstanding Research Publication Award from the AACJC Council of Colleges and Universities. She has received numerous other awards for her writing and research on teaching and learning in community colleges, and has been recognized as a Distinguished Graduate of the Community College Leadership Program. She is also a senior lecturer in the Department of Educational Administration at the University of Texas at Austin.

John E. Roueche is professor and Sid W. Richardson Chair, Community College Leadership Program at the University of Texas at Austin. He has written or co-written over 100 books, monographs, and articles, including *Teaching as Leading*, *Shared Vision*, and *Access and Excellence: The Open-Door College*, which received the 1987-88

Distinguished Research Award from the National Council for Student Development and the 1987-88 Distinguished Research Publication Award from the National Council for Staff, Program, and Organizational Development. *Shared Vision* received the 1990 Distinguished Research Publication Award from the Council of Universities and Colleges.